Charles Scott's

Analogy of Ancient Craft Masonry

to Natural and Revealed Religion

Charles Scott's

Analogy of Ancient Craft Masonry to Natural and Revealed Religion

Edited, corrected and annotated by
Saul M. Montes-Bradley II

Published by

TOBF Press

South Boston, Virginia, 2016

Printed in U.S.A.

ISBN: 0-9859632-4-7

ISBN-13: 978-0-9859632-4-8

To the memory of my good Brother

R∴W∴Roger K. Paul, 32°, KT
(1944-2016)

Cajun *extraordinaire.*
A good Mason, a good Christian.
Above all, a good Man.

CONTENTS

Foreword

In 1826, a group of Masons in Batavia, New York, were accused of murdering one of their own, William Morgan, allegedly for attempting to reveal the secrets of Freemasonry in an upcoming book. Despite obvious flaws in the accusation, and the fact that the so-called secrets had been in print for nearly two centuries, what became known as the *Morgan Affair* spawned the largest anti-Masonic movement this country has ever seen, including a national political party— the Anti-Masonic Party, the first 3rd party in the US, and the first to hold a national convention—that presented its own candidates in the 1832 elections, winning the delegates of the state of Vermont. Before 1840, the movement had run its course and petered out, and many of its members went on to the Whig party.

Nevertheless, the campaign of the Anti-Masonic party made serious damage to the Fraternity. Lodge membership dropped to historical lows, and anecdotal evidence abounds of Lodges kept open by a handful of Brethren in hopes of a better future[1]. The propaganda of the Anti-Masonic move-

---

[1] John C. Palmer, *Craft, Morgan and anti-Masonry*, The Little Masonic Library, Masonic Service Association, 1925, Vol. 7, cited in the Short Talk Bulletin of the Masonic Service Association, Vol. 11, No 3, March 1933: "The pressure was so strong that withdrawals by individuals and bodies were numerous. In 1827, two hundred and twenty-seven lodges were

ment caused many to view Masonry through the lens of their falsehoods, leading many Brothers to dedicate their efforts to dispel these misconceptions through a large body of Masonic works in the 1840s and 50s. It is in this context that one must view Brother Scott's analogy of Freemasonry and Christianity.

The reader would be best served by remembering that in no way does Brother Scott claim that Masonry is a form of Christianity. In his own words: *"Masonry is by no means intended to supplant the religion of the Bible."* The very title

---

represented in the Grand Lodge of New York. In 1835, the number had dwindled to forty-one.

Every Lodge in the State of Vermont surrendered its Charter or became dormant; and the Grand Lodge, for several years, ceased to hold its sessions. As in Vermont, so also in Pennsylvania, Rhode Island, Massachusetts, Connecticut; and in lesser degrees in several other states. The Masonic Temple was cleft in twain; its brotherhood scattered, its trestleboard without work; its working tools shattered."

As an example of the situation in any Lodges, W∴ Daniel P. Hannon was Master of Merrimack Lodge in Haverhill, Massachusetts, from 1827 to 1841 for lack of members to replace him. In 1827 Merrimack Lodge admitted ten members, in 1828 one, and Eben Bradley, in 1829, was the last member until after the reorganization. In 1892, at the 25th anniversary of Charles C. Dame Lodge of Georgetown, Massachusetts, Dr. Oliver S. Butler thus remembered those days: *"This was the most perilous epoch in the history of Freemasonry in New England, and right well did our Brethren suffer and succeed. It may be interesting to the younger members of the Craft to know that the Masons of Georgetown and vicinity shared in the conflict and triumphs of that stormy crusade. In 1828, when the storm was at its height, a call was issued to all Masons in this vicinity inviting them to meet for mutual consultation at the house of Mr. Sewell Spofford, who received his degree in Merrimack Lodge in 1813. This was in main respects the most important meeting Masonry ever held in this vicinity and few of the most daring of our Brethren responded, finding their way to the house singly and by circuitous routes under cover of the darkness. The meeting continued all night and was deeply interesting. The following Master Masons were present: Dr. Longley, Master of Merrimack Lodge, of Haverhill; Dr. Johnson, Master of St. Mark's Lodge, of Newburyport ; David Gray, Master of St. Matthew's Lodge, of Andover; Judge Marston, of Newburyport, and about thirty others whose names we have been unable to obtain, some of them coming from Danvers and Salem. At this session A new degree was instituted called the Rebound Degree by which these Brethren bound themselves together by solemn vows, that after every other secret vow and right had been surrendered to their enemies, this one should remain sacred and inviolate."*

speaks to similarities to be found in both, not to the essence of either; to inspiration in one from the other, not to their assimilation. Indeed, Masonry defines itself as a system of Morality explained in symbols and veiled in allegory. These symbols were not created by Masons, but were in existence long before the Fraternity was conceived, and their use by diverse civilizations throughout history gives them different and, sometimes, even opposite meaning; the allegories used in Masonry come from a varied source of religious and philosophical sources. Indeed, Masonry is not a religion, nor does it aspire to be, and despite Brother Scott's assertion that *"The Masonic institution is, in fact, founded on the Bible,"* we can say that while there are indeed degrees solidly based on the Bible—both Old and New Testaments—, there are also those based on the Egyptian Mysteries, Mithraic rites, Zoroastrianism, Sufism, and Islam, to mention but a few[2]. In fact, the allegories taken from the Old Testament are not of Christian but Jewish tradition, and yet others—like the Book of Rachel—are of even older origin. Even those stories often considered Christian may have their origins in more ancient sources.

There is no question, for instance, that Christianity borrowed heavily from the Mithraic Rites. Even a cursory study will reveal striking similarities between them. The Eucharist, a sacrament in many Christian churches, will remind us of the degree of Father (*pir-e moghan*) in the rites of Mithras, in which the Heliodromus pours the wine of Divine Love (*Esheg*) into the cup (heart) of the Lion (*Leo*), and together with bread—representing the flesh of the sac-

---

[2] A thorough analysis is beyond the scope of this work, but we can mention that the 28th Degree in the Ancient and Accepted Scottish Rite of Freemasonry, for instance, derives its doctrine from Hermeticism, the Kabala and Magism; in the 29th, Hugh of Tiberias, Lord of Galilee, visits the court of Saladin, the Sultan of Egypt and Syria, and they instruct each other in their concepts of chivalry and religion; and the 31st, teaches the concept of Justice from "the accumulated history of human lawgivers—handed down from King Alfred the Saxon, Socrates, Confucius, Minos, Zoroaster, and Moses."

rificed bull in whose death there was life—the Lions enjoy their ritual meal. That bull sacrificed in the *tauroctomy,* the central act in Mithraic rite, is not an actual sacrificed animal: The bull that Mithras kills is his ego, just as Perseus killed the Gorgon and St. George the dragon.[3] Even in Celtic Druidism we find the origin of some Christian and, indeed, Masonic imagery.[4] Our Lodges are dedicated to the Holy Saints John, and it takes no effort to see that their days are Midsummer and the Winter Solstice. Light and darkness. In the *Sanas Chormaic,* a glossary from the 10th Century, we read that the Druids had the sun engraved in their altars, much as it decorates every Masonic Lodge today; and in *The War of the Gaedhil with the Gaill,* we read that high king Brian Boru held court near Dublin *ó nodlaic mór co nodlaic becc:* from great Christmas to little Christmas.[5] All of the references to the Word, from Christianity to Zoroastrianism,[6] can also be found in the Samkhiya philosophy of dualism (Mahat)[7]; and in the concept of Righteousness (*Maat*) as the foundation of human life[8] in the Egyptian cosmogony.

While there is no doubt that the founders of the Fraternity were Christians of various denominations attempting to find common ground at a time when such was more a rarity than the norm[9], there is also no doubt that Masonry

---

[3] Payam Nabarz, *The Mysteries of Mithras, The Pagan Belief that Shaped the Christian World,* Vermont, 2005, pp. 39-42.

[4] Vide: Thomas Paine, An Essay on the Origin of Freemasonry, London, 1826.

[5] Ronald Hutton, *The Stations of the Sun, a History of the Ritual Year in Britain,* Oxford University Press, 1996, p. 5.

[6] Vide: Maneckji Nusservanji Dhalla, *The Niayshes of Zoroastrian Litanies,* New York, 1908.

[7] Veeraswamy Khrishnaraj, *The Baghavad-Gita,* New York, 2002, p. 305.

[8] Maulana Karenga, *Maat, the oral Idea in Ancient Egypt,* New York, 2004, p. 5.

[9] If we consider strictly the historical—as opposed to legendary—origins of Freemasonry, we must come to the inevitable conclusion that the Fra-

transcends the particular beliefs of any one member of the Craft, always searching for that kernel of Wisdom to be found in all philosophies: That which unites us in a common bond. As Albert Pike remarked in Morals and Dogma: *"Masonry propagates no creed, except its own most simple and Sublime One; that Universal religion, taught by Nature and by Reason. Its lodges are neither Jewish, Moslem nor Christian Temples. It reiterates the principles of morality of all religions. It venerates the character and commends the teachings of the great and good of all ages and of all countries. It extracts the good and not the evil, the truth, and not the error, from all creeds; and acknowledges that there is much which is good and true in all."*[10]

Charles Scott was not attempting to establish the Christian nature of Masonry, though he cheerfully points to all the aspects of our system that do have a Christian origin, and more, those that have any correspondence or, as he calls it, similitudes. Rather, he was drawing a parallel between Christianity and Masonry that would allay the fears of some of his contemporaries, stoked by the outlandish claims of the Anti-Masonic movement, and to permit his fellow Christians to approach Masonry without fear or misconceptions.

---

ternity arose from the religious strife during the civil wars that devastated England in the 17ᵗʰ Century. The first initiation of which we have a record is that of Elias Ashmole in Warrington on 16 October 1646, though this does not preclude an earlier origin: Absence of evidence is not evidence of absence.

[10] Albert Pike, *Morals and Dogma of the Ancient and Accepted Scottish Rite of Freemasonry*, Charleston, 1781, p. 718. As for the often misquoted statement, in the Catholic Encyclopedia the following completes the quoted paragraph—supposedly underscoring the sectarian character of Freemasonry: *"There has never been a false Religion in the world. The permanent one universal Revelation is written in visible Nature and explained by Reason and it is completed by the wise analogies of faith. There is but one true religion, one dogma, one legitimate belief."* Instead, what Pike wrote is: *"Above all the other great teachers of morality and virtue, it reveres the character of the Great Master who, submissive to the will of his and our Father, died upon the Cross."* Quite a difference, indeed! See: Charles George Herbermann, *The Catholic Encyclopædia*, New York, 1910, Vol. 9, p. 779, and subsequent editions.

At this time, perhaps, we need to clarify an additional point: Brother Scott approached Christianity according to his own beliefs. He made no effort to smooth the edges of his own faith. His audience was not an ecumenical council but those who shared his theology in his own time. Theological differences, even among those who called themselves Christians in Scott's time, were as diverse then as they are today. Thomas Paine, the Revolutionary philosopher, once famously wrote that Christianity is defined in the negative. That is, that those who describe themselves as Christians tell us who they are not, but shed little light on who they are. We know that whoever calls himself Christian is not a Jew, a Buddhist or a Muslim; but we do not know if he believes in God as the head of the Trinity, or in a Triune God consubstantial with the Son and the Holy Spirit. We do not know if he believes in *two* sacraments (Lutherans, Reformed Evangelicals,) *three* (some Lutherans[11]), *six* (Dionysius the pseudo-Aeropagite), *seven* (Catholics, Orthodox), *nine* (some Catholics[12]), or *none at all* (Friends, Baptists, Unitarians). We do not know if he believes in the transubstantiation. We do not know if he believes Christ to be the Son of God, God, or a great teacher. We do not even know if he believes that justification, in a soteriological sense, can be attained through Works, Faith, or some combination of both. There are, in consequence, many who would today consider some of Brother Scott's statements as sectarian. And they would be right. But they would be right with the benefit of temporal distance. Brother Scott did not speak of a universal form of Christianity but of that which he and his audience shared. He was a Trinitarian, heavily influenced—to judge by the sources

---

[11] In *The Babylonian Captivity of the Church,* Luther starts by arguing that there are three sacraments (Baptism, Communion and Confession) only to come to the conclusion that there are two (Baptism and Communion).

[12] There is hardly any agreement among Catholic theologians as to whether Ordination is a single sacrament or three separate ones (diaconate, priesthood and episcopate.)

he quotes—by the evangelical movement of the Anglican (and Episcopalian) church. And it is in this light that one should read him. It is only under this prism that one can observe the profound and, indeed, beautiful analogies that Brother Scott draws between his Christian beliefs and the teachings of Masonry.

Of course, others may draw different conclusions—indeed, they will—, but the nature of Masonry is such that no one person may speak in its behalf, and we are left free to draw such conclusions as our abilities will permit. Free-masonry is a set of core Moral principles shared by people of the most varied religious and cultural mores, concentrating in that which we have in common. This openness in Masonry has led many to label it a *relativist system*[13]. Nothing could be farthest from the truth. Toleration implies no relativism. Mutual respect implies no agreement. A belief in freedom of conscience implies no indifference. In the words of Br∴ George Washington, *"It is now no more that toleration is spoken of as if it were the indulgence of one class of people that another enjoyed the exercise of their inherent natural rights..."*[14] Masonic Tolerance is, therefore, the acceptance that Truth is expressed in many forms—not , as erroneously affirmed by its detractors, that that Truth is unknowable or, worse, that there are many "truths"—, and that we are all entitled to enjoy our inherent rights without fear of persecution; not as a class benefitting from the indulgence of another, but of our own right. It does not mean, however, that all systems of morality or religion are equally true. Masonry takes no sides in this argument. As Masons, many of us believe that there is a True and Moral way to live our lives, and that parts of that Universal Truth can be glimpsed in all the religious and philosophical systems ever devised by man. We also believe that Truth is self-evident. That it can-

---

[13] See Appendix I, p. 281.

[14] George Washington, *Letter to the Hebrew Congregation at Newport*, 21 August 1790.

not be imposed on anyone, be it by force or by argument, and that only through a lifetime of dedication to knowledge can we ever hope to approach Truth in Wisdom. Brother Scott found it in his particular form of Christianity. Others will—and do—find it in their interpretation and practice of their own religions or, as Br∴ George Washington, in none at all.[15] But even those who disagree—and some may disagree strongly—with the finer points of Brother Scott's theology, will find valuable information in both his description and in his interpretation of Masonic teachings.

Br∴ Scott's lament in his first lecture rings as true today as the day he wrote it: *"The benign principles of Masonry, like*

---

[15] *The Literary Digest,* Vol. XXIV, No 22, 31 May 1902, p. 746: "Bishop White, whose church in Philadelphia Washington attended part of the time while there, wrote to a correspondent in 1835: 'In regard to the subject of your inquiry, truth requires me to say that General Washington never received the communion in the churches of which I am the parochial minister. Mrs. Washington was an habitual communicant.' And, again, in a letter to the Rev. B. C. C. Parker, reproduced in Bishop White's *Memoirs,* he said: 'I do not believe that any degree of recollection will bring to my mind any fact which would prove General Washington to have been a believer in the Christian revelation further than as may be hoped from his constant attendance upon Christian worship, in connection with the general reserve of his character.'

When not an attendant at Bishop White's church, Washington generally attended the Rev. James Abercrombie's church in the same city. Dr. Abercrombie's recorded utterances on the subject of Washington's religion, are of much the same character as Bishop White's. Indeed, it is stated (in the *Annals of the American Pulpit,* vol. v., p. 394) that on one occasion Dr. Abercrombie administered a public rebuke to Washington on account of his attitude toward religious Observances. 'I considered it my duty,' says the preacher, 'in a sermon on public worship to state the unhappy tendency of example, particularly of those in elevated stations, who uniformly turned their backs upon the celebration of the Lord's Supper. I acknowledge the remark was intended for the President, and as such he received it.' Dr. Abercrombie is also reported as saying emphatically to the Rev. Dr. Wilson of Albany: 'Sir, Washington was a Deist.'

General Greely, in an article on *Washington's Domestic and Religious Life,* writes: 'It is, however, somewhat striking that in several thousand letters the name of Jesus Christ never appears, and it is notably absent from his last will.'"

those of Christianity, have too often been perverted. Our most whole-some lessons are often disregarded; our laws and constitutions have been openly violated; and our landmarks purposely forgotten. Many unite themselves with the fraternity, with no higher aim than that of satisfying an idle curiosity, or with the design of gratifying some low ambition. There are others who expect to be invested with some won-derful secrets, and to witness the most mysterious evolutions. Having received the several degrees, they seem to be overcome with a spell of disappointment, and never dwell for a moment even on the beautiful and sublime emblems of the Order. They never look beyond the surface of the ritual or Masonic lectures, for those mysteries which are deeply enshrined within." This is perhaps the most compelling reason for rescuing these pages from undeserved oblivion. Led by his prose, we might venture past the surface and, lantern in hand, advance in the understanding of Masonic lectures and rituals. It matters not if we find ourselves in agreement or not. Whether one believes that King Solomon was a Ma-son or that the Fraternity did not see the light for millennia after he ceased to be, the careful exploration of our rites and symbols must force us to *think,* and in so doing, to ad-vance our own *knowledge.* Returning to Albert Pike: *"Howev-er the Mason may believe as to creeds, and churches, and miracles, and missions from Heaven, he must admit that the Life and character of him who taught in Galilee, and fragments of whose teachings have come down to us, are worthy of all imitation. That Life is an undenied and undeniable Gospel. Its teachings cannot be passed by and discarded. All must admit that it would be happiness to follow and perfection to imitate him. None ever felt for him a sincere emotion of contempt, nor in anger accused him of sophistry, nor saw immorality lurking in his doctrines; however they may judge of those who succeeded him, and claimed to be his apostles. Divine or human, inspired or on-ly a reforming Essene, it must be agreed that his teachings are far no-bler, far purer, far less alloyed with error and imperfection, far less of the earth earthly, than those of Socrates, Plato, Seneca, or Mahomet, or any other of the great moralists and Reformers of the world."*[16]

---

[16] Albert Pike, *op. cit.,* p. 718.

In the course of editing this work, I have been careful not to change his meaning, although I have extensively corrected spelling and some grammatical construction to make it easier for contemporary readers. I have also endeavored to find his original sources—and after considerable effort, succeeded—updating his citations to ensure that the reader can refer to them whenever necessary, and added notes to clarify some points or add new information which, in some cases, was not available in his time. I have also included biographical information that may shed more light on the author and his thought. Finally, I have organized the Lectures under titles related to their content to facilitate the order of their reading.

While Scott's work is available in facsimile editions, the lack of clarity in the sources and absence of any reference to the author—not to mention the poor quality of the print—makes its reading exceedingly difficult, hence the effort into this edition, the first of TOBF's Masonic Library, which we hope will help our Brothers find more light in Masonry.

Saul M. Montes-Bradley II
South Boston, Virginia,
July 2016

Masonic Engraving painted by J. Biggen c. 1798

LECTURE I.
Introduction to Masonry

"I will bring the blind by a way that they knew not; I will lead them in paths that they have not known: I will make darkness light before them, and crooked things straight: these things will I do unto them, and not forsake them."[17]

"What end can be more noble than the pursuit of virtue? What motive more alluring than the practice of justice? Or what instruction more beneficial than accurate elucidation of symbolical mysteries, which tend to embellish and adorn the mind?"[18]

---

[17] Isaiah 42:16

[18] Laurence Dermott, *Ahiman Rezon*, Philadelphia, 1855. Hereafter Ahi. Rez.

E. N.: The first Book of Masonic Law published by the Grand Lodge of Pennsylvania was *Ahiman Rezon abridged and digested: as a Help to atilt are or would be Free and Accepted Masons*. It was prepared by the Grand Secretary, the Rev. Brother William Smith, D.D., Provost of the University of Pennsylvania, and was almost entirely a reprint of Dermott's work; it was approved by the Grand Lodge November 22, 1781, published in 1783, and dedicated to Brother George Washington. It is reprinted in the introduction to the first or edited reprint of the Proceedings of the Grand Lodge of Pennsylvania, 1730-1808. On April 18, 1825, a revision of the Ahiman Rezon was adopted, being taken largely from Anderson's Constitutions. It took its name from the Book of Constitutions of the Grand Lodge of Ancient Freemasons in England. Its meaning, according to Mackey "the will of selected Brethren," and is a derived

"Then I looked abroad on the earth, and behold, the Lord was in all things,

Yet I saw not his hand in aught, but perceived that he worketh by means."[19]

The enlightened craftsman beholds in Freemasonry a wonderful institution. Founded, as it is, on the truths contained in the Holy Scriptures, its principles constitute a moral science, which surpasses every other in the world. It is a compact system of rites, ceremonies, emblems and types, which are designed to teach and elucidate the rules of moral action, and those great truths which remind us of immortality, and lead to the solemn contemplation of the mysteries of eternity. The several degrees of ancient craft Masonry are generally regarded as symbolical, and they contain permanent land-marks of everything beautiful and sublime in the government of God. And such is the nature and universality of our mystic language, that it cannot be exposed to any innovation or change. It is understood and spoken by the craft, wherever they are dispersed around the globe, and it forms a common medium of communication or intercourse among our brethren of all nations, tribes, kindreds, and tongues. And something exceedingly beautiful may be perceived in this, if the view proposed to be taken of the Order be founded in reason.

The true philosophy of Masonic work, when properly understood, will be found to consist in the grand design to teach those doctrines which essentially relate to the temporal and eternal destinies of our race. The cardinal elements of divine truth are sublimely evolved in our lodges by the means or use of certain allegorical rites and ceremonies. The thoughtful Mason, when he surveys the moral

---

from three Hebrew words: *zhiln*, meaning Brethren; manah, to appoint or select; and *ratzon*, will, pleasure or meaning.

[19] Martin Farquhar Tupper, A.M., *Tupper's Proverbial Philosophy*, Boston, 1851, p. 56. Hereafter Tupper.

machinery and its beautiful operations, becomes seriously impressed with the truth embraced in the doctrines of the immortality of the soul, the resurrection of the body, and the mystery of the eternal Godhead. Our system comprises the whole history of man, from the moment of his creation to the consummation of all things—from the beginning of time to the final judgment; and, therefore, must necessarily refer to the purity of our first estate,—our lost innocence,—and the only means of its restoration. Herein, consists, it is believed, the chief value and dignity of speculative Masonry, which is justly entitled to occupy an elevated ground, and command the enlightened consideration of the world.

If the institution be of ancient origin—if it existed at the building of King Solomon's temple, (of which there is plenary testimony furnished to every well-informed member of the craft,) then there is much reason to think that its types and remarkable events shadowed forth or mystically represented the glorious plan of redemption. We believe that our ancient brethren read in them the most cherished assurances of a coming Messiah, in an age then far off, as distinctly as they did in the types and prophecies of the old dispensation. It was the pleasure of an infinitely wise God, *"who worketh all things after the counsel of his own will,"* to dispense the light of truth in various ways. Some are brought to light in one way, and some in another. *"While the world was yet young,"* and transgression of recent origin, God vouchsafed to hold direct communication with our race, and furnished our fathers with intimations of redemption, and directed them in the forms of acceptable worship.[20] As time progressed, and population multiplied, and the world grew, the revelations of Heaven became more and more

---

[20] We have but faint traces of patriarchal religion; but we know that while the world was yet young, and evil only of recent introduction, God held intercourse with the fathers of humankind, and instructed them in the mode in which he would be worshipped. — Henry Melvill, B.D., *Sermons*, Vol. 1, New York, 1844, p. 298. Hereafter 1 Mel. Ser.

distinct, and thus more light was afforded. Then God's wonderful plan of salvation was gradually revealed. There were degrees or stages of heavenly knowledge; there were eras of Divine truth. At one period, the compasses were under the square; at another, one of its points was raised; and at another time, both were elevated. The merciful and glorious purposes of the Almighty were at last entrusted to the keeping of the House of Israel.[21] With his chosen people was deposited the truth, which, at first, was taught in their mystical rites, and afterwards by the second sight of the prophets. The sacramental treasures and shadows of the temple followed, and then the Day-spring on high dawned upon the world. So there were different *degrees* of the knowledge of *"the truth as it is in Jesus,"* but they referred to one Savior—Jesus of Nazareth. There are several degrees in Masonry; but the knowledge which the Entered Apprentice acquires only differs in degree from that of the Fellowcraft, while that of the Fellowcraft is a part of the same great light which shines so brilliantly on the mind of the Master Mason, and causes his soul to beat with the mighty *"pulses of eternity."* If, in the patriarchal age, traces of Divine truth were made visible in the firstlings of the flock, which were offered up on some rude altar, the Entered Apprentice may read, in the emblems which adorn his chart, some beautiful intimations of a heavenly dispensation. If the ancient and devout Jew beheld in the blood of the paschal lamb the blood of One which was shed to redeem mankind, the Entered Apprentice wears an emblem of innocence in which he may behold a memorial of the Lamb which was slain from the foundation of the world. If the Israelites loved to worship in that splendid temple which our ancient masters erected, and saw in its solemn pomps and ceremonies august types of the Redeemer, the Fellowcraft Mason, who has been advanced to the inner chamber of our moral edifice, and who has kneeled in reverential awe in the holy presence of the Deity, may rejoice

---

[21] Mel. Ser., p. 298.

in that enlarging faith which bids him look forward to the fullness of that greater light which illumines the holy of holies. If our being on earth be merely transitory,—if the human soul is destined to an everlasting duration in that boundless hereafter, where decay and time are unknown, then any system of moral and religious instruction should commend itself to the serious consideration of rational and immortal beings.

Masonry is by no means intended to supplant the religion of the Bible, or detract from the church of God; but as one of the outward aids of truth, it will often induce men to ponder upon the nature of the undying principle of life, and its relations to the other world. The Masonic institution is, in fact, founded on the Bible, as we hope to establish in the following pages. The Holy Bible is the first great light of the Order,[22] and the outlines of every degree which belongs to ancient craft Masonry, may be found in that wonderful volume.

Religion has its external aids and its outward symbols. The Lord multiplied visions and used similitudes by the ministry of the prophets.[23] The wise founders of the Masonic institution, were acquainted with the Almighty's mode of instruction, and hence our figurative or symbolical language. Solomon, who was our first Most Excellent Grand Master, adorned his writings with the richest meta-

---

[22] As more immediate guides for a Free Mason, the lodge is furnished with unerring rules, whereby he shall form his conduct. The book of the law is laid before him, that he may not say, through ignorance he erred; whatever the Great Architect of the world hath dictated to mankind as the mode in which he should be served, and the path in which to tread to obtain his approbation, whatever precepts he hath administered, and with whatever laws he hath inspired the sages of old, the same are faithfully comprised in the book of the law of Masonry. That book, which is never closed in any lodge, reveals the duties which the Great Master of all exacts from us; open to every eye, comprehensible to every mind; then who can say among us that he knoweth not the acceptable service? — Ahi. Rez., p. 145, note.

[23] Hosea 12:10.

phors, drawn, from the visible universe. All the inspired poets borrowed their similarities and sublime imagery from external nature. Mankind are creatures of sense and observation. Religion has its forms and ceremonies, its altars and its creeds. It is forever allied, too, to the exterior world or material nature. Rich are its associations with the earth. Judea is the native land of our Savior, and the city of David was his birth-place. He grew up in that holy land. He visited its towns and cities. He wandered in its valleys and sojourned on its hills. In that land of marvelous things he healed the sick, unstopped the ears of the deaf, opened the eyes of the blind, raised the dead, and established his kingdom forever. There, too, he died for our iniquities, was buried, rose again for our justification, and from thence ascended into glory. The influences of external nature are as necessary as they are wonderful. They often facilitate the improvement of the moral faculties, elevate the affections, and fill the heart with a lively sense of gratitude to God. Who can look upon the lofty mountain, and not feel the awful grandeur of Deity, who laid its everlasting foundation? Who can survey the valleys of earth, teeming with rich productions and waving with golden harvests, and not think of the goodness and mercy of the Lord? Who can feel the healthful rays of the charitable sun,[24] or listen to the kind rains descending, and not be haunted by a beautiful spirit of worship for Him, who bids the sun to shine and the rains to descend alike on the rich and the poor, the evil and the good? What Newton ever trode the heavens,

---

[24] Bishop Home, in one of his fragmentary pieces, says that "The end of knowledge is charity, or the communication of it for the benefit of others." This truth he illustrates by a passage from Milton:

> "Consider first that great
> Or bright infers not excellence: the earth,
> Though, in comparison of heaven, so small.
> Nor glist'ring, may of solid gold contain
> More plenty than the sun that barren shines;
> Whose virtue on itself works no effect,
> But in the fruitful earth; there first received
> His beams, inactive else, their vigour find."

and caught no glimpse of immortality? The wise men of the East were heralded by a star to the village of our Lord's nativity. The moon and her lovely train pour their gentle influences into the soul. The witching hour of night woos the mind to thought. The grave tells us of a great hereafter. The city of the dead makes us think of the city of our God. The coming or departing hour whispers something of immortality. The yellow leaf, the withered flower, and the running stream invite our souls to heaven, where joy can never fade, and peace is a perennial fountain. Autumn should teach us to prepare for death, while the falling leaves sound to the ear like notes of pensive music, or a funeral song.[25]

The benign principles of Masonry, like those of Christianity, have too often been perverted. Our most wholesome lessons are often disregarded; our laws and constitutions have been openly violated; and our landmarks purposely forgotten. Many unite themselves with the fraternity, with no higher aim than that of satisfying an idle curiosity, or with the design of gratifying some low ambition. There are others who expect to be invested with some wonderful secrets, and to witness the most mysterious evolutions. Having received the several degrees, they seem to be overcome with a spell of disappointment, and never dwell for a moment even on the beautiful and sublime emblems of the Order. They never look beyond the surface of the ritual or Masonic lectures, for those mysteries which are deeply enshrined within. None but an expert master can have the key with which the gates of the temple are unlocked, or be fur-

---

[25] The Scriptures contain many affecting images of the shortness of human life; but to understand those images fully, we should visit the country from which those images are drawn. Let the traveler visit the beautiful plains of Smyrna, or any other part of the East, in the month of May, and revisit it toward the end of June, and he will perceive the force and beauty of these allusions. — Hartley's Researches in Greece, p. 237. (E. N.: The Rev. John Hartley, M.A., *Researches in Greece and the Levant*, London, 1831).

nished with the means of entering the apartments of the building filled with heavenly treasures!

It is difficult to tell how the types of Masonry can escape the attention of anyone who has been raised to the sublime degree of a Master. The whole plan or design of the institution having been drawn from the volume of inspiration, it must necessarily contain types and symbols of the most significant character. The symbolical degrees seem to have been most ingeniously and wisely constructed, for the purpose of shadowing forth an event very similar to that which was typified in the old dispensation of God. The signs, tokens, emblems, and ceremonies of the degrees of Entered Apprentice and Fellow-Craft, direct the mind of the contemplative Mason to the future, or lead it to anticipate some mystery which would be revealed in the Master's degree. While the first two degrees prepare the mind for the reception of greater knowledge of traditional lore, they also contain many types of an event in which the eternal happiness of mankind was bound up.

We would not be misunderstood. Masonry can lay no just claim to a Divine origin, though one of its founders was inspired.[26] There is evidently a designed resemblance between the events which are represented in the several degrees. The types succeed each other in regular order. They naturally follow each other; though they may not be readily comprehended by the Entered Apprentice or Fellow-Craft in their complete typical signification. It has been supposed that many of the circumstances recorded in the Old Testament were not generally known to be typical, until the great

---

[26] Many, who know nothing of our rites or of the principles of Masonry, presume too much when they undertake to condemn the Order. They very frequently charge that it is substituted for the church; when, if they were Masons, they would soon be convinced that, while it is a handmaid to religion, it leaves everyone to worship God under his own vine and fig tree. It may lead the benighted Mason to the true light, as we shall endeavor to show; but, according to its rules, no man of unexceptionable morals, and who believes in the existence of God, can be rightfully excluded from knowledge of the mysteries.

event with which the future was charged had transpired; when the resemblance between them became so striking that the typical character of those circumstances could no longer be concealed.[27] So the intimations contained in the symbols of the first and second degrees may not be fully perceived by the Entered Apprentice and Fellow-Craft; but where is the Master Mason who can fail to observe the resemblance and intimate connection which exist between the degrees and the events they illustrate? The Master can comprehend the types, and trace out their signification. "The members of our society," says an eminent Mason, "at this day, in the third stage of Masonry, confess themselves to be Christians. The veil of the temple has been rent—the builder is smitten, and we are raised from the tomb of transgression".[28]

Prophetic writing is defined by Bishop Warburton to be a speaking hieroglyphic. Emblems or hieroglyphics were used long anterior to the invention of alphabetical writing; and it may be affirmed that all which is beautiful in the allegorical style of composition is derived from the hieroglyphical language of the ancients. The mysteries of our Order are couched in figurative or emblematical language, which has a hidden or internal sense similar to that which exists in the word of Revelation. The Scriptures, in many parts, may be regarded in both a literal and spiritual sense. So it may be affirmed that many of the emblems of Masonry may be viewed in a double sense. The regular lectures may often direct the mind to their literal meaning, and pass over in silence their spiritual or internal meaning. This internal sense of our mystic language is often "hard to be understood;" but with the aid of Divine truth much that ap-

---

[27] Townsend's Notes on the Types of the New Testament, p. 72. (E. N.: Rev. George Townsend M.A., *The New Testament, Arranged in Historical and Chronological Order, with Copious Notes*, London, 1837. Hereafter *Town. Notes*)

[28] The Rev. George Oliver, D.D., A *Dictionary of Symbolic Masonry: Including the Royal Arch Degree*, New York, 1855, p. 42. Hereafter *1 Ol. Land.*

pears difficult to comprehend will become clear. By the brilliant light of the new dispensation, the hidden or spiritual meaning of our emblems may be perceived, and that darkness which rests on the mind will disappear like mists before the rising sun. We know that there is a book *"written within and on the backside, sealed with seven seals."*[29] And no man in heaven, nor in earth, neither under the earth, has been able to open it; but the Lion of the tribe of Judah has prevailed to open and to loose the seven seals.[30]

The internal sense of our lectures or landmarks[31] finds its analogy in the sacred writings. The Garden of Eden actually existed, however much commentators and critics may have disputed as to the point of its location. It matters not whether it was in the third heaven, in the regions of the air, or on the earth. But although there is no reason to doubt that there was such a place as the terrestrial paradise, it was a type or pledge of the Eden of the skies. Adam and Eve were real persons, and the innocence of their first estate was emblematical of that purity which exists in heaven. *"The institution of marriage, the cause, bond, and cement of the social state, was probably designed to prefigure that harmony, order, and blessedness which must reign in the kingdom of God."*[32] Christ, speaking of himself, said: *"I am the living bread which came down from heaven: if any man eat of this bread, he shall live forever: and the bread that I will give is my flesh, which I will give for the life of the world."* The Jews were astonished at his words, and Je-

---

[29] Revelation 5:1.

[30] Revelation 5:3-5.

[31] There is a certain course of instruction in the Masonic degrees which are denominated lectures. The universal laws and universal language of Masonry are landmarks. There are certain local ceremonies, usages, &c., which are not landmarks. — Albert Gallatin Mackey, *A Lexicon of Freemasonry,* South Carolina, 1845, p. 178, 179. Hereafter *Mack. Lex.*

[32] Adam Clarke, *Commentary on Genesis,* probably from the 1836 London edition of *The Holy Bible, Old and New Testaments…Containing Critical Notes,* Genesis in Vol. 1 of 6. There was also an edition in New York in 1856, Gen. III. Hereafter *Clarke's Com. Gen.*

sus said unto them: "*Verily, verily, I say unto you, except ye eat the flesh of the Son of man, and drink his blood; ye have no life in you. Whoso eateth my flesh, and drinketh my blood, hath eternal life; and I will raise him up at the last day. For my flesh is meat indeed, and my blood is drink indeed. It is the spirit that quickeneth; the flesh profiteth nothing: the words that I speak unto you they are spirit, and they are life."*[33]

The secret or spiritual meaning of the Masonic emblems and work we will endeavour to present in a manner acceptable both to the fraternity and general reader. Some of our views may appear novel, but if they are fairly investigated, they will be found to be consistent with the principles of the Order and the doctrines of that sacred volume which is ever open upon our altars.

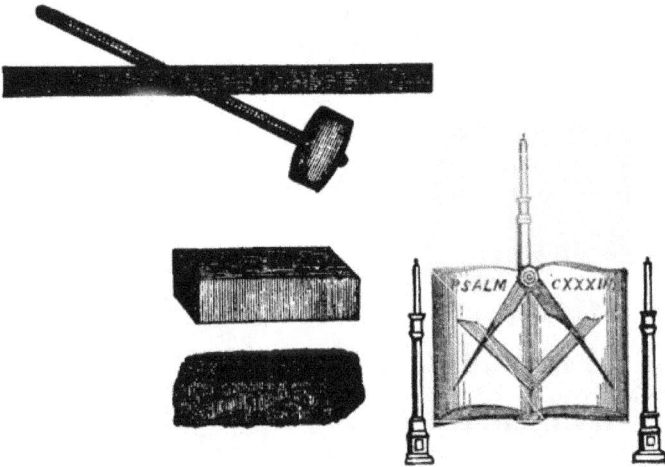

---

[33] John 6:53

LECTURE II.
The Initiation

Let there be light, said God, and forthwith light
Ethereal, first of things, quintessence pure,
Sprung from the deep, and from her native East
To journey through the aery gloom began,
Sphered in a radiant cloud, for yet the sun
Was not; she in a cloudy tabernacle
Sojourned the while.

Milton, Paradise Lost, 7.243-9

In the first degree, we are taught such useful lessons as prepare the mind for a regular advancement in the principles of knowledge and philosophy. These are imprinted on the memory by lively and sensible images.[34]

His thoughts kindle up his devotions; and devotion never burns so bright or so warm as when it is lighted up from within.[35]

---

[34] Ahi. Rez., p. 85.

[35] William Paley, *The Works of William Paley*, Philadelphia, 1836, p. 546, Sermon VIII. Hereafter *Pal. Ser.*

Worthy is the Lamb that was slain to receive power, and riches, and
wisdom, and strength, and honour, and glory, and blessing.[36]
Angels are round the good man, to catch the incense of his prayer,
And they fly to administer kindness to those for whom he pleadeth.[37]

No reflecting Mason can witness the initiation of a candidate, without being impressed with the intellectual and moral tendencies of the degree of Entered Apprentice.[38] It portrays the beauty, loveliness, and simplicity of a virtuous and holy life. The word candidate denotes one whose motives and intentions are pure. He represents one who has been long wandering in moral darkness, in the ways of sin and unbelief, but is desirous of receiving the light of wisdom and virtue; one who longs for the Spirit of truth to move upon the face of his degraded intellect, and bring forth the light of immortality. Darkness fearfully broods over the mysterious depths of the uninstructed mind, which is without form and void.[39] Nothing but the Spirit of righteousness can dispel the gloom, or illumine the solemn deep. A new creation must take place; a moral renovation pass over the long-neglected soul; a light must arise upon the benighted mind, that there may be called into being beautiful associations of thought and feeling. The candidate represents one whose soul must be born again, and become endowed with new hopes, new joys, new affections, new thoughts, new feelings and sentiments.[40] Evil must be

---

[36] Revelation 5:12

[37] Tupper, p. 55

[38] The first degree is well calculated to enforce the duties of morality, and imprint on the memory the noblest principles which can adorn the human mind. It is, therefore, the best introduction to the second degree, which not only extends the same plan, but comprehends a more diffusive system of knowledge. — Mack. Lex., p. 165

[39] 1 Mel. Ser., p. 361; also, George D'Oyly and Richard Mant, *The Holy Bible*, Cambridge, 1823, Vol. 1, Commentary on Genesis 1:2-3. Hereafter *D'Oyly and Mant's Com.*

[40] As God divided the light from the darkness—so he will separate the righteous from the wicked in the final day.

plucked up by the roots. There are evil desires which must be cast out of the temple, before it can be inhabited by that lovely tenantry which delight to dwell in a peaceful soul. Here, too, is taught the necessity and efficacy of prayer.[41] Around our mystic altars do Christian Masons devoutly kneel, and offer up their devotions to the Almighty Father of the universe. The fervent petition ascends, "that the candidate may not only become a true and faithful brother, but that he may dedicate himself and devote his life to the service of God; and that he might be endowed with a competency of divine wisdom, that by the secrets of our art he might be better enabled to display the beauties of holiness to the honor of God's holy name."[42] There is a tradition that no one could enter the mountain of the house for prayer and devotion, without adhering strictly to the established customs. No man could enter without pulling off his shoes or sandals; he could not carry into the temple any weapon, money, or metallic substance.[43] The temple was a house of peace, and "it was necessary," says Home, "that he should be divested of all worldly cares and affections; and having entered to pray and attend the service, he was to stand with his feet one even with the other, as a servant before his master, with all reverence and fear." To pray often and earnestly, putting all our trust in the Lord is the duty of every man and Mason.[44] The pious and prayerful man may pursue his journey through life, and fear no evil. It is our duty, as Masons, not only to pray for our selves, but for

---

[41] It has been well said of prayer, that prayer will either make a man leave off sinning, or sin will make him leave off prayer. — Pal. Ser., p. 1. All the ceremonies of our Order are prefaced and terminated by prayer, because Masonry is a religious institution, and because we thereby show our dependence on, and our faith and trust in God. — Mack. Lex., p. 243.

[42] Jeremy Ladd Cross, *The True Masonic Chart or Hieroglyphic Monitor*, New York, 1854, p. 13. Hereafter *Cross' Chart*.

[43] We brought nothing into this world, and it is certain we can carry nothing out. — 1 Timothy 6:7

[44] Faith is a Masonic and Christian virtue, and "prayer is the voice of faith."

our brethren, wherever they may be. The vows are upon us; and he who violates them departs from the ancient and acceptable custom of the Order. Then,

Let out thy soul, and pray!
Not for thy home alone;
Away in prayer, away!
Make all the world thine own.
Let out thy soul in prayer;
Oh, let thy spirit grow!
God gives thee sun and air;
Let the full blossom blow! [45]

The Fraternity are taught the necessity of appealing to the throne of Heaven, before entering upon any important undertaking. To the Father of all we must ask for strength and power to support us in every trial, duty, and emergency in life. It is not difficult for us to learn who taught us to pray, and how to pray. The Holy One prompts the sinful heart to plead for forgiveness, and ask for heavenly things. Jesus, while on earth, taught his disciples how to pray. The Masonic authority for praying before entering upon any important undertaking will be found in the Scriptures. Before Elijah attempted to restore the dead child of the Shunamite, he prayed unto the Lord. He knew and felt that all power resided with God, and that the departed soul could not return, unless He who had taken it away willed it to come back. Jesus prayed just before he raised Lazarus from the dead. In Gethsemane, it is recorded; he fell on his face and prayed. How often did He, while on earth, stretch forth his hands in holy prayer for our fallen nature. Solomon prayed at the dedication of the temple. And he kneeled down upon his knees, before all the congregation of Israel, and spread forth his hands toward heaven, and offered up his prayer. [46] The mourning Ezra fell upon his

---

[45] Arthur Cleveland Coxe, *Christian Ballads*, London, 1853, p. 47.

[46] 2 Chronicles 6:13

knees and spread out his hands to God in prayer.[47] And how affecting is the prayer of Stephen, in the trying hour of martyrdom! "He kneeled down, and cried with a loud voice, Lord; lay not this sin to their charge. And when he had said this, he fell asleep."[48] With his last breath he ended his prayer, and it went up in company with his soul to the home of the saints.

As rays around the source of light
Stream upward, ere he glow in sight,
And, watching by his future flight,
Set the clear heavens on fire;
So on the King of martyrs wait
Three chosen bands, in royal state,
And all earth owns of good and great
Is gather'd in that choir. [49]

That great theologian, Jeremy Taylor, said: "Prayer is the peace of our spirit, the stillness of our thoughts, the evenness of recollection, the seat of meditation, the rest of our cares, and the calm of our tempest. Prayer is the issue of a quiet mind and untroubled thoughts, it is the daughter of charity, it is the sister of meekness." Let us not forget

---

[47] Ezra 9:5.

Similar postures were adopted by most of the heathen nations that pretended to any kind of worship, when approaching the object of their adoration; which it is highly probable they borrowed from the people of God. Kneeling was ever considered the proper posture of supplication, as it expressed humility, contrition, and subjection. If the person to whom the supplication was addressed was within reach, the supplicant caught him by the knees; for, as among the ancients, the forehead was consecrated to genius, the ear to memory, and the right hand to faith, so the knees were consecrated to mercy. Hence, those who entreated favor, fell at, and caught hold of the knees of the person whose kindness they supplicated. — Thomas Hartwell Horne, *Introduction to the Critical Study and Knowledge of the Holy Scriptures*, 1836, Vol. 2, p. 131 (hereafter 2 Horne's Intro.) For other examples see *The Bible Cyclopædia*, London, 1843, Vol. 2, p. 1074. Hereafter 2 Pict. Dict.

[48] Acts 7:60

[49] John Keble, *The Christian Year*, Oxford, 1827.

that Masonry teaches us that it is our duty to pray; and that Jesus has instructed us all to pray. "Lord, teach us how to pray."

There is much beauty and sublimity in being brought masonically to light. The morning comes forth from her chamber of repose in the starry firmament, clad in a garment of light. The sun issues from his bridal apartments with a stately step, and takes up his daily walk in the heavens. Dark clouds and the wing of the tempest once rested on the holy mountain of Sinai, but a light was kindled on its summit, which threw a moral grandeur over all creation, and imparted knowledge of the goodness, mercy, and power of God. From the smitten rock of Horeb gushed a fountain of pure and limpid waters, and from the pent-up recesses of the rock and dark caves of the mountain, it came forth like some stream of life and light, to cheer and refresh our fathers in the wilderness. The House of Jacob walked in the light of the Lord. God lifts up the light of his countenance on our dark and fallen nature. He has given us the glorious light of the gospel, to enlighten our understanding. It is destined to penetrate the darkest corners of earth, and cast its luminous rays over the be nighted nations. God calls us "to walk in his light." The gospel points us to the day-spring on high. We read of the bright and morning star; the dawn of creation; and the morning of the resurrection.

> *The Saviour lends his light and heat*
> *That crowns his holy hill;*
> *The saints, like stars, around his seat,*
> *Perform their courses still.*

John Keble, *Christian Year*

Light, in a figurative sense, signifies a clear and luminous state of things.[50] What I tell you in darkness, that

---

[50] Light, true light, in the mind is, or can be nothing else but the evidence of the truth of any proposition. — Locke on Human Understanding, book 4, ch. 19. Freemasons travel in search of spiritual light, which can be found only in the East, from whence it springs; and having attained

speak ye in *light.*[51] Therefore whatever ye have spoken in darkness shall be heard in the light; and that which ye have spoken in the ear in closets shall be proclaimed upon the house-tops.[52] Light is the source of eternal truth. Light is life, and life is the light of men.[53] And the *light* shineth in darkness; and the darkness comprehended it not.[54] Who only hath *immortality*, dwelling in the *light* which no man can approach unto; whom no man hath seen, nor can see: to whom be honor and power everlasting. Amen.[55] Light is typical of the glory of the upper skies, or that brightness which encircles the throne of Jehovah. Christ is the true light to men; the true light on earth; and the true light in heaven. Do the brethren comprehend the meaning of being brought to *light? And God said let there be light, and there was light.*[56] How glorious is the privilege of being brought to

---

its possession, they are called the "sons of light." The light of Masonry is pure, as emanating from the source of all purity and perfection; and masons, remembering that they are brought out of darkness into light, are admonished to let the light which is in them so shine before all men, that their good works may be seen, and the great fountain of that light be glorified. — Mack. Lex., p. 182.

[51] Matthew 10:27.

[52] Luke 12:3.

[53] John 1:4.

[54] John 1:5.

[55] 1 Timothy 6:16.

[56] There are two great senses in which this passage may be understood: the one literal, the other allegorical. In ordinary cases, we object to giving a typical meaning to an historical statement, unless on the express warrant of other parts of Scripture. But though in this case, we have no such warrant, yet, forasmuch as the work of the Holy Spirit upon man is described as the extracting a new creation from the ruins of the old, we can hardly think that we deal fancifully with Scripture, if, in imitation of the early writers, we suppose a designed parallel between the natural and spiritual operations. — 1 Mel. Ser., p. 365.

Dr. Oliver says that the word light in the first chapter of Genesis means material light; but allegorically it referred to the Messiah, who is hence called by Zechariah and St. Luke, Oriens, or the East, from whence light springeth. In a tropological sense, it signifies divine grace; and ana-

light—to *reason*—to *truth*—to *wisdom*, and *love*—*the love of man and the love of God!* The Lord walketh in the light of eternity—his own pure light. There shall be no night there; and they need no candle, neither light of the sun; for the Lord God giveth them light.[57] The path of the just is as the shining light, that shineth more and more unto the perfect day.[58] The way of the wicked is darkness. The lamp of the wicked shall be put out. The light of the righteous rejoiceth.[59] Ye are the light of the world.[60] There is the beautiful light of Hope, burning by the side of those greater lights, Faith and Charity, which adorn the Christian's sky and radiate his path. Oh! How beautiful was that light which succeeded the darkness which rested upon the face of the deep! How great that light which arose on that dark and gloomy hour, in which Jesus died. What a glorious light of immortality illumined Joseph's new tomb, when the Son of Man came forth from his resting-place. It radiated the tops of the sacred mountains, and threw brightness over all the land of Judea. The Lord had arisen from the sepulcher and fulfilled the law.

Before a candidate for the secrets of Masonry is brought to light, why is it we pray[61] that he may dedicate the temple of his soul to God, and devote his life to the service of his Divine Master? It is surely not a vain and idle petition, signifying nothing. And how is it, that by the se-

---

logically, the glorious and eternal light in heaven. It was not, says Bishop Hall, the light of the sun, or stars, which were not yet created; but a common brightness only, to distinguish the time, and to remedy the former confused darkness.

[57] Revelation 22:5.

[58] Proverbs 4:18.

[59] Proverbs 13:9.

[60] Matthew 5:14.

[61] If I should never pray to Him or worship Him at all, such a total omission would be equivalent to this assertion: there is no God who governs the world, to be adored. — William Wollaston, *The Religion of Nature Delineated*, London, 1750, p. 25. Hereafter *Wollaston*.

crets of our art he may be better enabled to display the beauties of holiness? Brethren, who dwell together in unity, know how good and how pleasant it is to trace out the wonderful things which are to be discerned in our rites, and read those hieroglyphics bright, which none but craftsmen ever saw. They can stand, in thought, on the mountains of Zion, where the Lord commanded the blessing, even life for evermore, and look back upon the past, and forward to the great future; back upon Paradise *lost*, and forward to Paradise *regained*.

We are informed in our monitors, that the lamb-skin is a peculiar ensign of Masonry.[62] And why is it more honorable than the star and garter? And why ought everyone to wear it with pleasure to himself and honor to the fraternity? Because it is an emblem of innocence, and he who wears it should live unspotted from the world. It is worn in remembrance of that pure and holy Being, who suffered and died for our transgressions. It undoubtedly has reference to the Lamb that was slain from the foundation of the world. Our patron, Saint John the Baptist, spoke of *"the Lamb of God."* He spoke in a metaphorical sense, and referred to the Messiah, as one to be delivered over to death—as a lamb to be sacrificed for the sins of the world.[63] The prophet Isaiah beheld afar off the Lamb that was slain, and cried out: He is brought as a lamb to the slaughter, and as a sheep before her shearers is dumb, so he openeth not his mouth.[64] The people of God are often typified in the Scriptures under the

---

[62] The white apron and gloves are emblematical. They are not worn merely as insignia of the order, hut as badges of that innate innocence and purity of soul, which freemasons should always possess. Ahi. Rez., p. 150.

[63] The Scripture account of sacrifices leads us to conclude that they were instituted by Divine appointment, immediately after the entrance of sin by the fall of Adam and Eve, to be a type or significant emblem of the great atonement or all-sufficient sacrifice of Christ. Accordingly, we find Abel, Noah, Abraham, Job, and others, offering sacrifices in the faith of the Messiah that was to be revealed; and the divine acceptance of their sacrifices is particularly recorded. — 2 Horne's Intro., p. 117.

[64] Isaiah 53:7.

name of sheep, because of their mild, patient, and inoffensive nature. The lamb skin, then, is an appropriate emblem of the innocence of Jesus, and the meekness of his followers.[65]

The lamb, too, is of a social nature, and is emblematical of brotherly love. It is easily led. But there are *"lost sheep"*[66] spoken of in the Bible—those which have wandered far from their fold and shepherd. The apostles were sent to the lost sheep of the house of Israel. Christ called his own sheep by name and leadeth them out. The sheep should always listen to the shepherd's voice, and follow him and fear no evil. Jesus three times bade Simon Peter to feed his sheep. The repetition of the command is regarded as very beautiful in the Greek dialect. Jesus was called the lamb of God, not only on account of his spotless innocence, but in allusion to the lamb sacrificed for the Passover—he being the true Paschal Lamb, slain from the foundation of the world.

But the lamb-skin may be intended to remind us of one who suffered in being slain. It speaks of one that bled and died. And it behooved Christ to suffer. "The Messiah shall be cut off, said Daniel—chap. ix. 26—.They shall look on me, whom they have pierced."[67] Many were the types and prophecies of the sufferings of Jesus. The lamb-skin is, then, not only an emblem of innocence, but an emblem of suffering innocence. It is intended to remind us of that purity of life and conduct, which is so essentially necessary to gain admission into the celestial lodge above. We should always bear in affectionate remembrance, that pure Lamb

---

[65] The sheep, on account of its mild, inoffensive, and patient character, is used in Scripture to typify the people of God. — 2 Pict. Dict., p. 1228.

[66] The "lost sheep" is a particularly appropriate and beautiful simile, for an erring human being; for it is well known that a strayed sheep never finds its own way back. — 2 Pict. Dict., p. 1228.

[67] Zachary 12:10

of God, whose blood was shed to save a ruined and an apostate world.[68]

The working tools of an Entered Apprentice Mason are moral instruments. They are denominated the twenty-four inch gauge and common gavel. There is something quite appropriate in presenting a young operative in speculative science with those necessary instruments of his profession. With them he is directed to commence his moral work. If the operative mason, with the twenty four inch gauge, lays off his work, the free and accepted Mason applies it to a more noble purpose, that of judiciously dividing his time. It is an instrument divided into twenty-four equal parts, emblematical of the twenty-four hours of the day, and which are subdivided into three equal parts, whereby are found eight hours for the service of God, and a distressed worthy brother; eight for our usual vocations; and eight for refreshment and sleep.[69]

The common gavel is used in a moral sense, for the purpose of divesting our hearts and consciences of the vices and superfluities of life; to break off the rough edges of our evil dispositions, the better to prepare our souls for the Master Builder's use, and make them living stones for that glorious temple, which rests on the everlasting hill of eternity.

In these emblematical instruments[70] will be found the first rule for the government of our social and moral con-

---

[68] Masons, as one of their principles, profess innocence; they put on the white apparel, as an emblem of that character, which bespeaks purity of soul. — Ahi. Rez., p. 151. He that overcometh, the same shall be clothed in while raiment; and I will not blot out his name out of the book of life, but I will confess his name before my Father, and before his angels — Rev. iii. 5. White garments were not only an emblem of purity, and being in the favor of God; but also, as being worn on festival occasions, were tokens of joy and pleasure. — Horne's Intro., Sym. Index.

[69] Ahi. Rez., p. 146.

[70] Figurative language is very common in the Scriptures. They abound with

duct. In Masonic ethics or moral philosophy, a moral quality in human action is taken for granted. In directing the Entered Apprentice to divest his mind and conscience of the vices and superfluities of life, Masonry draws a line of distinction between good and evil—right and wrong. It teaches not only this distinction, but that the consequences of an evil action are very different from those of a good action; for it is requisite to *prepare* our souls as living stones for God's spiritual building. In directing us in the proper use of the gauge and gavel, it is considered that we are every way capable of perceiving the advantages of leading a moral life, and taking the necessary means to accomplish the end for which we were created. They must be used voluntarily and understandingly. Our nature is full of evil propensities and evil passions. But we are all accountable beings, and are bound to obey the moral law, or suffer the penalties of that law. Even long-neglected conscience will often admonish us of our duty to God; and if we would only listen to its monitorial voice, we would endeavor to divest ourselves of those pollutions which must necessarily impair the moral constitution.

Oh! How many thousands of workmen might be profitably employed in the vast quarry of our ruined nature! But how many blocks of thought are never taken even from their rude and natural state, which might have become polished ashlars, and been made ready for the building—for that house not made with hands eternal in the heavens. The rough ashlar is emblematical of our condition by nature—of our rude and ruined state—which must needs be polished and restored through our own endeavors and the blessing of God. A perfect ashlar is a stone made ready by the *hands of the workman*. And thus we are taught that every man has it in his power to shape his own destiny, being a, *free agent* and an accountable being. By diligence and labor he may *prepare* himself for the temple above. Every stone,

---

the most beautiful imagery. The discourses of our Savior are highly figurative.

before it can be taken thither, and laid in the blood of the Lamb, must be made ready.

Sometimes the speculative Master is represented as the builder of a spiritual edifice, and as one guided in his work by the rules and designs laid down by the Supreme Architect in the great books of nature and revelation, which constitute our moral and Masonic trestle-board. How beautiful and consistent are all the emblems and symbols of the Order! They all harmonize and agree with one another. They conflict in nothing. They instruct us in our social, moral, and religious duties. They inform us of the necessity and beauty of leading a godly, righteous, and sober life. Masonry has dedicated the Holy Bible to God.[71] It is his inestimable gift to man. It is the rule of our faith, and the only safe guide of our conduct. It reveals the true religion, and is the great light which would guide us to the city of our God.

One of the symbols in the third section of the chart of the Entered Apprentice is the Holy Bible, represented as being opened at the 133rd psalm of David, with the square and compasses resting thereon. That psalm contains a song of the degrees of David, and tells us of the benefit to be derived from the communion of saints. It is the adopted song of the Mason. It often sounded along the arches of the terrestrial sanctuary. Its sweet cadences and swelling notes made glad the city of the Lord, and resounded among the hills of Judea. It is still heard in our lodges: "Behold, how good and how pleasant it is for brethren to dwell together in unity! It is like the precious ointment upon the head, that ran down upon the beard, even Aaron's beard: that went down to the skirts of his garments; as the dew of Hermon, and as the dew that descended upon the mountains of Zion: for there the Lord commanded the blessing, even life for evermore."[72] And why is this psalm rehearsed

---

71 The Bible may be compared to a temple of wisdom, which should be dedicated to its author or builder, who is God.

72 Maundrell, travelling near Mount Hermon, in the year 1697, says: "We

during the ceremony of initiation? To answer this question, we should refer to the words of the psalm, and ascertain their meaning. We are told of the goodness and pleasure of those who dwell together in unity. The words breathe into our souls that spirit of friendship and brotherly love, which unites us into "a sacred band or society of friends, among whom no contention should ever arise, but that noble contention of who can best work and best agree." That psalm teaches us the doctrine of the communion of spirits, and how they dwell together in unity. It directs us to another and better land, where saints and angels live. It communicates the idea of a spiritual agency, or spiritual influences—of the existence of the cherubim and seraphim. It reminds us, too, of the mysterious unity of the Godhead. They agree, Three in One, and One in Three. There is a sublime picture of unity drawn by the inspired Job. He tells us of a time when the stars sang together—when "every one of them sang, and sang at the same time; and for the same reason, and the same song. There was one heart only in Heaven, and one voice." In another part of Scripture, we read of the harmony which reigns in that holy land. An angel appeared "to the shepherds at Bethlehem, and said, "Behold, I bring you good tidings of great joy, for unto you is born this day a Saviour." Suddenly, on the delivery of the message, "there was with the angel a multitude of the heavenly host, praising God." Again, we read of "the voice of much people in Heaven, saying, Alleluia;" others of the shining ranks take up the theme, and sing Alleluia, and then comes the swelling chorus of the skies: "Alleluia, for the Lord God Omnipotent reigneth."[73]

> *What sudden blaze of song*
> *Spreads o'er the expanse of heaven!*

---

were instructed, by experience, what the Psalmist means by the dew of Hermon, our tents being as wet with it as if it had rained all night." — 2 Horne's Intro., p. 25, note 3.

[73] Rev. Charles Bradley, *Practical Sermons*, New York, 1846, p. 72. Hereafter *2 Brad. Ser.* See also, Revelation 19:6.

In waves of light it thrills along,
Th' angelic signal given—
"Glory to God!" from yonder central fire
Flows out the echoing lay beyond the starry choir;
Like circles widening round
Upon a clear blue river,
Orb after orb, the wondrous sound
Is echoed on for ever:
"Glory to God on high, on earth be peace
And love toward men of love—salvation and release."

John Keble, *Christian Year*

Unity of sentiment and feeling among the fraternity is essentially necessary to social and intellectual pleasure. Without it, our institution would not long stand; but with it, the edifice rests upon an enduring basis. There is a spirit of union even in the signs, words, types, and emblems of the Order; and it diffuses itself throughout our social body, "like the precious ointment upon the head, that ran down upon the beard, even Aaron's beard, that went down to the skirts of his garments."

On the authority, then, of the Holy Bible, we are assured that there are pure and invisible agencies continually walking up and down this ruined segment of God's universe.[74] Their quiet steppings are in and about the sanctuary of the soul, and their calls are often responded to in the deep and low warnings of conscience. Notwithstanding God has afforded a full revelation of his mercy, and has pointed out clearly the way that leads to everlasting peace, we believe that he often gives his angels charge over us, and that these heavenly visitants find great delight in raising our minds to the source of truth. They would fix our thoughts on things eternal and the value of undying souls, which may become burning spirits around the throne, and forever dwell with them in unity.

---

[74] 1 Mel. Ser., p. 439, where this doctrine is ably sustained.

If, then, the 133rd psalm of David has become embodied in our lectures, and forms an essential part of the Entered Apprentice's degree, it follows that Masonry recognizes the doctrine of the communion of saints, and consequently, the existence of immortal beings. It would, also, allure our minds to the consideration of that *thrice illustrious* destiny, which constitutes the inheritance of the righteous, and fill us with an eager desire to partake of those pure enjoyments in the world of happy spirits. It indicates the unity of that bright companionship on high, and that mysterious brotherhood, who are continually giving *signs* of joy and *tokens* of love, and who ever de light to pronounce, in angelic accents, the name of the *omnificent God.* Then, how wisely would brethren act, were they to reflect more on the holy rites they administer, and the solemn ceremonies through which they pass, in the mystic temple of our worship!

On the tracing board is represented a mountain, on which are grouped or assembled a mystic band of *nine* faithful brethren. Our globe presents an undulating surface, consisting of mountains and valleys. "There are some mountains," says the eloquent Headley, "standing on this sphere of ours, that seem almost conscious beings; and if they would but speak and tell what they have seen and felt, the traveler who pauses at their base would tremble with awe and alarm; "And there are some mountains, which are consecrated in the traditional annals of the fraternity of Masons, and which will claim our special notice, when we come to speak of those strange scenes which were enacted in and about Jerusalem. For some wise, but inscrutable reason, the Almighty selected the summits of mountains[75] for the grandest displays of his mercy and power. On Sinai he thundered the law. The prophet Isaiah declared, that it should come to pass in the last days, that the mountain of

---

[75] The ancients celebrated worship on mountains and in groves, but it was prohibited when worship became idolatrous. — Emanuel Swedenborg, *Heavenly Arcana*, Boston, 1843, p. 47, n. 2722. Hereafter *Heav. Arc.* See also 2 Horne's Intro., p. 101.

the Lord's house shall be established in the top of the mountains, and shall be exalted above the hills; and all nations shall flow unto it.[76] Again: They shall not hurt in all my holy mountain.[77] Here the holy mountain evidently means the church of Christ in that coming day, "When the earth shall be full of the knowledge of the Lord." The prophet Daniel spoke of the stone that smote the image, and became a great mountain and filled the whole earth. It was on Mount Carmel that the prophet Elijah stood before Ahab and a mighty congregation of men, and fearlessly proclaimed: "How long halt ye between two opinions? If the Lord be God, follow him; but if Baal, then follow him." And then was witnessed an awful and grand display of Divine triumph over an idolatrous priesthood; and the followers of Baal were overwhelmed and utterly confounded. Baal could not answer the vain appeals and ceremonies of his blind disciples. But the Lord God answered his holy prophet; for the celestial fire descended and consumed the burnt sacrifice, and the wood, and the stones, and the dust, and licked up the water that was in the trench. And when all the people saw it, they fell on their faces: and they said, "The Lord, he is the God; the Lord, he is the God".[78] It was on the brow of a mount that Christ wept over Jerusalem, and on the mount he delivered his memorable sermon, which shall live after the hills are consumed. The judgment fire shall distil the curse from the ground. Then the new earth will appear, and the beautiful images of that sermon will be seen in all the land.

The sepulchral monuments of the great have often been erected on hills and mountains. The ancient temple arose, in all its pride and magnificence, on Mount Moriah, which is an intrinsic part of the Mount of Crucifixion. And our most interesting Masonic legends consist of incidents

---

[76] Isaiah 2:2.

[77] Isaiah 11:9.

[78] 1 Kings 18:38-39.

which occurred on that mountain which was baptized with the costliest blood, and fertilized with imperial gore. It stands shielded, and, as it were, forever protected by a whole amphitheatre of mountains, which rise up before it, sublimely typifying the Christian Church, which will ever defy the storms of persecution and tempests, raised by evil spirits, when they shall wander from the land of perdition. God is our refuge and strength, a very present help in trouble. Therefore will not we fear, though the earth be removed, and though the mountains be carried into the midst of the sea.[79]

---

[79] Psalms 46:1-2.

LECTURE III.
Wisdom, Strength and Beauty

Our institution is said to be supported by Wisdom, Strength, and Beauty. Its dimensions are unlimited, and its covering no less than the canopy of heaven.[80]

And he dreamed, and behold a ladder set up on the earth, and the top of it reached to heaven: and behold the angels of God ascending and descending on it.[81]

There is a ladder set up on the ground, but its top reaches to the summit of the mountain and to the gate of the city. Are you willing to go up, to leave the prison and to seek the palace?[82]

The Gentiles shall come to thy light, and kings to the brightness of thy rising.[83]

The globe shall be canopied by its far-spreading boughs.[84]

---

[80] Ahi. Rez., p. 139.

[81] Genesis 28:12.

[82] 1 Mel. Ser., p. 286.

[83] Isaiah 60:3.

[84] 1 Mel. Ser., p. 220.

The design of introducing scriptural passages is to furnish a scriptural defense of our institution, by showing that its language or ritual corresponds with the revealed word of God. The meaning of the Masonic emblems, the Great Light so fully explains, that we are forced to believe that the founders of the Order, whoever they were, must have been familiar with the language and doctrines of the Bible. It is confidently believed, that the truths of Freemasonry will be found to harmonize perfectly with those of revealed religion. There is this difference between them, however: the word of life teaches plainly, what Freemasonry often leaves to be discovered through study and investigation. But so remarkable is their correspondence that it is obvious that the Bible is the source of Masonic lore, or the strong foundation on which rests our moral edifice, which is said to be supported by "Wisdom, Strength, and Beauty.

In the language of our monitors, "it is necessary that there should be wisdom to contrive, strength to support, and beauty to adorn all great and important undertakings." And what great and important undertakings are here referred to? We may judge correctly of the force or proper construction of language, when it is viewed in connection with the subject matter, or in reference to other things of known signification with which it is associated. Were it said that the Christian church was supported by wisdom, strength, and beauty; there would be an appositeness in the remark, which would be observed by everyone. For, what undertaking is so great and so important, as that of rearing a moral temple on the ruins of our ancient nature? What so wise as the plan of redemption? What so strong as its firm foundations; and what so beautiful as the design of the building? Its plan is, indeed, wisdom; its foundation, strength; and its superstructure, beauty. The church militant and the church triumphant are both upheld and supported by a *Triune God*.

It will not appear difficult to determine the symbolical meaning of the supports of a lodge, which extend from east to west, and between north and south; whose covering is no less than a clouded canopy or starry-decked heaven; whose furniture is the Holy Bible, square and compasses; and whose ornaments are the Mosaic pavement,[85] the indented tessel, and blazing star. The pillars of Wisdom, Strength, and Beauty may be regarded as being symbolical of the Divine attributes. They that be *wise* shall shine as the brightness of the firmament.[86] The fear of the Lord is wisdom.[87] Get wisdom, get understanding.[88] How much better is it to get wisdom than gold.[89] He that getteth wisdom loveth his own soul.[90] Buy wisdom, and instruction, and understanding.[91] The fear of the Lord is the beginning of wisdom.[92] Fools die for want of wisdom.[93] Wisdom that is from above is pure, peaceable, and gentle.[94] St. John the

---

[85] As the steps of man are trod in the various and uncertain incidents of life—as our days are checkered with a strange contrariety of events— and our passage through this existence, though sometimes attended with prosperous circumstances, is often beset with a multitude of evils, hence is the lodge furnished with Mosaic work, to remind us of the precariousness of our state on earth. To-day our feet tread in prosperity—to-morrow we totter on the uneven paths of weakness, temptation, and adversity. Whilst this emblem is before us, we are instructed to boast of nothing, to have compassion, and give aid to those who are in adversity ; to walk uprightly and with humility; for such is this existence, that there is no station in which pride can be stably founded—all men, in birth and in the grave, are on a level. Whilst we tread on this Mosaic work, let our ideas return to the original which it copies; and let every Mason act as the dictates of reason prompt him, to live in brotherly love. — Ahi. Rez., p. 147, note.

[86] Daniel 12:3

[87] Job 28:28.

[88] Proverbs 4:5.

[89] Proverbs 16:16.

[90] Proverbs 19:8.

[91] Proverbs 23:23.

[92] Proverbs 9:10.

[93] Proverbs 10:21.

[94] James 3:17.

Evangelist heard the voice of many angels round about the throne saying, with a loud voice, Worthy is the Lamb that was slain to receive *power*, and *riches*, and *wisdom*, and *strength*, and *honor*, and *glory*.[95] The meaning of this passage is plain: *Wisdom* is ascribed to the Lamb of God on account of his *omniscience*, and *strength* is ascribed to him on account of his *omnipotence*.[96] Wisdom from above is that wisdom which flows from God, or that religion which was purchased by the precious blood of Jesus. God is *wisdom*, for he is *omniscient*.

But God is *strength* also. He is *omnipotent*. The Lord is my God, my *strength*, said David, praising his name.[97] The Lord is my *strength* and my shield.[98] The Lord is my *strength* and song, and is become my salvation.[99] It is God that girdeth me with *strength*.[100] The Lord is the *strength* of my life.[101] The Lord will give *strength* unto his people.[102] Ascribe ye *strength* unto God.[103] God is the *strength* of my heart.[104] The Lord is clothed with *strength*.[105] *Strength* and *Beauty* are in his sanctuary.[106] In the Lord Jehovah is everlasting *strength*.[107] With him is *wisdom*, and strength.[108] Then in Jah,

---

[95] Revelation 5:12.

[96] Clarke's Com. Rev. 5:12.

[97] Psalms 18:2.

[98] Psalms 28:7.

[99] Psalms 118:14.

[100] Psalms 18:32.

[101] Psalms 27:1.

[102] Psalms 29:11.

[103] Psalms 68:34.

[104] Psalms 73:26.

[105] Psalms 93:1.

[106] Psalms 96:6.

[107] Isaiah 26:4.

[108] Job 12:13-16.

Jehovah, is everlasting *strength*, power, and omnipotence. He is the fountain of all power. Commentators inform us that the Hebrew words translated *everlasting strength*, mean in the original text the *rock of ages*, which they say was Christ.

But the Lord is *beauty*. His beauty may be seen in all his works. In the landscape, and on the mountain; in the fields and forests; in the rivers, on the lakes, and on the seas; in the grass and flowers; in the firmament, adorned with stars; in the laws of nature; in the delicate workman ship of man; in the machinery of God's moral government; in his mercy and goodness; in the plan of salvation; in his sufferings; in his death, and resurrection, and ascension. He sitteth in the *south, which is at the right hand of the throne.*[109] Son of man, set thy face toward the south, and drop *thy word* toward the south.[110] Then let us worship the Lord in the beauty of holiness. David desired to dwell in the house of the Lord all the days of his life, to behold the *beauty* of the Lord, and to inquire in his temple.[111] So shall the king greatly desire thy *beauty*: for he is thy Lord; and worship thou him.[112] He is called the King in his *beauty.*[113] Then, the Lord is a pillar of wisdom, a pillar of strength, and a pillar of beauty. He is wise, strong, and beautiful. He is wise, for he is omniscient; he is strong, for he is omnipotent; he is beautiful, for he is omnipresent in mercy, goodness, and truth.

The pillars of wisdom, strength, and beauty are thus explained by an eminent Mason and divine: The plan of

---

[109] There were three words in the Hebrew used to signify south. One of these words literally meant, "in the presence of," and one signified that which lies to the right hand. The meaning of the other is uncertain — Thomas Broughton, *Historical Dictionary of all Religions*, London, 1741, South. Hereafter Eccl. Dict.

[110] Ezekiel 20:46. Judaea lay to the south of Chaldea, where the prophet Ezekiel stood. — 2 Home's Intro., General Index.

[111] Psalms 27:4.

[112] Psalms 45:11.

[113] Isaiah 33:17.

Solomon's temple was the effect of wisdom derived from above; the execution, the application of strength; and its curious and rich workmanship, was effected by the application of beauty, derived from a union of two countries, in the person of an expert architect named Hiram."[114] These pillars, the same author thinks, bear a reference to an edifice of much greater sublimity and beauty than the temple. Our ancient brethren illustrated these pillars in the following manner: The mighty pillars on which Masonry is founded, are those whose base is *wisdom*, whose shaft is *strength*, and whose chapter is *beauty*. The *wisdom* is that which descends from above; and is first pure, then peaceable, gentle, and easy to be entreated; full of mercy and good fruits; without partiality, and without hypocrisy. The *strength* is that which depends on the living God, who resisteth the mighty, and scattereth the proud in the imagination of their hearts; who giveth us power to resist and to escape all temptations, and to subdue all evil appetites. A *strength* which is a refuge to the distressed. A bond of unity and love amongst brethren, and of peace and quiet in our own hearts. Our *beauty* is such as adorns all our actions with *holiness*; is hewn out of the rock which is Christ, and raised upright by the plumb of the gospel; squared and leveled to the horizontal of God's will in the holy lodge of St. John; and such as become the temple whose maker and builder is God.[115]

But we would bid the brethren to look on the church of God. Its principal supports are wisdom, strength, and beauty. It was planned by the omniscient Jehovah, established for ever by his omnipotent hand, and adorned with beauty by our omnipresent Savior, who crowned its pillars with emblems of *unity*, *peace*, and *plenty*. The church is the temple of the Lord. Jesus is the builder. The Almighty determined in a council of the Trinity that his only begotten

---

[114] 1 Ol. Land., p. 155.

[115] 1 Ol. Land., p. 155, note 4.

Son should be the builder, and bear the glory. There is wisdom, strength, and beauty in its wonderful proportions. And it will endure forever. It is a spiritual, and, therefore, an immortal edifice. How strong its foundation, bow wise its plan, how beautiful the church of the first-born![116] We survey the material universe of God, and behold its wisdom; we gaze on the splendid canopy of the heavens, which is strong and lofty; on the firmament, that azure roof of the temple of nature, made beautiful with suns and stars; but the church of our Lord and Master is more glorious in wisdom, and more excellent in strength and beauty.

The universality of Masonry should remind us of that time when prophecy will be fulfilled, and all shall know God, from the least even unto the greatest. As in every clime Free Masons may be found, so in every land will the song of redemption be heard. Look on that clouded canopy, adorned with a fret-work of mystic stars, where we are told all good Masons expect to arrive at last, by the aid of the theological ladder,[117] which Jacob in his vision saw, reaching from earth to heaven. The rounds of that ladder are called Faith, Hope, and Charity, to which we must cling tenaciously, if we would reach the skies. The Mason is

---

[116] Does beauty make a building glorious, a noble plan and excellent workmanship? O what so beautiful as the church of the first-born? What so perfect as its salvation and happiness? — 2 Brad. Ser. p. 265; D'Oyly and Mant's Com., Zechariah 6:13; 1 Corinthians 3:16; 2 Corinthians 6:16; 1 Peter 2:5.

[117] There is a real visible ladder, said Hume, whose foot, though placed on the earth among the lowest of the creation, yet leads us, by steps, in contemplation of created things, up to God, the invisible creator of all things — Vide 1 Ol. Land., p. 273, note. The rounds of the Masonic ladder are named, and they are Faith, Hope, and Charity: because Masonry is founded upon faith in God, hope of immortality and charity to all mankind. But of these the greatest is charity; for faith ends in sight, hope terminates in fruition, but charity extends beyond the grave. It is by the practice of these virtues that the Mason expects to find access to Him who is the subject of faith, the object of hope, and the eternal fountain of charity. —Mack. Lex., p. 150.

taught to have faith in God, hope in immortality, and charity for all mankind. Let the eye rest on the tracing-board of the degree of Entered Apprentice, and there will be seen an emblem of Jacob's ladder resting on the *brow of a mount* and extending to heaven. If it be emblematical of that which Jacob in his vision beheld, whatever will be found typical in Jacob's dream will be also found in the emblematical ladder. And he dreamed, and behold a ladder set up on the earth, and the top of it reached to heaven: and behold the angels of God ascending and descending on it. And Jacob awaked out of his sleep, and he said: Surely the Lord is in this place; and I knew it not. And he was afraid, and said, how dreadful is this place! This is none other but the house of God, and this is the gate of heaven.[118]

It is important to bear particularly in mind the great fact connected with the life and history of Jacob. It constitutes an essential link in the chain of testimony. He was the depositary of the heavenly promises, and through him was the genealogy of the Messiah to be traced: "In thee and in thy seed shall all the families of the earth be blessed." From his loins was to spring a great and merciful Deliverer. We are then prepared to consider of the nature of the vision. We cannot question its reality. The fact is taken for granted. And why did God visit the wanderer in his sleep? Why disturb the repose of his wearied limbs? The answer will be found in the object of the vision. It was emblematic of a great truth, which the Almighty deemed important for Jacob to know. It was a beautiful, and, we may also add, a sublime representation of the communication which would be opened between earth and sky—a symbolical revelation

---

[118] Genesis 28:12-17. The vision of Jacob has afforded a variety of notions in regard to its signification. Dr. Clarke thought that its primary design was to point out the providence of God; secondly, the intercourse between heaven and earth, and the connection of both worlds, by the means of angelic ministry; thirdly, it was probably a type of Christ, in whom both worlds meet, and in whom the Divine and human nature are conjoined. — Clarke's Com. Gen. 28:12, and D'Oyly and Mant's Com. on same verse.

of the means of salvation, and of the providence of God.[119] And when we observe, says an eminent scholar and divine, that one great object of the celestial manifestation was the renewing with Jacob the promise made to Abraham and Isaac, we will be quite prepared to expect in the vision a revelation of the Messiah himself. Jacob had just secured the distinction of being the progenitor of Christ; and God is about to assure him, in the words of the original covenant with his fathers, that in his seed should all the nations of the earth be blessed. How natural, then, that some intelligence should be communicated in regard of the Christ; so that while the patriarch knew himself the depositary of that grand promise in which the whole world had an interest, he might also know, so far as consisted with an introductory dispensation, what the blessings were which the promise insured.[120] In this view, all the authorities agree. Then, the ladder which Jacob saw in his vision was typical of the Messiah, by and through whom alone can we ascend into glory.[121] By clinging to the rounds of the ladder, we may climb to a home on high. The smiling virtues of the gospel are faith,[122] hope, and charity. Without these, no man can be called a true Christian. Without them, he has no well-founded assurance of being finally saved.

It has been thought, and very reasonably, too, that Christ referred to the ladder of Jacob in the conversation he held with Nathanael:[123] "Verily, verily, I say unto you,

---

[119] 2 Brad. Ser., p. 100; D'Oyly and Mant's Com. Gen. 28:12.

[120] Mel. Ser., p. 284.

[121] The ladder was set up on the earth, and the top of it reached to heaven; for God was manifest in the flesh, and in Him dwelt all the fullness of the Godhead bodily. Nothing could be a more expressive emblem of the incarnation and its effects. Jesus Christ is the grand connecting medium between heaven and earth, and between God and man. — Clarke's Com. Gen. 28:13.

[122] In many of the transatlantic lodges, faith is represented by an emblem of a *cross*, or the form of a female bearing the same emblem.

[123] Vide 1 Mel. Ser., p. 280, Clarke's Com., and D'Oyly and Mant's Com.

hereafter you shall see heaven open, and the angels of God ascending and descending upon the Son of man." "Here," says Melvill, "the Redeemer appears to identify himself, as the Son of man, with the ladder: the angels are to ascend and descend on the one even as they did on the other." Then, it appears that Jacob's ladder symbolically conveyed the idea of a coming Savior, and the rounds of the ladder the means by which a brilliant intercourse is kept up between earth and heaven. It is worthy of remark, that the revelations which the Almighty made of himself or his purposes to our ancient fathers, were intended not only for them, but for all generations. Did he give the law to Moses on Mount Sinai, amidst the confused noise of the elements? For posterity were the tables of the law prepared, and the commandments promulgated amid the thunders of Sinai. Did Jehovah descend into the olden temple and dwell beneath the wings of the cherubim? For us did the Divine Presence rest on the mercy-seat. The All-seeing Eye of God, which looked down upon the exile reposing on a rock, was at the same moment fixed upon the solitary village of Bethlehem and the young child sleeping in the manger, "who was to reign over the house of Jacob forever." The Almighty had already commissioned the angel to deliver to the shepherds abiding in the field good tidings of great joy. His eye, as he stood above Jacob's ladder, was fixed on a far-off age.

It is thought, therefore, that the emblematical ladder, which adorns the Masonic chart, communicates the same useful lessons, or typifies the same events as did Jacob's ladder. It was emblematic of an all-protecting Providence and our great Deliverer;[124] and teaches the thoughtful

---

Gen. 28:12.

[124] This ladder, according to the sense of the best interpreters, is an emblem of Divine Providence, which governs all things. Its being set up on the earth denotes the steadiness of Providence, which nothing can unsettle: its reaching up to heaven signifies that it extends over all things: the several steps of the ladder are the motion and action of Providence: the angels going up and down show that they are the great ministers of

craftsman a lively sense of God's eternal presence. May he not well exclaim when his eye rests upon the Masonic ladder, in the language of Jacob: "Surely, the Lord is in this place, and I knew it not."

The life of a Mason, speaking in reference to the ceremonies through which he passes and the degrees he takes, is truly an eventful one. If God led Jacob through many trying and varied scenes, dark and mysterious are the ways which lead to the secret apartments of our mystic temple. If Jacob was made afraid, who did not tremble when he was initiated into the solemn rites of our Order, or was led by a way he knew not. But Jacob had no cause to fear, nor has he who enters into a lodge in search of its mysteries. There are none to threaten or alarm. No dark revels or midnight orgies are practiced in a lodge. No words of wrath or condemnation are heard, and no inquisitorial questions asked. The candidate hears of peace, brotherly love, relief, and truth. He is taught to reverence God's holy name, and never to mention it but with that reverential awe which is due from a creature to his Creator—to implore his aid in all laudable undertakings, and esteem him as the chief good. From God alone all blessings flow, and through him mercy and grace descend, like angels from their home of glory. We are instructed to fix our hopes on high, and rely on God; to be of good cheer, and try to climb the ladder whose "top is in the utmost heavens: it rests on the throne of Jehovah, but its foot stands on the earth; and not in some inaccessible mountain of it, but here by our side."[125] The angels are beckoning us all to our native skies. Would that the response could go up: "*We come—we come. Your call shall be obeyed. Your voices animate us as they steal down in solemn and beautiful cadence. We will share with you the throne and the dia-*

Providence, always employed in the preservation of the just: their ascending, represents their going up to receive Divine commands; and their descending, their coming down upon earth to execute them. — D'Oyly and Mant's Com., Genesis 28:12.

[125] 2 Brad. Ser., p. 103.

dem."[126] It has been stated that the Mosaic pavement, indented tessel,[127] and blazing star, constitute the furniture of a regular and constitutional lodge. The Mosaic pavement is emblematical of human life, checkered with good and evil. But it possesses a signification far more sacred. It is the opinion of an enlightened English Mason that it referred to the doctrine of man's redemption, which pervades the whole system of Masonry: We call it Mosaic, said he, because it was used by Moses in the floor of the tabernacle; but for what reason did Moses adopt it? My opinion is that it was in allusion to the redemption of the Israelites from their bondage, by the pillar of fire on the one side, and the pillar of cloud on the other; or, in other words, *light* and *darkness*. *Light*, and thereby *salvation* to the then church of God; and darkness and destruction to her enemies. A beautiful type of the gospel, which, when it appeared as a light to lighten the Gentiles, was to the Jews a stumbling-block, like the cloudy pillar; but to believers, the now true church of Christ, the power of God unto salvation, as was the pillar of fire. It is but reasonable, then, to suppose, that Moses adopted the checkered pavement in the tabernacle with the same view that Solomon adopted the two pillars in the porch way of the temple, as a memorial to the children of Israel of the happy deliverance of their forefathers from Egyptian bondage by the memorable pillar of fire and cloud, or light and darkness; which was evidently a type of human redemption through that Being who had *two* natures, Divine and human, as opposite as the light and darkness of the Mosaic pavement.[128] This pavement, we are informed, is a representation of the ground floor of King Solomon's temple; the indented tessel, that beautiful tessellated border which surrounded it; and the Hazing star in the centre is commemorative of the star which appeared to

---

[126] 1 Mel. Ser., 284.

[127] The indented tessel is the ornamented border which surrounds the Mosaic pavement. — Mack. Lex., p. 144.

[128] 2 Ol. Land., p. 155, note 40.

guide the wise men of the East to the place of our Savior's nativity.[129] Here, then, is a clear recognition by Christian Masons of that Divine Being, by and through whom we can alone hope for eternal life and light. Since the days of the Messiah, the emblematical character of the blazing star has been clearly perceived and fully recognized. Genuine Masonry has at no time taught any false doctrine. The tradition of the Order is a pure channel of communication. Masonic knowledge is transmitted orally from generation to generation. Our landmarks are those of truth. The waves of time can never efface them. The rains may descend, and the floods beat upon them, but they will only deepen the lines and make more visible the signs and tokens of wisdom. As ages roll on, and the nearer the fullness of time approaches, the truth will become more distinct, and men will more willingly acknowledge the sublime principles we teach. The time has already come when our bright craftsmen seem determined to examine every landmark and tradition, and search for every hidden meaning in the emblems of the institution. Many are gazing on our obscure firmament, like some moral astronomers, eager for discovery, and eyeing its splendid group of stars. A misty cloud hangs about our Masonic canopy, but there is a star-lit rainbow in it.

---

[129] The star in the East some have affirmed to have been of the same nature with those that have their proper place and motion in the celestial orbs; but although that omnipotent God, that made the sun stand still at one time and go back at another, cannot be denied to have been able to have commanded any of the stars upon such a message and employment, yet that he actually did so, is not necessary for us here to assert, there being otherwise sufficient reasons to persuade us that this was not a real star of the same kind with those heavenly bodies, but only a bright meteor, formed by the immediate power of God into the resemblance and similitude of a star, and so by a singular act of his providence, used and directed for the great purpose of heralding the Messiah. — Robert South, *Sermons Preached upon Several Occasions*, London, 1744, Vol. 4, p. 387 (hereafter *South's Ser.*); 1 Brad. Ser., p. 173.

Moses has declared that stars, from the very earliest period, have been *for signs and for seasons.*[130] There are the eleven stars, which Joseph beheld in his dream. There is the star of wormwood. Stars are often used as symbols of eminent persons: I will give him the morning star.[131] At the dawn of creation the morning stars sang together, and all the sons of God shouted for joy.[132] This transaction occurred in heaven. Earth was not the scene of such happiness and joy. Those *morning stars* were probably angels,[133] and other bright beings which existed long before this world was made, or the Spirit brooded upon the waters. They dwelt around and about the throne, before light arose upon the bosom of darkness. They were the sons of God, and they worshipped him forever. What myriads of stars and suns, angelic beings, made up the bright hosts of heaven, the shining population of the skies. How many of those morning stars sang for joy at the creation! Those angels of beauty and light beheld the great work go on beneath the exquisite skill and genius of the Divine Architect. They were present when its foundations were laid, and obtained an audience of the Master's work.

> *Him all his train*
> *Followed in bright procession, to behold*
> *Creation and the wonders of his might.*

> Milton, *Paradise Lost 7.221-723*

---

[130] There is a tradition mentioned by Plutarch that the stars of Castor and Pollux appeared on each side of the helm of Lysander's ship, when he first set out against the Athenians. — John & William Langhorne, *Plutarch's Lives*, Worcester, 1804, Vol. 2, p. 334. Hereafter *2 Plutarch's Lives.*

[131] Revelation 2:28.

[132] Job 38:7.

[133] That the morning stars meant holy angels — See D'Oyly and Mant's Com., Job 38:7. We read in Daniel, that they that be wise shall shine as the brightness of the firmament; and they that turn many to righteousness as the stars forever and ever — Daniel 12:3. St. Paul says one star differeth from another star in glory — 1 Corinthians 15:41.

They beheld it ascend in all its beautiful and sublime proportions. They looked with admiration on its pillars of Wisdom, Strength, and Beauty. They saw it completed, and holy were their rejoicings; for when the head-stone of the splendid Temple was brought forth, all the sons of God shouted for joy.

Masonry celebrates the creation of the world. An account of it is the first piece of history to which the attention is directed. We are reminded of the verity of the history, while a great moral truth is elicited from it. The Mason may dwell with delight on that lovely creation which takes place in the new-born soul, when the Holy Spirit moves upon the depths of its original pollution. Oh! Methinks there are songs in heaven at such new and moral creation— the new birth of the inner man. Do not saints and angels sing together, and all the sons of God shout for joy over a redeemed sinner? Answer me, ye spirits who dwell in light inaccessible! Shine, ye stars of glory upon our benighted souls! There is a Star of stars! It is a Star in the East, which will lead us to the garden and to the temple. It is the Star of Bethlehem—our blazing star—the Star of Jesus. It shines in the midst of the Mosaic pavement—in the midst of human life, checkered as that life is with good and evil. It is an emblem of mercy. It has shone down on all time and all generations: And, lo, the star, which they saw in the east, went before them, till it came and stood over where the young child was.[134] It was the same star which was spoken of by Balaam the prophet:[135]

---

[134] Matthew 2:9.

[135] A star shone in heaven, above all other stars; and its light was incomprehensible; and its novelty struck terror. All the rest of the stars, with the sun and moon, were the chorus of this star; and that sent forth its light above all. And there was trouble when this novelty came, so unlike to all the others. Hence all (the power of) magic was destroyed: ignorance was taken away; the old kingdom was abolished; God being manifest in the form of a man, for the renewal of eternal life. Thence began what God had prepared. — Epistle of Ignatius, see William R. Whittingham, *Epistles of Clement of Rome*, New York, 1846 (Clem. Epist.), p. 64.

"There shall come a star out of Jacob
And a sceptre shall rise out of Israel."

And the star which adorns our moral edifice is emblematical of that star. And would it not be wise in us to be guided by its light? It goes before us. It is a prophetic star. It points to a strange and mysterious event, which is revealed in the third degree. The Entered Apprentice will see it again in the holy of holies. "It stood over where the young child was." Who can doubt the meaning of this Masonic emblem? It casts its mild and gentle light over every apartment of the building. It will bring light out of darkness; but we must not forget that the Messiah came first to his own, and his own received him not. He was promised to the Gentiles long anterior to his coming. The Gentiles shall come to thy light, and kings to the brightness of thy rising.[136]

Have we nothing here for serious thought and contemplation? We may derive profitable instruction from the confidence and faith of those astronomers—wise men of the East[137]—which journeyed to the city of David. We may admire their moral greatness and sublime courage. Why did they visit the manger? When they arrived at the consecrated spot, they said: "We are come to *worship* him." Where is our *faith*? Do we trust in God? Have we *hope* in immortality? *Charity* for all mankind? Do we believe in the doctrines of the Holy Bible? They are the doctrines of our Order. If we reject them, we will repudiate our ancient institution. We may destroy the edifice, as some monument of ancient folly, and on its ruins never build again. But let us pause and consider. It is the work of master spirits. It is a splendid

---

[136] Isaiah 60:3.

[137] Magi was the appellation given among the Persians to priests, wise men, philosophers, and others, who devoted themselves to the study of the moral and physical sciences, and who particularly cultivated astrology and medicine. They enjoyed the highest consideration. The wise men from the East, who came to worship the infant Messiah, were philosophers of this description — 2 Home's Intro., Hist. In. 435.

monument of wisdom, and rests emphatically on the mount of vision.

We may look again on our clouded canopy, and that mount on which rests, emblematically, Jacob's ladder. We perceive a rude altar represented on the mount. It may refer to the altar which Jacob set up at Bethel, and on which he reposed when he had his vision, that altar from which he looked up and saw the stars shining out and the angels ascending and descending on the ladder. And why is our moral firmament clouded? Why is it not a clear and bright canopy? Why does the top of the ladder seemingly penetrate the clouds, beyond which are supposed to glitter numberless stars, though the mystic seven are only visible? The whole scenery represented is of a typical character. The revelation is, however, *dark* and *symbolical.* The top of the ladder is lost in the clouds. There were rays of truth—scintillations of wisdom—but the brightness of the new dispensation will illumine the firmament and dispel the clouds.[138]

On the left of the foot of the ladder may be observed a print of the trunk of a tree, perhaps in tended to represent the trunk of the olive, with the branch of the wild olive engrafted in it: And if some of the branches be broken off, and thou, being a wild olive tree, wert grafted in among them, and with them partakest of the root and fatness of the olive tree, boast not against the branches.[139] The old

---

[138] The learned brother Hutchinson thought that the degree of E∴ A∴ was symbolical of the first knowledge of the God of nature in the earliest ages of man, or, in other words, of the patriarchal dispensation. — The rev. George Oliver, Masonic Library, Philadelphia, 1855, p. 180. Hereafter, *Mas. Lib.*)

[139] Romans 11:17. The branches which were broken off are emblematical of the nation of the Jews, who have wandered far from their ancient home—the land of the holy sepulcher—and are scattered among the nations; they have been cut off on account of their unbelief. The wild olive is an emblem of the Gentiles, who have been grafted among them, (that is, brought to the knowledge of the truth,) and with them partaken of the root and fatness of the tree—the spiritual privileges of

branches are all broken off, but the natural branches, we are assured, will be again grafted into the parent stock, and then the tree shall grow and flourish again, and its boughs will overshadow the whole earth.

We are informed that there were figures of olive trees in the temple, and that the door-posts, as well as the images of the cherubim, were made of olive wood. David sung of the olive. In describing a happy household, where family devotions were daily offered up to God, he says: Thy wife shall be as a fruitful vine by the sides of thine house: thy children like olive plants round about thy table.[140] The innocent dove, sent out from Noah's ark in search of dry land, returned from its mission with an olive leaf in its mouth. The olive branch is an emblem of peace. David, in the 52nd psalm, breaks into the following strain: But I am like a green olive tree in the house of God: I trust in the mercy of God forever and ever. Oh! When the great day of wrath comes—when there shall be a war of elements—may the angels of the Lord wave over us that olive branch of peace which grows on the everlasting mount, near the throne of the Highest. There is also represented on the tracing board, a range of holy mountains, and there too are the cedars of Lebanon, clad in the emblems of immortality. The vale of Eden leads to the mountain of the cedars. What glorious associations and what dear memories gather, like angels, around and about us, when we look through the dark backward of time to by-gone ages, and wander, in imagination, among the hills and valleys of renowned Judea.

---

the Jewish nation.

[140] Psalms 128:3.

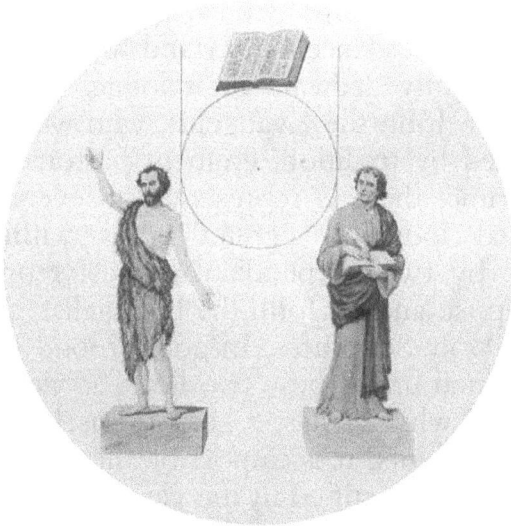

LECTURE IV.
The Point within the Circle

The Grand Master, having reached the east, strikes thrice with his mallet, and, after profound silence, dedicates the lodge, "in the name of the Great Jehovah, to whom be all glory and honor." [141]

I have surely built thee an house to dwell in, a settled place for thee to abide in forever. [142]

He took the golden compasses, prepared
In God's eternal store to circumscribe
The universe and all created things. [143]

I was an hungered, and ye gave me meat: I was thirsty, and ye gave me drink: I was a stranger, and ye took me in: naked, and ye clothed me: I was in prison, and ye came unto me. [144]

---

[141] Mas. Lib., p. 280.

[142] 1 Kings 8:13.

[143] Milton, Paradise Lost, 7.225-227.

[144] Matthew 25:35.

Lodges were anciently dedicated to King Solomon, he being the first Most Excellent Grand Master. Masons professing Christianity dedicate their lodges to St. John the Baptist, and St. John the Evangelist, who were, as we have been informed by tradition, eminent patrons of the craft. Since their time, there is represented in every regular and well-governed lodge, a certain point within a circle, embordered by two perpendicular lines, representing St. John the Baptist, and St. John the Evangelist; and upon the top rest the Holy Scriptures. In going round this circle we necessarily touch upon these two lines, as well as the Holy Scriptures; and while a Mason keeps himself circumscribed within their precepts, it is impossible he should materially err.[145] We are fully justified in the view which we are trying to present of the symbols and ceremonies of the Order. Why are lodges throughout Christendom dedicated to our patron saints? They are esteemed as beautiful examples for imitation. They are hallowed in our Masonic annals. It is an immemorial custom of the fraternity to celebrate the anniversaries of these saints. The Christian era was a propitious time to dedicate to them our lodges, and there is something exceedingly appropriate in the usage, if our views of Masonry be correct. How intimately connected are all the events of the world; how wonderfully allied the ages which have departed; how continuous is that great father of rivers, flowing on to eternity, upon whose vast depths the Spirit of the Almighty moved from the beginning. Age is connected with age, century with century, and event with event. The clock which strikes the knell of the passing moment, announces the living hour. Each sun that sets gives assurance of the coming morn. The present is associated with the past; the present and past with the future, and the future with the great hereafter. The mighty developments of this age; its lofty interpositions of mind; the sublime progress of thought, advancing with a "dominant step" to the boundless regions of truth and philosophy, are allied with other

---

[145] Cross' Chart, p. 17.

days, and especially with that period in which our saints
lived and preached "the truth as it is in Jesus." Not only the
age in which they taught, and the country in which they
lived, with its beautiful landscape, but the wonders of that
age and country; the miracles wrought by Christ and his
apostles; the fulfillment of prophecy; the birth of the Son
of Man ; all the days of his holy pilgrimage; the doctrines
which he taught; the object of his sacred mission; his cross
and passion, death and burial, resurrection and ascension,
by which was consummated the amazing plan of redemption, rise up before us with their ever-widening and ever-
deepening influences. We wander in thought through the
deserts where "the Baptist grew and waxed strong in the
Spirit, and where he dwelt until the day of his showing unto
Israel." We behold him in his simple and rustic attire, advance from the solitude of nature, a messenger of peace,
with glad tidings on his lips, and speaking in the language
of authority: "Repent ye, for the kingdom of heaven is at
hand!"[146] So perfect was his character, so lovely his life and
manners, that "all men mused in their hearts concerning
him, whether he was the Christ." But he was the forerunner
of Jesus. Malachi, the last of the prophets beheld him coming. Isaiah looked down from the heights of prophecy, and
saw him advancing from the vales of the future. The spirit
of that ancient prophet even heard his voice, "crying in the
wilderness, Prepare ye the way of the Lord: make straight in
the desert a highway for our God." "Verily, I say unto you,
that among them that are born of women, there hath not
arisen a greater than John the Baptist." His pure manners,

---

[146] The spirit of prophecy came upon John, when he was about thirty years
of age: this was the time appointed in the law for the commencement
of their ministry, by the priests and Levites. He preached in the deserts,
where the greatest multitudes passed; he wore a garment of camel's
hair, the most coarse and common garment, similar to that worn by the
prophets of old, to express his contempt for the vanities and ostenta-
tions of life. His food was the spontaneous produce of the country,
showing his self-denial, and the subjection of all his appetites. His days
were passed in the wilderness, far removed from the world, preparing
and preaching the way of the Lord. — Town. Notes, p. 44.

his faithful reproofs, his earnest admonitions,[147] and sublime teachings, are enough to make us all fall in love with virtue. He was the chosen herald of the mightiest event that ever transpired. Having been made acquainted with Jesus by the Holy Ghost, he bore testimony to him as the Christ. Other prophets had testified of the Lord before his coming. John beheld him face to face. The fathers in Israel looked with the eye of faith to a remote age for our Redeemer, and saw him in every type and symbol, in the blood of every sacrifice, and in every cloud of incense which ascended from their altars. John was familiar with his Master, and served him with all *freedom, fervency* and *zeal.* If other gifted ones viewed through a spiritual medium the Son of Man when he had not yet appeared in the flesh, John, while administering the holy rite of baptism to the Divine Builder, beheld the Holy Ghost descend and rest upon him, and heard a voice crying from heaven—This is my beloved Son in whom I am well pleased. John came preaching in that voice, which, full many centuries before, had sounded in the ears of the prophets; and he pointed our fallen nature to the star-paved way to paradise.[148] But brief was his sojourn, and summary his departure. He was cast by the cruel and unjust Herod into prison: he had no companion but his God. To gratify revenge and a most strange request, he was sentenced to the block.[149] A martyr to his faithfulness, his immortal soul was glorified in heav-

---

[147] All the exhortations of John refer to the spiritual dominion of the Messiah over the hearts and consciences of men. He never once speaks of it as a temporal or earthly power. — Town. Notes, p. 44.

[148] The death of John was painful, but momentary; it was sudden, but it could not find him unprepared. He had kept the faith, and preserved a conscience void of offence. He had done his duty, and waited daily and hourly, we may be sure, for his departure. He was now, therefore, called off from his station with honor, to quit the well fought field for the palace of the Great King; to refresh himself after the dust and toil and heat of the day, by bathing in the fountain of life and immortality. — Robert Sears, *Bible Biography*, New York, 1842, p. 326. Hereafter *Sears' Bible Biog.*

[149] The Baptist was beheaded in the year of our Lord 31.

en, ere his head had rolled on the ground, or was delivered to the foolish damsel in a charger. The terrors of an execution could not shake the courage of our saint, nor chains wear away the elasticity of his noble spirit, about to join the white-robed multitude. After the heat and toil of the day, he was called off from his station with profit to himself and honor to the Lord. His soul vacated its temple of flesh, to be raised to the sublime regions of truth, that it might be exalted to the mysteries of the Godhead. It passed the lofty arches of eternity in search of the purity of our first estate, and found in the sanctuary above *long lost innocence.*

That lowly spirit and humble heart, so beautifully depicted in our ritual adorned the life and character of the Baptist. His fame was very great, but he met all ranks and sects upon the level, ever acting upon the plumb, and parting with them on the square. And before entering upon his ministry, he served a proper time in the forests, subduing his passions and improving himself in moral Masonry. But when he came forth from solitude, where did he announce the Redeemer of Israel? *On the banks of the River Jordan.* It is the most celebrated stream mentioned in the annals of the Fraternity. It was on the margin of that river that he *prepared* men for the *reception* of Christ. They must needs be baptized in its waters, if they would bathe in the fountain of immortality. Masonic tradition, which is considered a pure channel of communication, informs us that this eminent and pious father was a member of the craft, or patron of the Order. The fact, as transmitted from an unknown period, there seems to be no room to contradict, though many have doubted its verity. The principles which the Baptist proclaimed, and the truths he preached, constitute the strong foundation on which the Masonic edifice rests. This we know. John was the *forerunner* of Christ, and testified to the Divinity of Jesus. It is sufficient for us to be assured that he was the herald of salvation, and that the doctrines he taught are those which Masonry elucidates. In the holy of holies of our temple is an ever-present Deity. The name of Jehovah is shrined in its *unutterable* language, and syllabled in the mysteries of the sanctuary. We believe that our ancient brethren continually looked forward to the one event "which stands associated with all that is glorious in the dominion of Christianity." *They* read and heard the words of prophecy, and longed for their fulfillment. *John* beheld the *light* which was come, and the glory of the Lord which was to arise upon Israel. He looked abroad upon the moral firmament when the Sun of Righteousness arose in the East with healing in his wings. *They* stood upon some Pisgah of Hope, and wished for the milk and honey of the Promised Land. *John* stood upon the summit of Calvary, and from that consecrated hill, in view of Jerusalem, he fixed his gaze on the celestial city and the holy mountains. *They* worshipped *Jehovah.* John beheld in the solemn enactments and ceremonies which were displayed on Moriah, blood-stained traces of the Savior of the world. The devout Baptist, in seeing the antitype, could still appreciate the type. In the blood of the victim and the incense of the altar were couched the mysteries of the temple worship. And when our fathers in Israel entered the holy precincts of the sanctuary and gazed on its typical furniture, or saw the sheaf of the wave offering, or hearkened to the silver trumps as they ushered in the jubilee,[150] their souls were transported to a far-off future, when all that was symbolical should be made manifest in the Lord our Redeemer. And thus we perceive that Masonry is forever linked with the past, and associated with a land of the loftiest and holiest recollections.[151] There is no stronger proof that St. John the Evangelist was a Free Mason, than we have that the Baptist was one. It is taken for granted that they both were either members of the institution, or patrons of it, mainly because

---

[150] Henry Melvill, B.D., *Sermons*, Vol. 2, New York, 1844, p. 48. Hereafter *2 Mel. Ser.*

[151] It is called the Holy Land, because it was chosen by God to be the immediate seat of his worship, and was consecrated by the presence, actions, miracles, discoveries, and sufferings of the Lord Jesus Christ; and also, because it was the residence of the holy patriarchs, prophets, and apostles. — 2 Home's Intro., p. 13.

we are so informed by tradition. Dr. Oliver says: that Calmet positively asserts that the Evangelist was an Essenean Freemason,[152] or belonged to a secret theological society with mystic rites and Masonic emblems. It is also stated, but with what truth we cannot say, that in the time of the Evangelist Masonry declined for the want of an acknowledged head, and that the craft held a meeting to take into consideration their deplorable condition. We are informed that they met in the city of Benjamin, and appointed a committee of seven to proceed to Ephesus and solicit St. John the Evangelist to accept the office of Grand Master. The Saint, although he was advanced in life, and much occupied in the discharge of his ministerial duties, yielded to their solicitations; and ever since that period, lodges have been dedicated to the Saints John.[153]

If the Evangelist were a mason, he must have been exceedingly bright, for he was made acquainted with many *mysteries*. He undertook to describe the "unutterable things" of heaven, and for this purpose adopted the use of *symboli-*

---

[152] The Essenes were a set or class of Jews known to exist in the time of our Savior. They lived together and separated themselves from the world, and adopted a system of principles and manners of their own. Our knowledge of their belief and habits is chiefly derived from tradition.

[153] From the building of the temple of Jerusalem to the Babylonian captivity, lodges were dedicated to King Solomon; and from thence to the coming of the Messiah, they were dedicated to Zerubbabel, and from that time to the final destruction of the temple, they were dedicated to St. John the Baptist. But owing to the general confusion which took place under the reign of Titus Vespasian, Freemasonry fell much to decay. Most of the lodges were broken up, when it was at length agreed upon by several who convened for that purpose, that a certain number should be deputed to wait on St. John the Evangelist, (who was then Bishop of Ephesus,) and solicit the favor of his patronizing the fraternity by taking on himself the acting part of Grand Master. He returned for answer, that although he was then advanced in years, (being upwards of ninety,) yet, having been in the early part of his life initiated into the society, and always having it much at heart, he would cheerfully comply with their request. And from that time down to the present day, lodges have been dedicated to the Baptist and to the Evangelist. — Ahi. Rez.; Scrip. Illus., p. 18.

cal or *figurative* language. The Apocalypse, many divines have thought, was designed to supply the place of that continued succession of prophets which demonstrated the continued providence of God to the Jewish and the patriarchal churches. The *figurative* language of this wonderful book has never been understood, for it contains the profoundest mysteries; and there is much spoken of which will only be revealed to them who are raised to the world of eternal life. Much of it is the language of prophecy, referring to events, some of which it is supposed have already happened, and some which will hereafter occur on the *ground floor* of the universe; while much which is written in it is typical of the glorious truths to which the righteous will be brought to light in the *third* heavens.

The circle, in all ages has been viewed as an emblem of God and eternity. The Lord sitteth upon the *circle* of the earth, and the inhabitants thereof are as grasshoppers.[154] He prepared the heavens, and set a compass upon the face of the deep.[155] The circle is a wonderful figure. It has attracted the attention of the world, and puzzled the greatest mathematicians. While it has challenged the profoundest study, it has caused some very ingenious results. How many have labored to *square* the circle or find its quadrature; and how many, in the progress of their eager study and calculation, have been ready to cry out, Eureka![156] But alas! Their efforts were vain. The circle is a significant emblem of Dei-

---

[154] Isaiah 40:22.

[155] Proverbs 8:27.

[156] The Forty-Seventh Problem of Euclid was an invention of our ancient friend and brother, the great Pythagoras, who, in his travels through Asia, Africa, and Europe, was initiated into several orders of priesthood, and raised to the sublime degree of Master Mason. This wise philosopher enriched his mind abundantly in a general knowledge of things, and more especially in geometry and Masonry. He drew out many problems and theorems, and among the most distinguished, he erected the forty-seventh problem of Euclid, which in the joy of his heart he called Eureka—signifying, I have found it. — Brad. Ser., on Masonry, p. 98.

ty. It can never be squared.[157] And God is past finding out. Who by searching can find out God? Who can tell up the sum of his power? Who can calculate the strength of the Almighty's arm, which set a compass upon the face of the deep? He sitteth upon the circle of the heavens, and with what instrument can we take his altitude? His steppings are in the terrible march of the earthquake, and the light of his countenance is abroad in the heavens. We may hear his voice in the thunder, and perceive in the lightnings the flash of his wrath. But what is the language of the circle? It tells us of an incomprehensible God; the mysteries of eternity; and the power and love of God, which are circular, for they are from everlasting to everlasting. Long before He laid the foundations of the earth or studded the firmament with stars, He loved our race. Before Adam and Eve sprang from beneath the touches of the Divine Artist, they and their posterity were the especial favorites of heaven. Salvation was planned in the councils of eternity; and the great design of redemption was drawn by the Sovereign Master of the universe, on the tracing-board in his own Holy of Holies. Jesus, the carpenter's son, of the tribe of Judah, was commissioned to superintend the work, and to erect a temple of finished and sublime architecture. The Christian Mason delights to survey its stately proportions, and wander in thought through its splendid apartments. The spirit of pure worship lingers about its invisible altars. Truth, like some anointed priest, is there arrayed in long and flowing robes. There the sweet incense of accept able prayer is ascending. Pure voices are "quiring to the young-eyed cherubim," whose outstretched wings are above the mercy-seat. The silver trumps are sounding for the general jubilee. And we may behold, in fancy, some new fire coming down from the skies to consume the offerings and sacrifices, when the

---

[157] The problem of the quadrature or squaring of the circle is stated to have been recently solved by a citizen of the State of New-York. We shall wait for the proof of such an unparalleled achievement in science. It is also said, that the discovery has shown that an equilateral triangle is precisely the opposite figure to a square.

glory of the Lord shall fill the house of the Lord; when all the earth shall worship and praise the Lord, saying, for he is good; for his mercy endureth forever.[158] The office of brotherly love[159] is enforced in the Masonic lectures. And *whence came* the moral lesson? From the temple of the skies—from the Holy of Holies of the New Jerusalem. Brotherly love is a *Christian* affection. The word *brother*, as used in the Bible, has an enlarged signification. James and Joses, and Simon and Judas, are called the brothers of Jesus. While the Lord hung upon the cross, there stood by him his mother, and his mother's sister, and Mary Magdalene; and when Jesus therefore saw his mother, and the disciple standing by, whom he loved, he saith unto his mother, Woman, behold thy son! Then saith he to the disciple, Behold thy mother! And from that hour that disciple took her unto his own home.[160]

Love is one of the most beautiful affections of the human heart.[161] Who does not love his father and mother, his brothers and sisters? We love our children with a love "which passeth all understanding." Who loves not the companion of his bosom, the Eve of his domestic garden? Will not his soul cleave unto her—will he not love her and speak kindly unto her?[162]—And does not the upright Mason love virtue? Does he not love to look upon those beautiful sisters, which adorn our chart—*Temperance, Fortitude, Prudence,* and *Justice?* In their gentle forms he may read the excellence of the Christian system. Charity is love, and the

---

[158] 2 Chronicles 7:1-3.

[159] Brotherly love, relief, and truth constitute the motto of our Order. They prove that a society which could adopt them can only be formed on the principles of virtue. — Mack. Lex., p. 36.

[160] John 19:25-27.

[161] To love, in Scripture, signifies sometimes to adhere, to cleave to, as in Genesis 34:3; 2 Pict. Dict., p. 789. It is the excellence of the Christian system that ennobles, regulates, and directs this passion to proper objects, and moderates it within due bounds. — Ibidem.

[162] Genesis 34:3.

greatest of the Christian graces. And now abideth faith, hope, charity, these three; but the greatest of these is charity.[163] Now the end of the commandment is charity out of a pure heart, and of a good conscience, and of faith unfeigned.[164] Though I speak with the tongues of men and of angels, and have not charity, I am become as sounding brass, or a tinkling cymbal.[165] God is love. And who does not love to dwell upon the beauties of nature? Who does not love to listen to the droppings of the sanctuary, and the steppings of the Great Spirit; to gaze upon the grandeurs of the universe, the glories of the sun, and the glittering troop ever marching in the skies. Nature loves and praises God. Every flower smiles a fragrant God. Every garland crowns a God. The still streams of thought gently murmur God. Imagination's rolling cataracts thunder God. Conscience oft, with a trembling tongue, answers God. And reason, from the height of some great argument, looks down and responds Almighty God.[166] To relieve the distressed is a moral duty incumbent on all men; but it is one particularly enjoined on the Masonic fraternity. In a popular sense, relief is denominated charity. To soothe the unhappy, is beautiful: "Blessed are they that mourn, for they shall be comforted." To restore peace to the broken-hearted, and bind up their wounds, is the duty of a Mason: "Blessed are the merciful, for they shall obtain mercy." It is our duty to succor the poor and needy: Thou, O God, hast prepared of thy goodness for the poor.[167] And the poor shall never cease out of the land.[168] The rich and the poor meet to-

---

[163] 1 Corinthians 13:13.

[164] 1 Timothy 1:5.

[165] 1 Corinthians 13:1.

[166] See lecture of the writer, published in Southern Reformer, at the city of Jackson.

[167] Psalms 68:10.

[168] Deuteronomy 15:11.

gether; the Lord is the maker of them all.[169] The poor have the gospel preached to them.[170] It is heavenly food.

Masonic Charity is a *secret*, but an active *spirit*. It might be compared to a stream flowing from the fountain of a pure heart. It reaches the wretchedness and want of all the brethren. Its gentle aid is felt particularly among those of the "mystic tie," or the "favored few;" for they fall "directly within the sphere of our good offices." There are physical as well as moral benefits in the dispensations of charity. In giving aid and comfort to distressed and worthy brethren, or their widows and orphans, the benefactors and the recipients are benefited. The words "distressed and worthy brethren" mean those who are in actual need or physical want; for any member of the craft who is able to work and will not, cannot be considered an object of charity.[171] He is unworthy in the eye of Masonry.[172] And such is the Scripture doctrine; for we are told, if a man will not work, neither shall he eat. Masonry inculcates industry, and teaches every man the necessity of relying on his individual exertions for support. If a brother be indolent, he deserves reproof, and it is our duty to give it. We are bound to do

---

[169] Proverbs 22:2.

[170] Matthew 11:5.

[171] The misplacing of a benefit is worse than the not receiving of it; for the one is another man's fault, but the other is mine. The error of the giver does oft times excuse the ingratitude of the receiver; for a favor ill-placed is rather a profusion than a benefit. It is the most shameful of losses, an inconsiderate bounty. If we give only to receive, we lose the fairest objects of our charity—the absent, the sick, the captive, and the needy. — Lucius Annæus Seneca, *Seneca's Morals*, Edinburgh, 1776, ch. 5, *Of Benefits*, p.33

[172] As dependence is one of the strongest bonds of society, mankind were made dependent on each other for protection and security, as they thereby enjoy better opportunities of fulfilling the duties of reciprocal love and friendship. Thus was man made for social and active life, and he that will so demean himself, as not to be endeavoring to add to the common stock of knowledge and understanding, may be deemed a drone in the hive of nature, a useless member of society, and unworthy of our protection as Masons. — Brad. Ser., on Masonry, p. 96.

what sound morality requires, which is, "to provide such a person with labor, and pay him accordingly." But in all cases of sickness or other afflictions of Providence, the rules of the Order require us to extend relief; or alleviate, as far as we can, their physical condition. The benefactors and recipients are both improved. "The Christian religion considers charity as a means of moral cultivation." Charity is a virtue which may be exercised in secret, and the acts of Masonic benevolence are never made public.

But there is another sense in which we may aid and assist our brethren. If they are in darkness, it is our duty to furnish them with Masonic and moral instruction. If we see a brother falling into evil and wicked habits, we should give him timely admonition, and keep him, if possible, from moral ruin, by whispering in his ear good counsel, and advising him upon the points of fellowship. We should remonstrate with him face to face, and never talk evil of him behind his back; but visit him and give him all necessary instruction; and, if wandering from the path of rectitude, inform him of his error, and turn him from the way of evil and mischief.

To be good and true is one of the first injunctions of the Order. Truth is a Divine attribute, and the foundation of every virtue.[173] Truth is indestructible, because eternal. The Christian church is founded on truth. God is truth, as well as love. Solomon's temple rested on *triple* foundations: so does the Masonic edifice. God is *truth*, and he is a *Triune God*.

Let us, then, as a band of brothers, be good and true to each other; faithful to our trust and faithful to the confidence reposed in us. Let us all work by those designs which our Master Builder in heaven has drawn for us; and then we will be able to present finished specimens of work, such as are needed for the completion of the temple above. And when we come to die—when the beams and rafters of our

---

[173] Cross' Chart., p. 18.

earthly tabernacles shall be torn down by the destroyer, and the foundations of nature give way—when dust shall return to dust, ashes to ashes—good angels will *pass on* our souls, as *living stones* made ready for the house of the mountain of God. We should all be pious laborers; apprentices, bound to learn the Christian's trade. The Bible is our square, our compasses, gavel, and gauge—level, trowel, and plumb line; and if we are true to ourselves and our God, our work will be good work and square work. The earth is our Zarthan and Lebanon. Let us diligently hew the living rock, and prepare our souls to be laid up in the heavenly temple.

Temperance   Fortitude   Prudence   Justice

LECTURE V.
The Cardinal Virtues

Let thine eyes behold the things that are equal.[174]

How poor, how rich, how august,
How complicate, how wonderful is man! [175]

If he know not the relations in which he stands to others, and have not the means of knowing them, he is guiltless. If he know them, or have the means of knowing them, he is guilty.[176]

There are emblematical steps delineated on the tracing board.[177]

The form of a lodge is that of an *oblong square*, and a lodge is usually situated due east and west. The sun rises in the east and sets in the west.[178] The east has been called the

---

[174] Psalms 17:2.

[175] Edward Young, *The Complaint,* Edinburgh, 1775, p. 5

[176] Francis Wayland, *The Elements of Moral Science,* Gould, Kendall and Lincoln, 1840, p. 75

[177] Ahi. Rez.

[178] All knowledge, all religion, and all arts and sciences have travelled, ac-

place of light. The garden planted eastward in Eden denoted intelligence and love. A star in the east heralded the birth of the Messiah. It conducted the wise men of the east to the place of his nativity. The Son of man was crucified in the east. Christianity arose in the east and travelled to the west. The tabernacle of Moses was an oblong square. It was situated due east and west.[179] So was Solomon's temple. The tabernacle was surrounded by an oblong court. Its tent was oblong. An east wind blew upon the Red sea and divided its waters. Moriah was situated in the *east* of the *northern part* of Zion. The brook of Cedron took its rise not far northward of Jerusalem, and having passed by that city, it then takes an eastwardly direction. Solomon's temple fronted to the east. It is a Masonic custom to inter the dead with their faces to the east. They must rise to meet the Son of man in his coming. The Lord will appear in the east with all his holy angels, when he shall come to judge the nations; and then the reanimated dust of the sepulchers shall rise up and march to the great white throne; and rivers of fire shall rise from the east to west. As the lightning cometh out of the east, and shineth even unto the west; so shall also the coming of the Son of man be.[180] It is worthy of remark that our Lord, says a learned commentator, in a most particular manner points out the very march of the Roman army: they entered into Judea on the east, and carried on their conquest westward. A very gifted and spiritual man said that the east denotes the Lord; charity from the Lord; a state of truth, and a state of love.

---

cording to the course of the sun, from east to west! From that quarter the Divine glory at first came; and thence the rays of Divine light continue to diffuse themselves over the face of the earth. From thence came the Bible and through that the new covenant. From thence came the prophets, the apostles, and the first missionaries, that brought the knowledge of God to Europe, to the isles of the sea, and to the west first. — Clarke's Com., Ezekiel, ch. 43.

[179] The tent itself was an oblong square, thirty cubits in length, and ten in height and breadth. The oblong court was an hundred cubits long and fifty broad. — 2 Home's Intro, p. 96.

[180] Matthew 24:27.

Masonry regards all men alike. All men are brothers.[181] All are equal, and all immortal. All are walking upon the common level of time. All journeying to the grave, or that bourne from whence no traveler returns. All flesh of men will go down to the dust, but arise again at the last day. We all stand in need of spiritual comfort and spiritual nourishment. It is not the external, but internal qualifications, which constitute the Christian. The genius of Masonry would commune with the inner man, and hold converse with the spirit. It would illustrate all the *signs* and *tokens* of mercy, and the sublime truths connected with our immortal nature. It would bid us work diligently, masonically, faithfully, and charitably. It would remind us of corruption, but assure us of incorruption. That, this mortal shall put on immortality, then shall be brought to pass the saying that is written, Death is swallowed up in victory.[182]

Masonry regards no man on account of his worldly wealth or honor.[183] The poor, as well as the rich, may knock at the door of our temple, and gain admission. All are welcome, if found worthy, to receive light. This is strictly scriptural: Seek and ye shall find; ask and ye shall receive; knock and the door shall be opened unto you. Masonry, from her ample treasures, makes full provision for the poor. And one of the objects of the Messiah was to judge the poor. He shall judge thy people with righteousness, and thy poor with judgment. He shall judge the poor of the people; he shall save the children of the needy, and shall

---

[181] Christians are denominated brethren. I beseech you therefore, brethren, by the mercies of God, that ye present your bodies a living sacrifice, holy, acceptable unto God, which is your reasonable service. — Romans 12:1. And when we had finished our course from Tyre, we came to Ptolemais, and saluted the brethren, and abode with them one day. — Acts 21:7.

[182] 1 Corinthians 15:54.

[183] The level is an emblem of equality. In the sight of God all men are equal; subject to the same infirmities; hastening to the same goal; and preparing to be judged by the same immutable law. — Mack. Lex., p. 181.

break in pieces the oppressor.[184] The poor and the deceitful man meet together: the Lord lighteneth both their eyes.[185]

The art or science of Freemasonry opens up a universal field for meditation and thought. There is not a sign, symbol, token, word, or ceremony, which does not afford some moral lesson. The social, intellectual, and religious advancement of man is its chief design. Man may be said to be one of the lesser lights of the Order; and his wonderful faculties of body and soul are made to argue his lofty destiny. The candle was lighted at the blaze of immortality which the Scriptures kindled in our lodges. And fire is a symbol of the Deity.[186] Put out the light of the Bible—that great light—and all the lesser lights will become extinguished.

> *"Put out the light and then—put out the light—*
>
> * * * * * * * * * * * *
>
> *I know not where is that Promethean heat*
> *That will that light relume."*

---

[184] Psalms 72:2-4.

[185] Proverbs 29:13.

[186] And the Lord went before them by day in a pillar of cloud, to lead them the way; and by night in a pillar of fire, to give them light. — Exodus 13:21.

The Lord descended upon Mount Sinai in fire. — Ibidem 19:18.

The sight of the glory of the Lord, in the eyes of the Israelites was like a devouring fire. — Exodus 24:17.

The Lord talked with Moses in the Mount out of the midst of fire. — Deuteronomy 5:4.

And the mountain burned with fire. — Ibidem 5:23.

It is said that Numa built the temple of Vesta where the perpetual fire was to be kept, in an orbicular form, not intending to represent the figure of the earth, but the frame of the universe, in the centre of which the Pythagoreans place the element of fire. — 1 Plutarch's Lives, p. 146. Fire was one of the elements of Druidical worship.

Put out the light, and all the stars will fall, one by one, from our moral firmament. The mystic star in the centre of the Mosaic pavement will disappear forever. It will no longer radiate the checkered scenes of life; no longer conduct our thoughts to Bethlehem; or illuminate our way to the holy of holies. But the Bible is a great and shining light. It will burn forever and ever. The breath of inspiration has kindled many sacred lights. The angel of the Lord appeared unto Moses in a flame of fire.[187] And the Lord went before our fathers in Israel in a pillar of fire to give them light.[188] And there came out a fire from before the Lord, and consumed upon the altar the burnt offering and the fat: which when all the people saw, they shouted, and fell on their faces.[189] At another time, when our ancient Master, Solomon, had made an end of praying, the fire came down from heaven, and consumed the burnt offerings and the sacrifices and the glory of the Lord filled the house of the Lord.[190] How many lights are burning upon and around the altar of the Most High! How many lights has revelation kindled on the earth! The heavens are shining with the glorious manifestations of God; while rivers of light flow, as it were, from beneath the very throne of Jehovah. The tops of the mountains shine with truth. Let the Great Light[191] burn on. It shines brightly on our altars, and it affords such a steady emission of Divine wisdom, that all may see and understand it.

---

[187] Exodus 3:2.

[188] Exodus 13:21.

[189] Leviticus 9:24.

[190] 2 Chronicles 7:1.

[191] Emphatically, is the Bible called the greater light of Masonry; for, from the centre of the lodge, it pours forth upon the east, the west, and the south, its effulgent rays of Divine truth. The Bible is used among Masons as the symbol of the will of God, however it may be expressed. — Mack. Lex., p. 35.

There is a book who runs may read,
Which heavenly truth imparts,
And all the lore its scholars need,
Pure eyes and Christian hearts.

John Keble, *Christian Year*

We have said that man is one of the lights of Masonry. It is true. If he be just in the discharge of his duties, faithful in his work, and diligent in polishing his soul, he will become, through the assistance of the Holy Spirit, a righteous man, whose light will shine more and more unto the perfect day. If Masons would only do their duty, or live up to the doctrines of our institution—the doctrines of the Holy Bible— a *new order* of things would appear. Let, then, every one place a sentinel at the door of his heart—a *tyler* at the outer avenue of the temple, to keep off the *cowans* of our corrupted nature, and those *clandestine* passions, which would intrude themselves into the sanctuary of the soul. Let no thought *pass* or *repass* without the permission of enlightened conscience; let the mind be always *duly* and *truly prepared* to worship God, and *every way worthy and well qualified* to enter into communion with the Spirit. Then we may hope to be invested, *after death*, with the secrets of the sublime hereafter; and the Master of the house will bid us come in.

"Oh ye, that in these latter days
Our citadel defend,
Perchance for you, the Saviour said
I'm with you to the end:
Stand therefore girt about, and hold
Your burning lamps in hand,
And standing, listen for your Lord,
And till he Cometh—stand!
"The gates of hell shall ne'er prevail
Against our holy home,
But, oh, be wakeful sentinels,
Until the Master come!
The night is spent—but listen ye;

For on its deepest calm,
What marvel if the cry be heard,
The marriage of the Lamb!"

Are you a Christian Mason? Never be ashamed to answer, I *am*. It is a beautiful and Christian response. I AM is the ancient name of Jehovah. How simple and how grand are those words. In the language of a learned bishop, God does not say, speaking in reference to his people, I am their light, their life, their guide, their strength, or tower, but only, I *am*. He sets, as it were, his hand to a blank, that his people may write under it what they please that is good for them. As if he should say, are they weak? I am strength. Are they in trouble? I am comfort. Are they sick? I am health. Are they dying? I am life. Have they nothing? I am all things. I am wisdom and power; I am justice and mercy; I am grace and goodness; I am glory, beauty, holiness, eminency, super-eminency, perfection, all-sufficiency, eternity, Jehovah, I *am*. Whatsoever is amiable in itself, or desirable unto them, *that I am*; whatsoever is pure and holy; whatsoever is great or pleasant; whatsoever is good or needful to make men happy, *that I am*.[192]

The cardinal virtues[193] are explained in the degree of Entered Apprentice; but it is beyond the design of our work to enlarge upon them, or do anything more than show whence they were derived, or upon what authority they have been made a part of the Masonic system. The practice of temperance, justice, prudence, and fortitude is forcibly enjoined in both the Old and New Testaments. Temperance stands at the head of the Masonic virtues.[194] It

---

[192] William Beveridge, The Theological Works of William Beveridge, Oxford, 1842, Vol. 1, p. 244, sermon XIII.

[193] The illustration of these virtues is accompanied with some general observations peculiar to Masons. — Brad. Ser., on Masonry, p. 65.

[194] It may be interesting to the friends of the cause to know, as a mere matter of history, that the first Temperance Society on record was established by the Free Masons of Italy, just a century since. On the 8th of April, 1748, Pope Clement XII. issued his celebrated Bull forbidding

does not merely mean the restraining of our sensual appetites or physical enjoyments, but it is the keeping, says Cicero, of our words and actions within the due limits of order
and decency[195]. Solomon, than whom no man could better
judge, spoke of this virtue as necessary to control our sensual indulgences: When thou sittest to eat with a ruler, consider diligently what is before thee: and put a knife to thy
throat, if thou be a man given to appetite. Be not desirous
of his dainties: for they are deceitful meat[196]. But we should
be temperate in all things, if we would obtain the mastery
in all things. There is no law against meekness and temperance[197]. A man is temperate, when he is filled with the Spir-

---

the practice of Freemasonry by the members of the Roman Catholic
church. Many of the Masons of Italy continued, however, to meet; but
for the purpose of evading the temporal penalties of the Bull, which extended in some instances to the infliction of capital punishment, they
changed their exoteric name, and called themselves Xerophagists. This
is a compound of two Greek words, signifying "those who live without
drinking." This title they selected, because they then introduced a
pledge of total abstinence into their by-laws; and hence the Free Masons of Italy may claim the honor of having taken the initiatory step in
that great reformation which has since done so much good to mankind.
— Anon.

E. N.: It is to be noted that since the time of Clement XII very little has
changed in some respects. In 1983, Mons. Ratzinger, Prefect of the
Congregation for the Doctrine of the Faith (Grand Inquisitor), ratified
the excommunication (approved it in 1981 under Cardinal Seper.) of all
Catholics who joined a Masonic Lodge *ipso facto*—i.e. by the mere act of
joining a Lodge—, excommunication reserved to the Holy See—i.e.
only the Pope can lift it. The order was confirmed by Pope John Paul II
and published the same year. Mons. Ratzinger became Pope Benedict
XVI at the death of John Paul II and, since no papal action has
changed it, it remains a very certain fact of Canonical Law. As in the
past, many Catholic masons continue to patronize their lodges. Fortu-
nately for them, there are no longer corporal punishments associated
with their "grave sin." The text of the Declaration can be found in its
entirety in the Appendix II, on page

[195] Marcus Tullius Cicero, *Three Books of Offices or Moral Duties*, translated by
Cyrus R. Edmonds, London, 1850, p. 11 Book 1, ch. 5. Hereafter *Cic.
Off.*

[196] Proverbs 23:1-3.

[197] Galatians 5:23.

it; for, says the Scripture, be not drunk with wine, wherein is excess; but be filled with the Spirit.[198] Paul bid Titus to be *sober, just, holy, temperate; holding fast the faithful word,* as he hath been taught.[199] All the virtues are materially dependent on each other, yet each has its respective set of duties arising from it.[200] Their observance is commanded by the Divine law; and however successfully we may escape human punishment for their violation, there is a day of reckoning when we must account for both sins of omission and commission.

Fortitude is that noble and steady purpose of mind, whereby we are enabled to undergo any pain, peril, or danger, when prudentially deemed expedient.[201] In the language of Cicero, it is that greatness and unshaken resolution of a truly brave and invincible mind. Patience is nearly allied to fortitude. If we are faint in the day of adversity, our strength is small. The patient in spirit are better than the proud in spirit.[202] We are exhorted to be patient in tribulation.[203] We have all need of patience. He possesses true fortitude who can resist all temptation to do evil. That mind is brave and invincible, that can defy the assaults of the tempter and his ingenious machinations. He is strong and magnanimous, who can overthrow sin and hold it up to the derision of the world. Sin is one of the works of the devil, and so is death; but he that overcomes the first, will prove victorious over the second. Death will be then deprived of its sting, and the grave of its victory: "And for this purpose was the Son of man manifested, that he might destroy the works of the devil." And the man that can suc-

---

[198] Ephesians 5:18.

[199] Titus 1:8-9.

[200] Cic. Off. b. 1, ch 5.

[201] Cross's Chart, p. 19.

[202] Ecclesiastes 7:8.

[203] Romans 12:12.

cessfully encounter the prince of darkness has true Christian magnanimity and fortitude.

Prudence is that virtue which prompts us to inquire after truth in regard to all things connected with our happiness in this life and that which is to come. Such is the idea communicated in Proverbs: Every prudent man dealeth with knowledge.[204] The simple inherit folly: but the prudent are crowned with knowledge.[205] The wise in heart shall be called prudent.[206] A prudent man always looks ahead. He examines the ground on which he stands; he weighs his thoughts; ponders on all his actions, and looks to their probable consequences. A prudent man generally foresees evil. And wisdom will make men just. Justice does not merely consist in rendering to everyone his due, or giving to every man that which is his own; in being faithful to all our civil engagements, or in never violating any of our promises. It has a higher and more exalted meaning. We are deeply indebted to God; and we know that we can never pay him what we owe. Christ's Sermon on the Mount contains a beautiful definition of justice, when viewed in connection with our social relations: Therefore all things whatsoever ye would that men should do to you, do ye even so to them: for this is the law and the prophets.[207] The Almighty cannot pervert justice. It is the duty of all men to be temperate, patient, prudent, and just. The Ruler of heaven and earth has so commanded, and it is an eternal and unchangeable law.

It must be apparent to every member of the craft, that there exists a preconcerted connection between all the emblems or symbols of our Order.[208] The connection will be-

---

[204] Proverbs 13:16.

[205] Proverbs 14:18.

[206] Proverbs 16:21.

[207] Matthew 7:12.

[208] The system of masonry is arranged in lectures, which are divided into

come still more evident as we progress in the elucidation of Masonry. Design is apparent in all our ceremonies. Types may be regarded as similitudes to some person, event, or thing, which is to occur. They prefigure something which will transpire; and lead the mind to contemplate or expect something, which will happen in the future. Such was the nature of the types of the Messiah and his kingdom. The Entered Apprentice, when he is initiated, is left in a state of expectancy. Knowledge of the first degree prepares him for the reception of more light or information. Knowledge of the first *makes him ready* for the second degree, which will, by and by, be seen to be an apt state of preparation for the third or sublime degree of a Master Mason.

Typical or symbolical elucidations will be observed in all the degrees; and the light which they afford will be concentrated at last in one remarkable event, which event is of itself a sublime type of a more sublime and august event or transaction, as we expect to establish. Every emblem or type of Masonry finds its analogy in the Bible. There are Masonic steps, and they are *numbered*: Now thou numberest my steps, said Job.[209] In David's psalm of thanksgiving, he sung: Thou hast enlarged my steps under me, that my feet did not slip.[210] The steps of a good man are ordered by the Lord: and he delighteth in his way.[211] None of his steps shall slide. In the church's complaint, she is made to sing: Our heart is not turned back; neither have our steps declined from thy way.[212] Order my steps in thy word, says the Psalmist.[213] It was a wise saying of Solomon: A man's

---

sections, and the whole is a regular system of moral truth represented in allegory.

[209] Job 14:6.

[210] Psalms 18:36.

[211] Psalms 37:23.

[212] Psalms 44:18.

[213] Psalms 119:133.

heart deviseth his way: but the Lord directeth his steps.[214] O Lord, I know that the way of man is not in himself: it is not in man that walketh to direct his steps.[215] In Romans, mention is made of those who walk in the steps of the faith of our father Abraham.[216] *And Christ suffered for us, leaving us an example that we should follow in his steps.*[217] Our Savior, on a memorable occasion, said unto Peter: *Follow me.* These words, according to the most able interpreters, meant that Peter should not merely emulate the virtues of Christ, but that he should conform to Him in the manner of his death. The disciple, when he was carried out to be crucified, *was girded about his body, and his hands were stretched forth.*[218] If our Master suffered, we must suffer; if he experienced trials and temptations, we must also; if he died, so must we die; if his life and death present to our view a finished picture of *virtue, fortitude,* and *integrity,* unparalleled in the history of the universe, his example is indeed worthy of our imitation; and it is our duty to follow his steps, as nearly as we can, in the way he travelled before us. This we must do to gain admission into the sanctuary, whither he was taken. And he who will try to follow in his steps will find a mystery: We would not that any should be ignorant of this mystery.[219] He who has the secret will always keep it. We read of the preaching of Jesus Christ, according to the revelation of the mystery, which was kept secret since the world began.[220] The mystery was the truth of the gospel—a knowledge of Jesus Christ—the preaching of Jesus Christ, which was not made plain under the patriarchal or Levitical dispensations. That which was only *shadowed* forth in the early history of

---

[214] Proverbs 16:9.

[215] Jeremiah 10:23.

[216] Romans 4:12.

[217] 1 Peter 2:21.

[218] John 21:18.

[219] Romans 11:25.

[220] Romans 16:25.

the world was *brought to light* in the gospel; and that which is typified in the two first degrees of Masonry is made manifest or clear in the third degree. There is a mystery spoken of in Corinthians: But we speak the wisdom of God in a *mystery*, even the *hidden* wisdom which God ordained before the world unto our glory.[221] There are *stewards*[222] of the mysteries of God.[223] St. Paul spoke as though he understood all mysteries and all knowledge. He *followed in the way of the Lord.* He that speaketh in an unknown tongue, said he, speaketh not unto men, but unto God. What a beautiful illustration of this sentiment is found in the Royal Arch Degree. In Colossians, we are told of the mystery which had been *hid from ages and from generations, but now is made manifest to the saints.*[224] And what was the riches of the glory of this mystery among the Gentiles? It is, Christ in you, the hope of glory. There are three things recorded in this remarkable passage: first, there is the *mystery* of Christ; then Christ is the *hope* of glory; and lastly, Christ in you is the *hope* of glory.

---

[221] 1 Corinthians 2:7.

[222] Steward, one who manages the affairs or superintends the house hold of another, as Eliezer of Damascus did that of Abraham. — Genesis 15:2. Great confidence was reposed in those who held such an office: and hence St. Paul describes Christian ministers as the stewards of God over his church and family. — 2 Pict. Dict., 1253. There are certain officers of a regular lodge called stewards, in whom great confidence is reposed by the brethren, and their duties are strictly defined.

[223] 1 Corinthians 4:1.

[224] Colossians 1:26.

LECTURE VI.
The Entered Apprentice

The weight and force of the united testimony of numbers, upon abstract mathematical principles, increases in a higher ratio than that of the mere number of such witnesses. [225]

We know of no scriptural method of addressing transgressors, but as free agents; and we abjure, as unsanctioned by the Bible, every scheme of theology which would make men nothing more than machines. [226]

To make daily progress in knowledge and virtue is our constant duty, and expressly required by our general laws. [227]

Despise not what is wonderful, when all things are wonderful around thee.

From the multitude of like effects thou sayest, behold a law. [228]

---

[225] Thomas Starkie., *Practical Treatise of the Law of Evidence*, London, 1833, Vol. 1, p. 489. Hereafter Star. Ev.

[226] 1 Mel. Ser., p. 100

[227] Ahi. Rez. E. N.: E∴A∴, 2nd section.

[228] Tupper, p. 69

The force of moral testimony[229] depends greatly upon the number of circumstances and coincidences, and their consistency; as the force of human testimony, in our courts of justice, depends chiefly upon the number of witnesses and their consistency in the narration of their story.[230] The emblems, symbols, &c., of Freemasonry, may be termed moral witnesses. There is no just ground to suspect their integrity, having lived for ages, and never varied in their evidence. That which they have at all times spoken, will bear the same construction and meaning. They direct the mind to the contemplation of our social and eternal destinies. The series of deductions which have been and may be drawn from them concur, and the order in which the emblems and types are introduced, enhance materially the strength of the evidence. The uniform construction which enlightened craftsmen in all ages have given to them, evince their meaning, and establish, in our estimation, their scriptural character. Invariably awakening the same train of thought and reflection, and pointing to particular circumstances of known biblical signification, they furnish a body of coincidences which can only be accounted for upon one of two grounds or suppositions: either the points on which they agree are true or they are not. If they be true, a consistent moral system is the result; if untrue, or, in other words, if the construction which they have received, singly and collectively, be the mere creation of the imaginations of men, then there is nothing in the Order worthy of our pur-

---

[229] In courts of justice matters of fact are proved by moral evidence alone; by which is meant not only that kind of evidence which is employed on subjects connected with moral conduct, but all the evidence which is not obtained either from intuition or from demonstration. — 1 Green. Ev. 4. E. N.: Simon Greenleaf, *A Treatise on the Law of Evidence*, Boston, 1842, Vol. 1.

A presumption of any fact is, says Lord Tenterden, an inferring of that fact from other facts that are known; it is an act of reasoning; and much of human knowledge on all subjects is derived from this source. (Sir F. Burdett, 4 Barn. & Ald. p. 161. E. N.: as quoted in *The Law Magazine*, Vol. VI, Jul.y-October 1831, London, 1831, p. 358, notes.)

[230] 1 Star. Ev., p. 485.

suit or investigation. It is, then, neither an art nor a science. It would amount to an idle and senseless thing. But such a view of the Order cannot be maintained upon any known rule of logic. It has stood the test of ages, and the severest trials. Many of the wisest and best of mankind, from its origin down to the present day, have been faithful and devoted craftsmen.[231] Many have exemplified, in their walk and conversation, its sublime doctrines; while many have been brought to knowledge of the true light—the light of the gospel—through its instrumentality. There are multitudes who have traced their first serious impressions to the period when they were initiated into the Order, or were raised to the degree of a Master. Those who have been fully made acquainted with the machinery of the institution, or its moral lessons, have felt the silent work of reform going on within them. In the first degree, the foundation stone of moral improvement is symbolically laid; and laid, too, in reference to the location of the sacred Mount, whereon the temple of Solomon stood, and the grandest events of time were enacted. Moriah[232] was situated northeast of the city of Jerusalem.

There is evidently design in every department of our moral work. The agreement in all our emblems or symbols, in referring to our immortal nature with its thrilling associations, cannot be wisely regarded as the result of chance or accident. The founders of the institution, doubtless, had some great end or design in view, or its foundations would

---

231 Melancthon, Locke, Newton, Chalmers, Burns, Hutchinson, Preston, Washington, Warren, Green, Clinton, Jefferson, Madison, Franklin, Jackson, and a host of other worthies who might be named, were members of the fraternity. The Masonic aprons of Washington and Warren were worn in procession on the recent occasion of laying the cornerstone of the monument now being erected to the memory of the Father of our country.

232 A hill on the north-east side of Jerusalem. In the time of David, it stood apart from the city, and was under cultivation; for here was the threshing-floor of Araunah, the Jebusite, which David bought, on which to erect an altar to God. — 2 Samuel 24:24-25; 2 Pict. Dict., p. 889.

not have covered the earth and its roof formed a cloudy canopy. Freemasonry otherwise would never have extended from east to west, and between north and south; its supports would not have been wisdom, strength, and beauty. Its splendid furniture, its beautiful ornaments, its movable and immovable jewels, all correspond with the moral design and architecture of the mystic building. Such is the consistency and fullness of the testimony. If one symbol or emblem constituted our only witness, and it stood alone and unsupported, there could be little or no satisfactory proof of the moral and religious tendency of the institution; but when there are many witnesses *in and about the temple*, and they all agree, the additional and concurrent testimony adds to the credibility of our view, and verifies it. The coincidences are natural and important. They agree in points obviously material, and even in minute or remote points, which were not likely to be material, or in matters of importance not easily perceived, but which evidence design[233]. Partial variances, if any exist, are of little moment, unless they be of so prominent a nature as to falsify the deductions from the uniform and consistent character of the symbolical representations. "I know not," said Dr. Paley, "a more rash or unphilosophical conduct of the understanding, than to reject the substance of a story, by means of some diversity of the circumstances with which it is related. The usual character of human testimony is substantial truth under circumstantial variety. This is what the daily experience of courts of justice teaches. When accounts of a transaction come from the mouths of different witnesses, it is seldom that it is not possible to pick out apparent or real inconsistencies between them. Those inconsistencies are studiously displayed by an adverse pleader, but oftentimes with little impression on the minds of the judges. Numerous, and sometimes important variations present themselves; not seldom also, absolute and final contradictions;

---

[233] 1 Star. Ev., p. 486.

yet neither the one nor the other are deemed sufficient to shake the credibility of the *main fact*."

The degrees of ancient craft Masonry afford a vast number of important circumstances or significant allusions, interwoven and connected with each other, and also with natural and revealed truth, so that it would seem impossible to resist the conclusion to which they would conduct the thinking mind. There are also a number of dependent reflections and thoughts which arise out of the principles of Masonry, which coincide or agree in their minutest bearings and relations. The connection which exists between the symbols and the train of thoughts which they generate is as perceptible in a moral point of view as that which exists between a man's conduct and his motives, or between cause and effect. We have shown that the blazing star is one of the elements of our hieroglyphical language. We have said that it is emblematical of the star of Bethlehem; and what a sublime train of reflections it awakens in the mind. Our thoughts are fixed on the remembrance of that star winch arose in the east and travelled to the west, and which was as "beautiful as the young child to which it pointed." And by it we are *brought to the light* of many touching and sublime conceptions. The whole plan of God's amazing mercy and providence becomes visible. But the emblem is associated with other emblems, which give birth to similar thoughts and reflections united in sublime alliance; and the *whole, when put together*, make a tower of strength.

If the analogy which exists between the physical and spiritual kingdoms demonstrates a connection between the Author of nature and the Author of revelation, or prove that the God of nature is also the God of revelation, then, surely, there is much force in the analogy which is found to exist between the doctrines of speculative Masonry and spiritual truth, as found in the word of God. It is not intended even to intimate that this connection argues a particular or special relation between the authors of Masonry and the great Author of the book of Revelation. It simply shows that the principles of our Order are founded on the principles contained in the Bible. And while we seem to read the truth of revealed religion written in the book of Nature, the Bible has kindled our moral firmament and decked our clouded canopy with mystic stars. If we can gather testimony for the "truth as it is in Jesus," from the rocks which were rent on the day of crucifixion, we know that Masonry is associated with the mighty memories of the past, and the *rocks* and *mountains* of Judea. If the cross of Christ was erected on Calvary, on its adjacent hill were witnessed scenic representations of the death of the Savior. If He ascended from the summit of Olivet, the foot of the Masonic ladder emblematically reposes on the *brow* of a mount, and its top seems to penetrate beyond our vision. If He opened a communication between earth and heaven, we have shown that our theological emblem illustrates the same fact. If there exist "manifold appearances of design and of final causes in the constitution of the world," there are multiplied evidences of design manifested in our rites and ceremonies. The material world is "boundless and immense:" the Masonic world is illimitable in its dominions. The mind of the cultivated Mason is directed to the study of the visible universe, and may survey the bright fields of astronomy and investigate the laws of the planetary system. While the Master gazes on suns and stars pursuing their way in the heavens, he cannot fail to think of Him who made those suns and stars, and dwells in that inaccessible light which he made to shine in far lovelier canopies. He will ponder on Him which spreadest out the heavens, which maketh Arcturus, Orion, and Pleiades, and the chambers of the south.[234] Who can bind the sweet influ-

---

[234] Job 9:8-9.

The sacred writers rarely mention any of the constellations by name; because it is supposed that the heathen nations worshipped the hosts of heaven. — 2 Home's Intro., p. 187.

Bp. Patrick thinks that nothing more is intended by Arcturus, Orion, &c., than to point out to us that all the constellations of heaven obey

ences of Pleiades, or loose the bands of Orion[235]; who can bring forth Mazzaroth in his season, and Arcturus with his sons[236]. We may read, in the sacred pages, of the celestial hemisphere, the wisdom, strength, and beauty of the Almighty Creator; and while we are employed in the study of the science of astronomy, we will perceive unparalleled instances of wisdom and goodness; and through the whole creation trace the glorious Author by his works[237]. He telleth the number of the stars: he calleth them by their names.[238] And how many living orbs of light revolve the unseen depths of glory, in "radiant circles" round the central throne? The All Seeing Eye can number them at a glance and call them by their names. The material heavens have no language, and yet the inspired Psalmist calls on them to praise the Lord: Praise ye him, sun and moon: praise him, all ye stars of light. Praise him, ye heaven of heavens, and ye waters that be above the heavens.[239] The heavens declare the glory of God, and the firmament showeth his handiwork.[240] They call upon us, says Bishop Home, to translate their actions into our language, and copy their obedience in our lives, that so we may, both by word and deed, glorify, with them, the Creator and Redeemer of the universe.

Begin, my soul, the exalted lay,
Let each enraptured thought obey,

God in their several seasons; both those which we see, and those in the other hemisphere. St. Jerome delivers substantially the same comment.

[235] "The sweet influences" are the pleasant season of spring; "the bands" are the rigors of winter, when the earth is bound with frost. — Scott's Com. Job 38:31. St. Chrysostom, says Scott, explains Mazzaroth of the twelve signs of the Zodiac.

[236] Job 38:31-32.

[237] Cross' Chart, p. 24

[238] Psalms 147:4.

[239] Psalms 148:3-4.

[240] Psalms 19:1.

And praise the Almighty's name:
Lo! Heaven and earth, and sea and skies,
In one melodious concert rise,
To swell the inspiring theme.

Dr. Ogilvie.[241]

Masonry has its terrestrial globe as well as its celestial. Our artificial globes are spherical bodies, on the convex surface of which are represented the countries, seas, and various parts of the earth, the face of the heavens, the planetary revolutions, and other particulars.[242] Doubtless, these artificial globes were intended to assist the contemplative Mason in studying the material world, that he might be inspired with a due reverence for the Deity and all his works. The celestial and terrestrial globes have been most wisely adopted as emblems of the Order. The study of geography is particularly important to an accurate knowledge of the Scriptures. Sacred geography may be said to embrace the surface of the earth; not merely the Holy Land, with its mountains, plains, rivers, and cities, but all lands, rivers, and seas; for Christianity will yet spread over all the world. The religion of our Savior was designed to embrace, in its merciful and wonderful provisions, all nations. When "the apostles were commissioned to prosecute their evangelical labours, a new field of geography was opened by their ministry, far beyond the boundaries of the Holy Land, Babylon, Assyria, or Egypt." Ministers of Christ are now piously and zealously engaged in the great cause of humanity, and preaching Christ crucified in the most dark and remote regions. They have carried out to the heathen the volume of

---

[241] E. N.: Dr. John Ogilvie, D.D., a poet of some renown in his day, was the son of one of the ministers of Aberdeen, where he was born in 1733. He was educated at Marischal College, from which afterwards he received the degree of Doctor of Divinity. The venerable divine continued his useful parish labours till his death in 1814. In addition to his poems Dr. Ogilvie was the author of several works on philosophy and Christian ethics. See: James Grant Wilson, *The Poets and Poetry of Scotland,* New York, 1876, Vol. 1, pp. 246-248.

[242] Cross' Chart, p. 24.

our fathers' love and faith, and the time will surely arrive when its benign and civilizing influences will be witnessed in the dark places of the earth. Masonry, then, has incorporated into its system all that nature argues for its God. Whatever natural theology teaches is embraced in our universal science; whatever analogy exists between natural and revealed religion; or whatever may be the analogy of religion, natural and revealed, to the constitution and course of nature, it constitutes a portion of Masonic truth. If, therefore, natural religion teaches a future state of existence; that the government of God is one of rewards and punishments; that his government is a moral government; that there exists a state of probation or moral discipline, as Bishop Butler proved conclusively; then, all these truths are taught in the science of Masonry: for we have shown that Masons, as such, are enjoined to study all the works of God, that they may be inspired with reverence for their Creator. If there be any analogy between natural and revealed religion, that analogy is recognized in Masonry; and whatever proof there is in the world of nature of the Divine origin of the Scriptures, has been adopted also by the Order. If the consideration of the material universe lead us to believe that "there must be some scheme of Providence vast in proportion to it"—and if this little scene of human life in which we are so busily engaged lead us to contemplate "a much larger state of things," then, that science, which is universal, and cannot be understood without a knowledge of the material world or the constitution of nature, must embrace all the arguments, by way of analogy, which may be drawn from nature.

The degrees of Masonry illustrate the doctrine of a state of probation, trial, labor, or moral discipline. The Entered Apprentice must serve a proper time as such, before he can be advanced to the degree of Fellow Craft. He must learn to cultivate his moral and intellectual nature; to measure and divide his time properly; to guard against temptation and avoid evil; and to keep the door of his heart closed to every unholy desire. Such are his Masonic duties—such his moral work,—which he must perform before he can be taught to number and mark the immortal ashlar; for it must be polished before it can be either marked or numbered. In the due performance of such work, there are many trials and difficulties—many perplexities and troubles. Moral improvement is a gradual work. Faith precedes hope, and hope comes before charity. We must serve our Grand Master with *freedom, fervency*, and *zeal*. The first degree is preparatory to the second. The Entered Apprentice takes only the first step in Masonry, the second step is in the Fellow Craft's degree. They both teach probation, or the necessity of preparation to receive the sublime degree of a Master Mason.

It is believed that the principles which we profess inculcate the doctrine of free agency and the trust which we should always repose in God. No one can be made a Mason without his own deliberate consent or free will. He must seek admission voluntarily—uninfluenced by friends or idle curiosity.[243] He should come as one anxiously desiring to subdue his passions and to improve his social and moral being; with a sincere wish to be brought to knowledge of the truth; and that his soul might be imbued with the love of man and the love of God.

There were several stages or degrees in the creation of the world. When God divided the light from the darkness, he called the light Day, and the darkness he called Night. And the evening and the morning were the first day.[244] The

---

[243] The following questions must be answered affirmatively by a candidate previous to his initiation: 1st - Do you seriously declare, upon your honor, that, unbiased by friends and uninfluenced by mercenary motives, you freely and voluntarily offer yourself a candidate for the mysteries of Masonry? 2nd - Do you seriously declare, upon your honor, that you are prompted to solicit the privileges of Masonry by a favorable opinion of the institution, a desire of knowledge, and a sincere wish of being serviceable to your fellow creatures? 3rd – Do you seriously declare, upon your honor, that you will conform to all the ancient established usages and customs of the fraternity? (*Trestleboard.*)

[244] Genesis 1:4-5.

earth passed from one stage to another; *islands, and conti-nents, and waters, assuming different forms and proportions, and be-ing successively fitted up for different living tribes.*[245] The earth was at *first* without *form and void. Darkness* was upon the face of the deep. The Spirit moved or brooded over the waters, and then came *the light.*[246] God made the firmament before he made the earth, and the earth before he put lights in the firmament, and the waters before the living creatures which were to move therein, and the earth and air before he made the fowls and birds; and after he had made all other things and beings, and all nature was fair and beautiful, and pro-nounced good by the Almighty, then he said: "Let us make man in our own image, after our likeness, and let them have dominion over all." It seems, then, that the Mosaic account of the creation contains the doctrine of progres-sion: that one state of existence prepares the way for an-other; for one period of time, at the creation, was the pre-cursor of another. It teaches, that if God, in his infinite mercy and goodness, made earth and all that it contains, and made man and gave him dominion over all, then man is a creature of the loftiest destiny; and when he shall have passed through various states of moral culture, and per-

---

[245] 1 Mel. Ser., p. 360.

[246] The words, "And the earth was without form and void, and darkness was upon the face of the deep: and the Spirit of God moved upon the face of the waters," are regarded by many divines as being typical. They admit of a twofold application—to natural things and to spiritual. The work attributed to the Holy Spirit may serve as a type of that which this Divine agent came down at Pentecost to perform. The Gospel of St. John commences in the same strain and with the same sublime abrupt-ness as the book of Genesis: as though the historians of the New Tes-tament and of the Old had to give the narrations of similar creations. And, forasmuch as that moral change, which passes over those who become heirs of the kingdom of heaven, is described in the Bible as nothing less than a new creation, and is moreover ascribed to the agen-cy of that Spirit which brooded over the waters of the primitive chaos, there can, at least, be nothing unreasonable in the supposition that a typical character attaches, in some degree, to the scriptural account of the formation of all things. — 1 Mel. Ser., p. 361.

formed various degrees of service, would be raised at last to the world of spirits.

The Entered Apprentice is represented as one doomed to labor. He symbolizes a hewer of wood and drawer of water. And labor is a part of the original curse: In the sweat of thy face shalt thou eat bread.[247] It would seem, however, that man was not intended be an idle being, even if he had retained his first estate.[248] He was created an active agent, but his labor was a pleasing pursuit: He took the man and put him into the garden to dress it and keep it.[249]

The degree of Entered Apprentice may be looked upon in a twofold aspect. It may be typical of our lost innocence, or that which was forfeited at the fall of man. It may be also typical of that freedom, fervency, and zeal with which our first parents labored, before their transgression, to worship and adore their Creator, and in keeping and dressing the garden. Their labor consisted in moral and religious culture, pious meditation, and prayerful devotion to their Divine Creator. And "thrice happy were the happy pair."

> *Discovering in the wide landscape all the east*
> *Of Eden and Eden's happy plains,*
> *Lowly they bow'd adoring; and began*
> *Their orisons, each morning daily paid*
> *In various style; for neither various style*
> *Nor holy rapture wanted they to praise*
> *Their Maker, in fit strains pronounced or sung*
> *Unmeditated, such prompt eloquence*

---

[247] Genesis 3:19.

[248] Idleness was not allowed even in Paradise, filled as it was with all tailings pleasant to the sight and good for food. Adam, though he could know no want, nor be apprehensive of any scarcity, had yet an employment assigned him that he might keep his faculties in exercise, and manage his time and opportunities to the best advantage. Industry and righteousness are constantly united, and no man can be said to love or serve God, who does not endeavor to do good in his generation. — Sears' Bible Biog., p. 12

[249] Genesis 2:15.

Flow'd from their lips, in prose or numerous verse,
More tuneable than needed lute or harp
To add more sweetness.

Milton, *Paradise Lost*, 5.142-152.

Probation implies progression, and progression implies reward. If the labor of the Entered Apprentice is intended to refer to the fall of man, or the curse pronounced for his disobedience, then the industrious and Christian Mason has an assurance that the time will come when he will be called from his labor on earth to refreshment in heaven. Every Entered Apprentice who wrought at the building of King Solomon's temple, at its completion, would have been entitled to his reward, if found worthy, by being advanced, or rather invested with the secrets of the three Grand Masters. So, if we walk worthy of our vocation and faith fully serve our God, at the final consummation of all things—the day for the completion of the temple on high—we will all be rewarded abundantly for our pious labours.

The right of the Entered Apprentice to be advanced, or the Fellow Craft to be raised, depends, in strict principle, upon his proficiency in the degree which he has received. He should be able to exhibit a beautiful specimen of intellectual or moral work, to entitle him to receive wages, or to enter upon the study of the higher departments of science. The progress of knowledge is not confined in its results to the mere facts which we acquire, or the elements of truth; but it advances with a majestic step to other and higher regions of philosophy.[250] The understanding is enlarged for the more ready reception of other facts and other truths, when a wider field of observation is opened to the mind's eye, or a broader domain of reason. The human intellect cannot remain stationary. It must either advance or retrograde in power and strength. Such is the case with all our moral and social capacities. The soul, that eternal and active

---

[250] Aber. on Intel. Powers, p. 71. E. N.: surely a reference to John Abercrombie, *Inquiries Concerning the Intellectual Powers*, Boston, 1843.

principle, must be either improving its moral condition, or be heaping up wrath for the day of wrath. There are degrees of wickedness and degrees of virtue and holiness. One sinner differs from another sinner in the acts of disobedience. And "one star differeth from another star in glory."

We need not resort to the fact that our social and moral being is susceptible of the highest culture, to establish the progressive character of the human soul. Nature, when read by the Great Light of our Order, furnishes abundant proof of the soul's immortality. The disordered state of the spiritual world, contrasted with the regular and systematical order of the material, affords a strong presumption of another state, in which the moral evils which now exist will be corrected.[251] Out of the ruins of humanity may arise a new-born spirit, whose immortal nature will be capable of advancing higher and higher in the regions of bliss. The elements of truth contained in the degree of Entered Apprentice are but the rudiments of Masonic knowledge, but which are essential to be learned and understood, before one can with propriety be advanced to the higher degrees. So man in his present state may be looked upon as possessing only the rudiments of what he may become hereafter in a more expansive sphere of existence.[252] The Mason should look to the future—*mark his advancing steps to meet the Son of Man in his coming—the great Builder of the church of God.* Every step in life should be cautiously and considerately taken. We should *measure* our steps and mark the ground whereon we stand. It is scriptural and holy ground. The *plumb* admonishes us to walk uprightly in our several stations toward God and man[253]. We are all travelling on the *common level* of time, and we should not advance without a,

---

[251] Thomas Dick, *The Philosophy of a Future State,* London, 1847, p. 70, ch. 1, s. 8. Hereafter *Dick's Future State.*

[252] Idem p. 90.

[253] Cross' Chart, p. 22.

due guard to all our steps and actions, always keeping in view the *penalty* of the Divine law; for if we depart from the *line* of duty, or prove ungrateful to our heavenly Father, we will never be *raised*, through the strength of the Lion of the tribe of Judah, to a glorious immortality. It is well that we are probationers in time—"the pensioners on the bounty of an hour." Earth is the *floor* on which we must, if ever, work out our salvation. Here each one must lay his *corner-stone* of virtue and righteousness, upon which he is charged to erect a superstructure honorable to himself and profitable to his Master. The Entered Apprentice, in his preparatory state, may learn a lesson of humility, and to place but little value on worldly riches, or earthly grandeur—a lesson which is impressed upon his mind by symbolical ceremonies, too important in their character ever to be forgotten[254]. The Bible, which he is informed should be the rule of his faith, "is a symbol in Masonry of the will of God; and from the centre of the lodge pours forth its effulgent rays of Divine truth." It is the great light of God. All the lesser lights are doomed to expire. The sun will drop in darkness from his throne in the heavens; the moon will be turned into blood, or wane away, when doomsday comes; but the light of Divine Wisdom will burn brighter and brighter and forever and ever.

---

[254] Mack. Lex. E. N.: the same quote is generally found in the same terms in Preston, Oliver, Dermott and the majority of Masonic monitors still in use by all Grand Lodges.

LECTURE VII.
The Fellowcraft

The plumb-rule and level, united, represent the cross; the plumb, rule constituting the lower limb, and the level the upper and transverse limb; while the heavy setting maul would be a point within a circle.[255]

The temple of speculative masonry is built by piling precept upon precept, symbol upon symbol, instruction, explanation, admonition, example, and historical fact, like a series of polished and perfect stones, emblematically carved, marked, and numbered.[256]

Say, ancient edifice, thyself with years
Grown gray, how long upon the hill has stood
Thy weather-braving tower, and silent marked
The human leaf in constant bud and fall?
The generations of deciduous man,
How oft hast thou seen them pass away? [257]

---

[255] Willoughby of Birkenhead. E. N.: as quoted by Rev. George Oliver, *Historical Landmarks and other Evidences of Freemasonry*, New York, 1855, Vol. 1, p. 439, note 29 on Lecture XLVIII.

[256] Rev. George Oliver, *Historical Landmarks and other Evidences of Freemasonry*, New York, 1855, Vol. 1, p. 178, note 15 on Lecture XXXI.

[257] Hurdis. E. N.: Scott refers to James Hurdis (1763-1801), an English clergyman from Bishopstone, Sussex, who was appointed professor of po-

The Fellow Craft's degree, says a learned Mason, is one particularly devoted to science. Clothed with a white garment[258], the candidate for this degree advances to be invested with its deep and unutterable truths. Passing the porch of the temple, on his way to the inner chamber, he is taught our ancient and unerring method of distinguishing a friend from a foe[259]. His mind is fixed upon the wonders of nature and art. He is taught the difference between operative and speculative Masonry; and, by instruction and contemplation, is led to view with reverence and admiration the works of creation, and is inspired with the most exalted ideas of the perfections of his Divine Creator[260]. Extensive knowledge and cultivated genius enabled our ancient brethren to work out those beautiful and sublime designs which our revered master, Hiram, the builder, drew on his tracing-board. . It has been stated that, in the degree of Entered Apprentice every emblematical ceremony is directed to the lustration of the heart; in that of the Fellow Craft, to the

---

etry at Oxford University in 1793. Hurdis, an admirer and imitator of William Cowper, was rescued from oblivion in an article by William Taylor on the collective works of Dr. Sayer, published in the *The Quarterly Review*, Vol. XXXV, London, 1827, p. 175, which includes the poem here quoted (p. 203).

[258] The ancients were also wont to put a white garment on the person baptized, to denote his having put off the lusts of the flesh, and being cleansed from former sins; and that he had obliged himself to maintain a life of unspotted innocence. Accordingly, the baptized are, both by the apostles and the Greek fathers, frequently styled the enlightened, because they profess to be children of light, and engage themselves never to return again to the works of darkness. The white garment used to be delivered to them with this solemn charge: "Receive the white and undefiled garment, and produce it without spot before the tribunal of our Lord Jesus Christ, that you may obtain eternal life. Amen. — Eccl. Biog.; Mas. Lib., p. 151.

[259] The application which is made of certain words among Masons is as a testimony of their retaining their original word uninfringed, and their faith with the brotherhood uncorrupted. And, to render their words and phrase more abstruse and obscure, they selected such as by acceptation in the Scriptures and otherwise, might puzzle the ignorant by a double implication, — Hutchinson, Mas. Lib., p. 166.

[260] Mack. Lex.

enlargement of the mind.[261] This statement is emphatically true; but that enlargement of mind, that advancement in knowledge, or progress in science, may inspire our affections and advance our moral nature. Advancement in mind is advancement in the philosophy of the soul. "Every triumph of the intellect, imbued with the Spirit of God, in the field of physical science, is an achievement in moral science." Discoveries in the material or immaterial universe reveal the goodness and wisdom of Deity. The providential *designs* of God, the Architect of universal nature, show the merciful genius of our Master in heaven.

In a lodge of Fellow Craft Masons, the Bible should be opened upon the altar; and, by having reference to the chart, it would appear proper that it should be opened at the seventh chapter of the book of Amos, the 7th and 8th verses of which read as follows: Thus he showed me: and, behold, the Lord stood upon a wall made by a *plumb-line*,[262] with a *plumb-line* in his hand. And the Lord said unto me, Amos, what seest thou? And I said, a *plumb-line*. Then said the Lord, Behold, I will set a *plumb-line* in the midst of my people Israel: I will not again pass by them anymore. There is the following passage in second Kings: I will stretch over Jerusalem the *line* of Samaria, and the *plummet* of the house of Ahab.[263] Such was a part of the denunciation of God

---

[261] Mack. Lex.

[262] The rule, the plumb-line, the square, and the compasses are "emblematical of the conduct we should pursue in society; to observe punctually all our engagements; faithfully and religiously to discharge those important obligations which we owe to God and our neighbor; to be upright in all our dealings; to hold the scale of justice in equal poise; to square our actions by the unerring rule of God's Sacred Word; and keep within compass and bounds with all mankind, but particularly with a brother. — Ahi. Rez., p. 150.

God's judgments are sometimes represented by "a line" and "a plummet," to denote that they are measured out by the exactest rules of justice. — See D'Oyly and Mant's Com. on Amos 7:7. Also 2 Kings 21:13; Isaiah 28:17.

[263] 2 Kings, 21:13.

against Jerusalem for the idolatries of Manasseh. How dreadful is the use of the line and plumb, when strictly applied by the hand of the Almighty. How nicely will He plumb all our thoughts and deeds. If we do not walk *uprightly* before God and man; if we do not *raise* our thoughts *directly* to heaven, we shall have cause to tremble with fear; for our ungrateful souls will have refused the true worship when it was before us, and He will stretch over us the *line* of Samaria and the *plummet* of the house of Ahab. And when He comes to judge the world, will He not have a *plumb-line* in his hand, and will He not set a, *plumb-line* in the midst of all his people?

The plumb is an instrument made use of by operative masons for the purpose of erecting perpendicular hues. In speculative Masonry, it is one of the tools of the Fellow Craft. The plumb is also the jewel of the Junior Warden, and instructs us, says Mackey, symbolically, as the authority of this officer is exercised only in time of refreshment, when the brethren have ceased to labor, and are no longer within the lodge room; that then, more particularly, when the eyes of a censorious world are upon him, should the Mason walk *uprightly* and eschew evil. But does it not symbolically instruct us as to the authority of *Him, by and through whom we can come to the Father,* and that a time will arrive when the *earthly labours of the just will cease, and they shall be called to everlasting refreshment?*

The other instruments of the Fellow Craft have been adverted to incidentally. The square is an angle extending to ninety degrees, or the fourth part of a circle. It is not only one of the working tools of the Fellow Craft, but the distinctive jewel of the Master of a lodge.[264]

The square, then, is an angle extending to ninety degrees, or the fourth part of a circle. We have shown that the

---

264 Mack. Lex.

circle[265] is an emblem of Deity and eternity. Man has within him an *immortal part*. The *living soul* is an emanation from God. It is a *segment* of eternity. It may be compared to the *fourth* part of a circle, and may be said to belong to that which has neither beginning nor end. It is destined for an eternal duration. It is a part of the *Great Circle*, which has a *Common Centre*, that *Perfect Point* from which all perfect forms or figures are drawn. The great Geometrician, before time began,

> *Took the golden compasses, prepared*
> *In God's eternal store, to circumscribe*
> *The universe and all created things;*
> *One foot he centered, and the other turn'd*
> *Round through the vast profundity obscure,*
> *And said, thus far extend, thus far thy bounds,*
> *This be thy just circumference, O world.*

Milton, Paradise Lost, 7.225-31.

The square is also a significant emblem of virtue and morality. As by the application of the square the stone is tried and proved, so by the application of the principles of morality, each action of human life is judged, and approved or condemned.[266] Our moral work must prove *true* and *trusty*; it must be *square* work. If it is not such, it will be *rejected* and *cast among the ruins of sin*, and will never be taken from the fires which were kindled at the fall of man. It will there

---

[265] The square was the figure under which the Israelites formed their encampments in the wilderness, and under which they fortified or defended the holy tabernacle, sanctified with the immediate presence of the Divinity. — Masonic Lib. p. 176, n. The ground-plot on which the temple was erected was a square of 600 cubits. The court of the priests was a perfect square. The altar of burnt-offerings was 12 cubits square. The most holy place was a square of 20 cubits. Solomon began to build the house of the Lord in the fourth year. In the most holy place of Solomon's temple were four cherubim. The breastplate of judgment was four-square when doubled, and had four rows of stones, three stones in each row. There, are four Gospels. The Jews divided the night into four watches, and the day likewise.

[266] Mack. Lex.

remain for ever and ever; but the penal flames will never polish or burn off its rough edges. No angel of light will ever be sent to the ruins below, in search of any rejected stone, to bring it forth with shouting and praise.[267]

The level is an emblem of equality. All men are created equal. The level teaches particularly the equality of men in the sight of God. We are all heirs of immortality—all are journeying to the spirit land. All our brethren have travelled the way before us; some to the spirit land of glory and others to the regions of outer darkness. Let us all ask ourselves the solemn question, whither are we going? The Mighty Master will certainly square our thoughts and plumb our actions. We will all be judged by his righteous law. If we advance in the path of sin, it will surely lead us to that awful precipice, from which we must step into the profoundest woe.

The second section of the Fellow Craft's degree refers to the origin of the institution, and views Masonry under two denominations, operative and speculative.[268] The early

---

[267] There is a Jewish tradition concerning a certain stone, which, after having been by the builders of the second temple thrown aside among the rubbish, was at last found to be exactly fitted for the honorable place of a chief corner-stone. — George Horne, *A Commentary on the Book of Psalms*, London, 1826, p. 398. Hereafter Horne on Psalms.

[268] Ahi. Rez., p. 167.

By operative masonry, we allude to a proper application of the useful rules of architecture, whence a structure will derive figure, strength, and beauty; and whence will result a due proportion, and a just correspondence in all its parts. It furnishes us with dwellings and convenient shelters from the vicissitudes and inclemencies of seasons; and while it displays the effects of human wisdom, as well in the choice as in the arrangement of the sundry materials of which an edifice is composed, it demonstrates that a fund of science and industry is implanted in man for the best, most salutary, and beneficent purposes. By speculative Masonry, we learn to subdue the passions, act upon the square, keep a tongue of good report, maintain secrecy, and practice charity. It is so interwoven with religion as to lay us under obligations to pay that rational homage to Deity which at once constitutes our duty and our happiness. — Ahi. Rez., p. 168.

history of the Order, like that of the world, is involved in much obscurity, but our landmarks or traditions induce the belief that Masonry is of great antiquity. In its progress through many generations, some innovations may have been engrafted upon the system; but its fundamental principles remain unaltered. The internal evidence of Freemasonry, tending to establish its ancient origin, could not, perhaps, with Masonic propriety, be disclosed to the public eye.[269] There are but few bright craftsmen, we presume, who have investigated its history, and have not been convinced that it originated in a very remote age. Its ceremonies, language, signs, words, and usages are ancient. The traditions of the Order carry about them earmarks of antiquity; while the truth of many of them are confirmed by rabbinical traditions and other traditional evidence. Some of the principal facts engrafted into the body of Masonry must have been transmitted orally through many generations to King Solomon. But while we would avoid any absurd speculation, we feel warranted in stating that the symbolical degrees were perfected at the building of the first temple, or a short time prior to its completion. The Masonic lectures would seem to indicate that such was the fact. We know, says brother Mackey, from the traditions of our Order, that it existed in its present form at the building of Solomon's temple: and the enlightened brethren of the craft no longer hesitate to trace the birth of symbolic Masonry to that renowned spot, the threshing-floor of Oman the Jebusite.[270]

---

[269] Some distinguished members of the fraternity are of opinion that the secrets of the Order consist in signs and words. This opinion cannot be regarded as authority. But if it be a question of words, and names, and of your law, look ye to it; for I will be no judge of such matters. — Acts 28:15.

[270] Many distinguished Masons have claimed for the institution a more remote origin. Some have even contended that Adam was a Mason; but the Freemasonry of Adam consisted, according to Dr. Oliver's opinion, in the fact that he was created beautiful in body, glorious in mind, perfect in righteousness and true holiness, and without taint and sin. — 1 Ol. Land., p. 498. Some have thought that Noah, Enoch, and Peleg

There are historical traces of the existence of the Order in the age of King Athelstan. To prove this, we rely upon the most indubitable facts. Athelstan granted, about the year of our Lord, 926, a charter to his brother Edwin to

---

were Free Masons. And there are some curious legends concerning Enoch and Peleg. There is, in fact, a degree called the Noachites, or Prussian Chevaliers, from which the following legend has been extracted by Dr. Oliver. The descendants of Noah, notwithstanding God had appointed the rainbow as a token of the covenant that he would not again destroy the earth by an universal deluge, resolved to erect an edifice, which, by its height, should place them beyond the reach of Divine vengeance. For this purpose they assembled together in the extended plain of Shinar. They laid the foundation, and carried on the building for ten years; at which time God, seeing their pride, determined to interfere. He confounded their language; and, by this simple process, put an end to their design. Hence the tower was called Babel, which signifies confusion. Sometime after this, Nimrod began to establish degrees of rank amongst his subjects, which had not existed before. He built the city of Babylon, and arrogated to himself the honors of Divine worship. It was on the night of the full moon, in the month of March, that God confounded their language. And therefore, the Noachites held their great meeting on that particular night; and their common monthly meetings were only held when the moon was at full, and they used no other light in their lodges. After their language was confounded, and the people obliged to separate, each tribe pursued his own course. Peleg, who suggested the plan of the tower, and had been the grand architect during its construction, being struck with the force of conscience, condemned himself to a most rigorous penance. He migrated, with his followers, to the north of Germany, after having suffered great miseries and encountered great dangers in passing the mountains and plains in his way thither. In that part of the country which is now called Prussia, he took up his residence. Here he built a triangular temple, where he enclosed himself, that he might be at leisure to worship God and implore him to pardon his transgression. In the course of excavation in the salt mines of Prussia, A. D. 553, there was discovered, at the depth of fifteen cubits, the foundation of a triangular edifice, in the centre of which was a small pillar of marble, on which the above history was inscribed in Hebrew characters. A tomb was found, in which an agate stone was encrusted, containing these words: "Here were deposited the ashes of the grand architect of the tower of Babel. God showed him mercy, because he humbled himself." These monuments, says Dr. O., are in the possession of the King of Prussia. — 2 Ol. Land., p. 63, note. Vide article in *Masonic Portfolio*, Sept. No 1847, on the Antiquity of the Order. E. N.: Scott most probably refers to The Masonic Portfolio, a work of Wilkins Jannehill, who was for several years Grand Master of the G∴L∴ of Tennessee, and who was often quoted by Dr. Oliver.

open and hold a Masonic lodge.[271] And there are some old manuscripts extant, which inform us that the Order was introduced into Britain at the period of the Roman invasion, by Cæsar; therefore, it must have existed before that time in another land. The simple fact that it existed then, affords the strongest presumption that it has been transmitted to us through the lapse of ages reaching far beyond the time of the Roman invasion of Britain. Alfred, the father of English law and literature, was a Mason. He usually divided his time into *three equal parts.* One was employed in sleep and refection of his body by diet and exercise; another in the dispatch of business; a third in study and devotion: and that he might more exactly *measure* the hours, he made use of *burning tapers of equal length,* which he fixed in lanterns.[272] It is remarkable, that the division of the twenty four hours of the day into three equal parts by Alfred, and the purposes of that division, agree perfectly with Masonic usage. This king also encouraged the mechanic arts, which once had a very close connection with the operative part of the Order. He invited and encouraged men of science and art to settle in his dominions. He set apart a seventh portion of his revenue for maintaining a number of workmen, whom he constantly employed in architectural pursuits.[273] The Encyclopædia Americana says that Masonry was introduced into Britain by Alfred and Athelstan, and its members were encouraged for the purpose of building castles and churches. The language and sentiments of Alfred breathed the spirit of moral Masonry. His fertile mind perceived the beauty and force of our style, and drew from it many of his happiest figures. Speaking in reference to the kingly office in one

---

[271] Ahi. Rez., p. 5.

[272] 1 Hume's Hist. Eng., ch. 2, p. 97. E. N.: Undoubtedly refers to David Hume, *The History of England from the Invasion of Julius Cæsar to the Revolution in 1688.* E. N.: While I have been unable to find the edition used by Scott, the quote can be found in context in the London edition of 1822, Vol. 1, p. 107.

[273] Idem, p. 99. E. N.: Idem, Vol. 1, p. 109.

of his paraphrases, he says: There are materials for every craft, without which a man cannot work at his craft; and a king also must have his materials and tools. But all craft and power will soon be worn out and put to silence, if they be without wisdom. Whatever is done through folly, man can never make that to be a good craft. Therefore, I desired wisdom. This is now what I most truly say. I have desired to live worthily while I lived, and after my death to leave to men that should be after me, a remembrance in good works.[274] Up to the year 1720, there existed a very old manuscript, which contained the following particulars: St. Alban loved Masons well and cherished them much, and made their pay right good; for he gave them two shillings per week and three pence to their cheer; whereas, before that time, in all the land, a Mason had but a penny a day and his meat, until St. Alban mended it, and *he gott them a charter from the King and his counsell for to hold a general counsell, and gave it the name of Assemlie. Thereat he was himselfe, and did helpe to make Masons, and gave them good charges.*[275] St. Alban was a Christian Mason, and the first British martyr. It is uncertain who introduced the gospel of Christ into Britain. Bishop Short, however, assumes it as an undoubted fact, that Christianity was *established* there very generally, before the end of the second century; and he sustains his statement by Tertullian, who says: That the kingdom of Christ was advanced in Gaul and Britain, and that Christ was solemnly worshipped by the inhabitants.[276] There is a tradition that Bran, being led into captivity, heard the word at Rome, and delivered it on his return to his countrymen.[277] But this tradition is doubtful; and where there is so much uncertainty, we may indulge at least the speculation, that our Order,

---

[274] Edward Churton, *The Early English Church*, London, 1840, p. 193. Hereafter *Chur. Eng. Church.*

[275] Mas. Lib., p. 4.

[276] Thomas Vowler Short, *The History of the Church of England to the Revolution, 1688*, New York, 1849, p. 2.

[277] Robert Southey, *The Book on the Church*, London, 1859, Vol. 1, p. 9.

whose benign principles reflect the light of the Word, prepared for the more ready reception of the glad tidings of
salvation into Britain. Freemasonry existed in Britain,
though not generally, before the time of St. Alban; but he
was invested with its mysteries while he was in the service
of the Roman army. *And it was not until after he re turned from
the army, that he was converted to Christianity.* It is said, however,
that Alban was converted by a Christian priest who fled to
his house for safety and protection from the persecutors of
the day.

St. Paul, it has been supposed by some early church
historians, visited Britain in the year of our Lord 63; for
about that time he preached the gospel in Spain, and is said
to "have gone to the utmost bounds of the west." It should
be remembered, that in the early part of the first century,
Britain was partly in possession of the Roman colonies.
Now, Freemasonry was introduced into the British island at
the period of the Roman invasion conducted by Cæsar,
which took place in the year 55 B.C. Our institution may be
said to have been the pioneer of Christianity in that country, or to have paved the way to its introduction. Freemasonry, prior to the Roman invasion, was not known in Britain. It came, then, from Rome. So, the apostle Paul, after
his first imprisonment at Rome, is reported to have *travelled
to the west*, and preached the glad tidings of the gospel in the
islands that lie in the ocean.[278]

Mr. Westamacot, in concluding a course of lectures at
the London Royal Academy, in 1836, in remarking upon
the causes which tended to revive literature and the arts in
the Middle Ages, stated, that there were two principal causes: These were the Crusades, and the extension, or it might
be called the establishment of the Free Masons' institution
in the north and west of Europe. The adventurers who returned from the Holy Land brought back some ideas of
various improvements, particularly in architecture, and

---

[278] Chur. Eng. Church., p. 17.

along with these a strong desire to erect castellated edifices. This taste was spread into almost every country by the establishment of the fraternity of Free Masons, who had, it appears, under some peculiar form of brotherhood, existed for an immemorial period in Syria and other parts of the East, from whence some bands of them migrated to Europe; and after a time, a great efflux of these ingenious men, Italian, German, Spanish, French, &c., had spread themselves in communities through all civilized Europe.[279]

---

[279] Moore's Magazine, No. 1842, p. 215. (E. N.: This magazine, the work of Br.˙. Charles Whitlock Moore, was very popular in Masonic circles at the time. While the actual name was *Freemason's Magazine*, most references called it simply *Moore's Magazine*.

Some of our brethren have assimilated Freemasonry to the mysteries of Eleusis, which were instituted by Erectheus or Ericthonius, in honor of Ceres. Moderns know but very little in regard to the precise character of these mysteries, and that which we know should be sufficient to satisfy us that the rites and ceremonies of the Masonic institution are entirely different from those which were celebrated in the plains of Eleusis. Cicero entertained a very high opinion of the latter. The following account of their supposed ceremonies is given by Mr. Cumberland, in his Observer, a work spoken of as containing a great deal of valuable research: The Eleusinian mysteries, says he, were celebrated in the time of autumn, every fifth year, at Eleusis, where a great concourse of people met on the occasion. The ceremonies of initiation were preceded by sacrifices, prayers, and ablutions. The candidates were exercised in trials of secrecy, and prepared by vows of continence; every circumstance was contrived to render the art as awful and striking as possible: the initiation was performed at midnight, and the candidate was taken into an interior sacristy of the temple, with a myrtle garland in his hand; here he was examined, if he had duly performed his stated ablutions; clean hands, a pure heart, and a native proficiency in the Greek tongue, were indispensable requisites. Having passed this examination, he was admitted into the temple, which was an edifice of immense magnitude: after proclamation made that strict silence should be observed, the officiating priest took out the sacred volume containing the mysteries; these books were written in strange characters, interspersed with figures of animals, and various emblems and hieroglyphics. The initiated were enjoined to honor their parents, to reverence the immortal gods, &c. When this was finished, the priests began to play off the whole machinery of the temple in all its terror, &c. Severities were exercised upon the initiated by persons unseen. — 1 Tylter's Hist. p. 68, n. E. N.: The quote is from Lord Alexander Fraser Tytler Woodhouselee, *Universal History from the Creation of the World to the Beginning of the Eighteenth Century.*

The term ancient York Masonry is, at the present day, particularly used to distinguish genuine Freemasonry from that which is called spurious or clandestine. The term ancient York Masonry, however, originated in the fact, that Prince Edward summoned all the Masons in England, or Britain, to meet at York, where they accordingly assembled and established a general lodge, over which the Prince presided as Grand Master. He brought with him to the convocation, we are told, all the writings and records then extant—some in Greek, some in Latin, some in French, and other languages—from the contents of which the constitutions and charges of the ancient English lodge were framed.[280]

The design of referring to the antiquity of our institution must be apparent to the reader. We have merely glanced at the subject; for it would require a large volume to discuss it. The antiquarian will find abundant means of gratifying his curiosity in the compilation and writings of Dr. Oliver, Hutchinson, Webb, Cole, Tannehill, Chandler, and others, who have collected a vast amount of evidence touching the ancient origin of the Order.

I have been unable to find the edition used by Scott, but the citation can be found the London edition of 1835, Vol. I, p. 128, notes.

[280] Davis' Mon. p. 22. E. N.: Davis' Monthly can hardly be found anymore, but the same quote can be found in *Ars Quatur Coronatum*, Vol. IV, 1891, p. 113; widely available in Masonic libraries.

Charles Scott

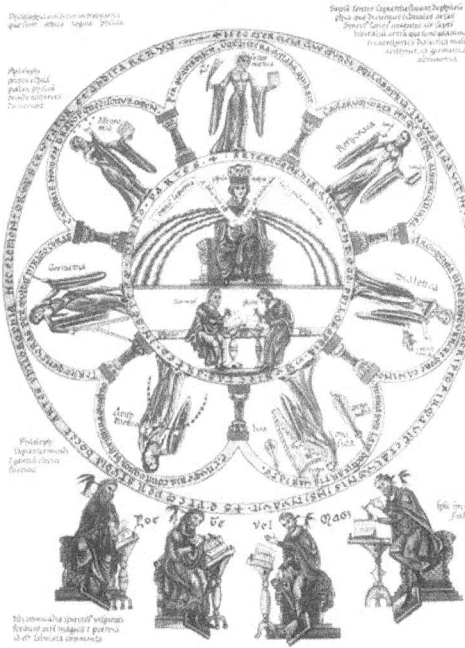

LECTURE VIII.
The Liberal Arts

The soul considered with its Creator, is like one of those mathematical lines that may draw nearer to another for all eternity without a possibility of touching it: and can there be a thought so transporting as to consider ourselves in these perpetual approaches to Him, who is not only the standard of perfection, but of happiness?[281]

Masonry includes within its circle almost every branch of polite learning, and under the veil of its mysteries is comprehended a regular system of science.[282]

And God blessed the seventh day, and sanctified it.[283]

---

[281] Joseph Addison, *The Spectator* No. 112, p. 72. E. N.: It can be found in *The Works of Joseph Addison, embracing the whole of The Spectator*, New York, 1837, Vol. 1.

[282] Ahi. Rez.

[283] Genesis 2:3.

And now I have sent a cunning man, endued with understanding, of Hiram my father's, the son of a woman of the daughters of Dan, and his father was a man of Tyre.[284]

And he reared up the pillars before the temple, the one on the right hand, and the other on the left.[285]

He will seek out the secrets of grave sentences, and be conversant in dark parables.[286]

The period stipulated for rewarding merit is fixed in the second degree, and the inimitable moral to which that circumstance alludes is explained. The celestial and terrestrial globes are considered, and their emblematical character, while the accomplished Mason is authorized to elucidate the liberal arts and sciences, the various orders of architecture, and the five human senses.[287] It is not presumed that any individual could master all these branches of study; but Masonry adapts itself to the various capacities and different tastes of men. If there be any truth in the beautiful conceptions of Dick and others that the sciences will engage the study of the redeemed in the world to come, what boundless tracts of knowledge and wisdom will open for ever to their heavenly vision. The human intellect is rendered capable of perpetual progress toward perfection; it may be ever advancing and never tiring—approaching nearer and nearer to God, the source of eternal wisdom and fountain of everlasting life, and always "enjoying felicity in every stage of its career." Thus would the genius of Masonry ever direct our thoughts to the contemplation of our immortal

---

[284] 2 Chronicles 2:13.

[285] Ibidem.

[286] Proverbs [sic]. E. N.: This quote is actually from the Book of Ecclesiasticus 39:3, included in the Apocrypha of King James' Bible until 1885. This book is also known as the Book of the All-Virtuous Wisdom of Joshua ben Sirach, or its shorter form, Sirach.

[287] Mas. Lib., p. 50.

natures and the consolations of religion. It is not the spirit of religion, as stated; though it would point to the light and bid us follow it. It may significantly direct our minds to Him who is both able and willing to save; but we can only experience righteousness through the gentle influences of the Holy One of the Godhead. It will remind us, too, that hope—the smiling prophet of the future—comes by faith. Well may we pause and consider whither we are going, and strive to add virtue to virtue and knowledge to knowledge. "A wide and unbounded prospect lies before us."

The eloquent Dick has ingeniously traced out the connection which exists between the intellectual and scientific pursuits of this life and those of a future state of being. He has discussed the objects on which the faculties of celestial intelligences will probably be employed, or the *sciences* which will be cultivated in the other world: and they are the sciences embraced in our Masonic lectures. And can it be that the Christian Mason will pursue eternally the study of those arts and sciences which constitute a portion of the degree of Fellow Craft? Some of them, we have high authority for believing; will be cultivated in the greatest perfection in that land of promised glory.[288] There, geometry,

---

[288] All the knowledge which can be attained in the present state is but a drop to the ocean, when compared with the treasures of wisdom and knowledge that may be acquired in the eternal world. The proportion between the one and the other may bear a certain analogy to the bulk of the terraqueous globe, when compared with the immensity of the worlds and systems which compose the universe. If an infinite variety of designs, of objects, and of scenery exist in the distant provinces of creation, as we have reason to believe, from the variety which abounds in our terrestrial system—if every world be peopled with inhabitants of different species from those of the other—if its physical constitution and external scenery be peculiar to itself—if the dispensations of the Creator toward its inhabitants be such as have not been displayed to any other world—if the manifold wisdom of God, in the arrangement of its destinies, be displayed in a manner in which it has never been displayed to any other class of intelligences—and, in short, if every province of creation exhibit a peculiar manifestation of Deity—we may conclude that all the knowledge of God, of his works and dispensations, which can be attained in this present life, is but as a faint glim-

the first and noblest of sciences, will be the subject of investigation; for by it the spirits of the righteous may discover the power, the wisdom, and goodness of God, and view with delight the proportions of the universe.[289] The science of form, beauty, magnitude, and numbers, will occupy, in some degree, those purified intelligences which dwell in heaven. And is there no heavenly music? The art or science of music is coeval with the creation of the world.[290] We know that the stars sang together then. Music is the language of feeling and sentiment. The stars which mingled their harmonious voices, and the sons of God which shouted for joy, were children of light and glory. Then, there was music in heaven, when this beautiful creation arose out of chaos. There is scriptural evidence that music was known and cultivated before the flood: His brother's name was Jubal: he was the father of all such as handle the harp and organ.[291] Miriam, the prophetess, and other women, understood and practiced this beautiful science; for we are told that she took a timbrel in her hand; and all the women went out after her, with timbrels and with dances.[292] David exhorted everyone to praise God with musical instruments: Praise him with the sound of the trumpet: praise him with psaltery and harp: praise him with the timbrel and dance: praise him with stringed instruments and organs: praise him upon the loud cymbals: praise him

---

mering of a taper, when contrasted with the effulgence of the meridian sun. — Dick's Future State, p. 52.

[289] Cross's Chart, p. 32.

[290] The art of music is probably coeval with the existence of our race, or at least with the first attempt to preserve the memory of transactions. We have positive evidence of its existence before the deluge. Before the invention of writing, the history of remarkable events was committed to memory and handed down by oral tradition: the knowledge of laws and of useful arts was preserved in the same way, and rhythm and song were probably soot found important helps to the memory. — Pict. Dict., p. 903.

[291] Gen. 4:21

[292] Exodus 15:20.

upon the high-sounding cymbals. Let everything that hath breath praise the Lord. Praise ye the Lord.[293] Then music is a proper vehicle for praising God. The hand of the Lord came upon Elisha when the minstrel played.[294] When David was returning from the field of his victory over the Philistines, the women came out from all the cities of Israel, singing and dancing, to meet King Saul, with tabrets, with joy, and with instruments of music.[295] And they answered one another as they played, and said, Saul hath slain his thousands and David his ten thousands. Then music is a means of national rejoicing. Music was brought to great perfection under the administration of our grand master, King Solomon. The worship in the first temple consisted chiefly of songs of praise.[296] The notes of love rang through its hallowed apartments, and floated in gentle cadences along its *secret* arches. Our ancient brethren chanted, then, the inspired psalms of David. How rich, how solemn, how happy were those strains of music which arose like "a concord of sweet sounds," at the dedication of the temple! There were the priests, one hundred and thirty of them, to sound with trumpets: and with them stood, at the *east* end of the altar, the Levites, arrayed in *white* linen, having cymbals, and psalteries, and harps.[297] The trumpeters and sing-

---

[293] Psalms 150:3-6.

[294] 2 Kings 3:15.

[295] 1 Samuel 18:6.

[296] Music, of all pleasures the most intellectual, that glorious painting to the ear, that rich mastery of the gloomier emotions of our nature, was studied by the priesthood with a skill that influenced the habits of the country. — George Croly, Salathiel, A *History of the past, the Present and the Future*, London, 1827, Vol. 1, p. 23 (42). It was always cultivated among the Jews with much care, and was employed, not only about the tabernacle and temple, but also in the common scenes of domestic and social life. — John W. Nevin, *A Summary of biblical Antiquities*, Philadelphia, 1829, Vol. 1, p. 194. Hereafter *Bib. Antiq.*

[297] Musical instruments of the Jews were of three general kinds: such as had strings, such as were played upon by blowing, and such as were sounded by being struck. Of the first class were the harp and the psaltery; of

ers were as *one*. Their music was as *one sound*, praising and thanking the Lord. And when these worshippers lifted up their *voice* with the trumpets, and cymbals, and instruments of music, and praised the Lord, the glory of the Lord filled the house of God.[298] Music, then, appropriately constitutes a part of our beautiful and sublime rites. It was cultivated by our masters. It was a means of praising God in the ancient temple. And is not the human heart a strange instrument of music? "It is a harp of a thousand strings." Let our voices sing to that sweet instrument, and "give forth its slumbering harmony." How often has the hand of the unseen Spirit swept over its strings, and moved the voice to swell its tide of melody! Oh let us respond to the touches of the Spirit, and fill our souls with praise! "Christ and his apostles" sung a hymn "ere they went out to the Mount of Olives."[299] And there are songs in heaven. The song of Moses and the Lamb floats in glorious notes through the arches of the celestial temple, and echoes along the undulating hills of eternity. And shall *we* ever hear that music, behold that temple, or survey those hills? Does the good genius of Masonry answer? Its voice is still. Angels of mercy, answer! Bright train of religion, Faith, Hope, and Charity, answer us! May we all hear that song of redeeming love! If we can only ascend the ladder by its beautiful rounds, we shall hear the swelling tide of joy as it rolls by the throne of Jehovah.

---

the second, the organ, the pipe of different sorts, the horn, and the trumpet; of the last, the most common were the cymbal and the tabret or timbrel. — Bib. Antiq., Vol. 1, p. 194.

[298] 2 Chronicles 5:12-14.

[299] In that solemn hour, when the Paschal supper was just closing, and our Lord "sang a hymn" with his disciples, before he went forth to the last scene of his trial and agony, we know, from the voice of tradition and the concurrence of all antiquity, that he adopted, as was natural, the particular form always made use of by the Jews at the end of the Passover. It was called the Great Hallel, or hymn of praise, and consisted of Psalms 115 to 118 inclusive. — Kip's Double Witness of the Church, p. 97. The Importance of Music in Praising God. — 1 Mel. Ser., p. 464.

The subject of creation is again brought to our notice in the Fellow Craft's degree: "In six days God created the heavens and the earth, and rested upon the *seventh day*; the *seventh*, therefore, our ancient brethren consecrated as a day of rest from their labours; thereby enjoying more frequent opportunities to contemplate the glorious works of creation, and to adore their great Creator."[300] We cannot be too often reminded that the Holy Ghost is not only the author of the Holy Scriptures, but that creation is the great work of his power. Masonry reminds us again and again, that, as the Spirit called out of chaos the universe, form out of that which was without form and void, light out of darkness, so must the same Spirit, the Comforter, brood over the depths of sin and transgression, before light can arise out of darkness. He alone can call form of beauty and loveliness out of the melancholy void. Masonry, in so frequently referring to the creation, intended, it is thought, to impress upon the mind its *typical* character, and that it shadowed forth the redemption of man. The value or dignity of the new creation is commensurate with the stupendous work of the universe. Both were intended for the glory of God, and to display his handiwork. And does not the Christian Brother, whose soul has felt the gentle broodings of the Spirit over the dark and gloomy waste of sin, know something of this new creation? In being brought to the glorious light of the gospel, is he not conscious that the same gracious Spirit which moved upon the face of the deep in the beginning, brooded also over the depths of his benighted soul? " How majestically will the Spirit sit upon the flood of death," as it comes sweeping by the dwelling of the Christian, to bear him on its bosom to the vast ocean of eternal light, where he will meet his Savior walking on its deep waters, and saying: *"Fear not—it is I!"*

The Masonic rite, then, of being brought to light, is not only typical, as we have shown, of a new born soul, but

---

[300] Cross' Chart, p. 24.

necessarily typifies a *Mediator*, through and by whom we may, if found worthy, be raised to essential bliss. Then we may pass the porch of the inner chamber, on our way to the holy of holies, and cross the waters above the firmament, for the *Word* will be with us. And there, and there only, will be found a Sabbath day of eternal rest. The veil which covers the mind of the Fellow Craft may be removed when he goes into the holy of holies. Moses took the veil from off his face, when he entered into the tabernacle before the Lord.[301] It was then that he received a "new irradiation" of glory. The veil was emblematical of the obscurity of the legal dispensation, and the manifested glory of the Lord was typical of the glory of the Messiah. The veil which covers the face of the Fellow Craft Mason may be said to be removed, when he is admitted into the *"sanctum sanctorum,"* when he receives a new irradiation of the truth in the solemn and mysterious developments of the third degree.

God ceased from his labours upon the seventh day, and the seventh day is one consecrated in the annals of our Order. The number seven is a mystic number. Seven stars deck the Masonic canopy. The chief reason why it was venerated by ancient craftsmen was doubtless because God hallowed the seventh day in the beginning. God *then* sanctified it. Seven is called a perfect number, and it is a sacred number. Dean Woodhouse says that seven is a number expressive of *universality, fullness, and perfection.* There was the seventh consecrated year of jubilee. Noah admitted the clean beasts by sevens into the ark. There were seven golden candlesticks; seven sabbatical years; seven years of famine; and there were seven priests, who blew the seven trumpets about the walls of Jericho. There are seven thunders spoken of in the Revelation of St. John. We read that in the midst of the elders stood a lamb having seven eyes. There were the seven churches of Asia, the angels of which

---

[301] Exodus 34:34.

were the seven stars, in the right hand of Him who is the first and the last; of Him that liveth and was dead, and is alive for evermore, and hath the keys of hell and death; and which themselves were the seven golden candlesticks, in the midst of which He walked.[302] The book of seven seals had seven rolls; *"so that"* says Bishop Newton, *"the opening of one seal only laid open the contents of one roll."* At the opening of the seventh seal there was silence in heaven about the space of half an hour.[303] In short, the number runs throughout the Scriptures, and is associated with the most remarkable events. This number was held in veneration among many nations of antiquity, particularly among the Hebrews was it regarded sacred. "The Pythagoreans," says Mackey, "called it a venerable number, because it referred to creation, and because it was made up of two perfect figures—the *triangle* and the *square*."[304] It has been wisely adopted into the body of Masonry; for on the seventh day God ended his work which he had made; and God blessed the seventh day, and sanctified it: because that in it he had rested from all his work which God created and made.[305] Every Mason is taught to look upon the Sabbath as a day which should be specially devoted to rest and worship. Our patron Saint, while he was an exile and a prisoner in the isle of Patmos,

---

[302] Revelation 2:1.

[303] Revelation 8:1.

[304] Noah received *seven* days' notice of the commencement of the deluge, and was commanded to select clean beasts and fowls by sevens, *seven* persons accompanied him into the ark; the ark rested on Mount Ararat in the *seventh* month: the intervals between dispatching the dove were, each time, *seven* days. The walls of Jericho were encompassed *seven* days by *seven* priests, bearing *seven* rams' horns. Solomon's temple was dedicated in the *seventh* month, and the festival lasted *seven* days; the candlestick in the tabernacle had *seven* branches; and the tower of Babel was said to have been elevated *seven* stories before the dispersion. — Mack Lex., p. 283. That seven, seventy, and seventy-seven denote what was holy and sacred; that seven days denotes the beginning of temptation; that seven denotes what is full and entire. — Vide Heav. Arc., n. 395, 433, 728, 2928.

[305] Genesis 2:2-3.

consecrated the Sabbath to meditation and prayer. It was on the Sabbath day that he felt the full light and power of the Holy Spirit. He says: *"I was in the Spirit on the Lord's day."* It was on that day that he heard distinctly the voice of Heaven, saw visions of glory, and conversed with angels, who seemed as "palpable to feeling as to sight." On that day—a day on which our Lord triumphed over death and hell—St. John beheld our Lord standing in the midst of the golden candlesticks; and he had in his right hand seven stars; and out of his mouth went a sharp two-edged sword; and his countenance was as the sun shining in his strength.

It is a notable fact, that the knowledge of the Sabbath was at one time lost, and so was the knowledge of God *lost.*[306] The holy Sabbath, as we read in Nehemiah, was made known to the Israelites; and, when God delivered them from bondage, he restored to them the knowledge of the Sabbath.[307] Was not the Sabbath, then, a typical day? The knowledge of it was lost, but was regained. It is typical of a day of heavenly rest and refreshment. And as there are six days of labor and one of rest, are not the six days of labor emblematical of our probationary state, which should be devoted to pious work, in order that we may enjoy a day of eternal rest? If, then, the six days of labor and one of rest partake of a typical character, Masonry has adopted their typical character, which is truly sublime. Our work in time borders on eternity. No geographical line has ever been mapped out between the two kingdoms. The *light* of the great future breaks upon the soul along the unknown

---

[306] As wickedness increased in the world, and the true worship of God was corrupted by an almost universal idolatry, so the solemn day of his worship was neglected likewise. And though it may have been revived after the flood, and continued in some parts of Abraham's family, yet in their Egyptian slavery the observation of it appears to have been interrupted. But God renewed the commandment to the Israelites. — D'Oyly and Mant's Com., Exodus 16:23.

[307] Exodus 16:23.

margin of the grave; and corruption is closely allied to in-corruption and mortality to immortality.

Theologians inform us that "the old Sabbath com-memorated creation; the new, a spiritual creation, made sure in the resurrection."[308] The Son of man is Lord also of the Sabbath.[309] Jesus Christ is God of the Sabbath. He is God our Creator. John tells us so: "In the beginning was the *Word*, and the *Word* was with *God*, and the *Word* was *God*. The same was in the beginning with God. All things were made by him; and without him was not anything made that was made."[310] And the knowledge of Jesus, like the Sabbath, was *lost* to the world. *He was in the world, and the world was made by him, and the world knew him not.* He *came to his own, and his own received him not.*[311] If, then, Jesus is the Lord of the Sabbath, and he made it and sanctified it, and it is a day of rest, and is so regarded in our landmarks—a day for contemplating the works of nature and adoring God—is not the way of the Man of Sorrows in our temple? This question is one worthy of the most serious consideration. Are the Scriptures true? The book of the law was found in the temple. Was that book inspired? Our ancient Masters answered this question long ago, and have transmitted their testimony to us through the channel of tradition. A faithful brotherhood have whispered it in the ears of each succeed-ing clan. Those of the Fraternity, who were passing off the

---

[308] The Jewish Sabbath was in commemoration of the exodus out of Egypt; the Christian Sabbath of a more excellent deliverance. — 2 Pict. Dict., p. 1064. We regard it as a fact of considerable importance, in proving the Divinity of our holy religion, that from the time of our Redeemer's resurrection, his disciples commemorated that event by a weekly Sab-bath. — McOwen on Sabbath, p. 54 [E. N.: Peter McOwen, *On the Sabbath,* Methodist B.C.]. The observance of Sunday as the Sabbath was first passed into a law (according to Eusebius,) by Constantine the Great, A. D. 321, and made general throughout the Roman Empire. — 1 Eccl. Dict., p. 1165.

[309] Luke 6:5.

[310] John 1:1-3.

[311] John 1:10-11.

stage of life, told it to others who were to take their places: and thus the truth has been sent on from generation to generation.

The pillars which were erected at the entrance of the porch of Solomon's temple cannot fail to attract our attention. "Moreover," says Josephus, "this Hiram made two hollow pillars, whose outsides were of *brass*, and the thickness of the brass was four fingers' breadth, and the height of the pillars was eighteen cubits, and the circumference twelve cubits; but there was cast with each of their chapiters *lily* work, that stood upon the pillar, and it was elevated five cubits, round about which was net work interwoven with small palms made of brass and covered the lily work. To this, also, were hung two hundred pomegranates, in two rows. The one of these pillars he set at the right hand, and called it Jachin, and the other at the left hand, and called it Boaz."[312]

It is supposed that these pillars had reference to the pillar of cloud by day and the pillar of fire by night,[313] which

---

[312] The following description is given of those famous pillars in 1 Kings 7:15-22. And he came (Hiram, the widow's son) to king Solomon, and wrought all his work. For he cast two pillars of brass, of eighteen cubits high a piece: and a line of twelve cubits did compass either of them about. And he made two chapiters of molten brass, to set upon the tops of the pillars: the height of the one chapiter was five cubits, and the height of the other chapiter was five cubits: and nets of checker work, and wreaths of chain work, for the chapiters which were upon the top of the pillars; seven for the one chapiter, and seven for the other chapiter. And he made the pillars, and two rows round about upon the one net work, to cover the chapiters that were upon the top, with pomegranates: and so did he for the other chapiter. And the chapiters that were upon the top of the pillars were of lily work in the porch, four cubits. And the chapiters upon the two pillars had pomegranates also above, over against the belly which was by the net work: and the pomegranates were two hundred, in rows round about upon the other chapiter. And he set up the pillars in the porch of the temple: and he set up the right pillar, and called the name thereof Jachin: and he set up the left pillar, and called the name thereof Boaz. And upon the top of the pillars was lily work: so was the work of the pillars finished.

[313] That by a pillar of cloud by day and pillar of fire by night, denoted heav-

went before the Israelites in the wilderness; and that they were intended as memorials of God's promises.[314] The Israelites, who followed the pillar of cloud by day and the pillar of fire by night, typified the followers of Jesus Christ, and teach us that if we presume to depart from the rules of the true faith, we must inevitably perish. And where is the thoughtful Fellow Craft, who, when his eye rests upon the emblematical pillars of Masonry, does not remember the promises, which the Lord made to his people, and how faithfully they have all been performed. These pillars should continually remind us of the goodness of our heavenly Father and his kind providence.

The fruit of the pomegranate tree is said to be beautiful and delicious, and its exuberant seeds juicy and rich.[315] The spies from Eshkol brought with them *three* kinds of fruit, *grapes*, *figs*, and *pomegranates*.[316] The leaves of the pomegranate tree are of livid green, and stand opposite to each other, narrow and spear-shaped, about three inches long and half an inch broad in the middle. The flowers come out of the branches *singly* or *three* together. Frequently, one of the larger terminates the branch, and beneath that are *one*, *two*, or *three* smaller buds, which continue a succession of blossoms for some months, giving a continued brilliancy to the gardens in which they grow.[317] Then how beautiful is the emblem of the pomegranate! The lily is one of the fairest of flowers, and a native of the East.[318] In the 14th chapter of

---

en: that the former denoted a state of illustration, tempered by the obscurity of truth—the latter a state of obscurity, tempered by illustration from good. — Heav. Arc., n. 8108.

[314] George Oliver, *The Star in the East*, London, 1825, p. 104.

[315] The pomegranate tree is common in Palestine and other parts of the East. — 2 Eccl. Dict., p. 1062.

[316] Numbers 13:23.

[317] Eccl. Dict., p. 1062.

[318] Lilies are natives of the East, and are found plentifully growing in the fields. — Hosea 14:5; Matthew 6:28; 2 Eccl. Dict. p. 767. Horne states that lilies were never known to grow wild in Palestine. — 2 Horne's In-

Hosea, which contains a promise of God's blessing, is the following passage: "I will be as the dew unto Israel: he shall grow as the *lily*, and cast forth his roots as Lebanon." Lilies are mentioned in Christ's Sermon on the Mount: And why take ye thought for raiment? Consider the lilies of the field, how they grow; they toil not, neither do they spin: and yet I say unto you, that even Solomon in all his glory was not arrayed like one of these[319].

> *Emblem of Him in whom no stain*
> *The eye of Heaven could see,*
> *In all their glory monarchs vain*
> *Are not arrayed like thee.*
>
> Bp. Horne.[320]

Some authors have supposed that the work in form of a lily on the pillars of the temple was work in form of the lotus, which greatly resembled the lily; but there is reason to doubt this opinion.[321] Christ, in speaking of the lily, seems to have had his mind fixed on Solomon and the lily work which adorned the pillars of the temple. The lily, from its *whiteness*, was considered by the ancients as an emblem of *purity*. The spirits of the just must be arrayed like the lily; for we read in Revelation of the *white-robed multitude*, which St. John beheld about the throne of God.

The pillar which was set up on the right hand in the porch, and which was called Jachin, denoted establishment, (Jachin, that is, he shall establish) and the left hand pillar denoted strength (Boaz, that is, strength)[322]—The learned

---

tro., 35, n. 8. The lily is repeatedly alluded to in the Scriptures, as an emblem of purity. It occupied a conspicuous place among the ornaments of the temple furniture. The brim of the molten sea was wrought with flowers of lilies. — Mack. Lex., p. 182.

[319] Matthew 6:28.

[320] E. N.: While Scott attributes this poem to Bishop Horne, it is in fact by Nealer. See: *Christian Melodies*, Second Edition, London, 1837, p. 28.

[321] 2 Pict. Dict., p. 767.

[322] Clarke's Com.; 1 Kings 7:21.

commentator believes these pillars to have been emblematical; for, notwithstanding their names, they supported no part of the building. Those who would seek admission, or gain an audience in the holy of holies of our mystic temple, *must pass by the representatives of these pillars.* Mark well the entering in of the house.[323] The pillar of cloud by day and of fire by night were the visible means of the deliverance of the Israelites[324] Christ is the means of deliverance from sin, that which makes bondsmen of us all. *It is by Him we must pass,* if we ever reach the skies.

The pillars, Jachin and Boaz, were cast in the plains of Jordan, in the *clay ground between Succoth and Zarthan.*[325] Mark, they were cast *between* Succoth and Zarthan, and in *clay* ground. Why is the place and the manner of casting them so particularly described? Why tell us they were cast on *clay* ground, and *between* Succoth and Zarthan? We have a Masonic reason: The Christian church—the whole plan of redemption—is founded upon the *human* nature of Christ, and man was fashioned out of the dust—clay ground. The Son of God is the *second person* in the holy Trinity, and *between* the Father and the Holy Ghost. The pillars were not intended merely for ornament, though they were fine specimens of architecture. They were cast *hollow,* says Josephus, and were intended to subserve some useful purpose. And Hiram, the builder, cast them. King Solomon sent and fetched Hiram out of Tyre. He was a widow's son, of the tribe of Naphtali, and was filled with *wisdom* and *understand-*

---

[323] Ezekiel 14:1.

[324] It has been supposed that Solomon, in erecting the two pillars called Jachin and Boaz, had reference to the pillar of cloud and the pillar of fire which went before the Israelites in the wilderness; and that the right hand or south pillar represented the pillar of cloud, and the left hand the pillar of fire. — Mack. Lex., p. 235. The first piece of workmanship in which Hiram Abif was engaged, was the construction of these brass pillars. They were designed, says Pyle, to bear allusion to the two memorable pillars of fire and of cloud which conducted the Israelites from Egypt.

[325] 1 Kings 7:46.

ing, and *cunning*, to work in all works in brass, that were durable. In second Chronicles he is spoken of after this manner: "Did Hiram his father make to King Solomon." The words *Hiram ab*, or *Hiram abif*, are those contained in the original language.[326] The word *ab* or *abif* means father. It is often used, said Dr. Clarke, in the Hebrew to signify *master, inventor, chief operator*. The name, says brother Mackey, given to the chief architect in the lodge, is derived from the Hebrew words *Hiram abif*. The most literal translation of *abif* is *father*. It is a word of endearment. Remember the language of St. Paul: Ye have received the *spirit of adoption*, whereby we cry *Abba, Father*. And it was by adoption that the builder is called Hiram abif. He was one of the founders of our sublime institution—of our symbolical or ethical system. At least, upon his works and life it mainly rests. And was not there something typical in the very name of our ancient master? Would it be fanciful to say that it typified the two natures of Christ, the human and Divine, that *Hiram* was typical of the former, and *Abif* of the latter? The Christian church is founded upon the human and divine nature of Jesus Christ.

How powerfully is truth elucidated in our lodges, and yet there are many among us and of us upon whom it has made no lasting impression! They take now no thought of the future; but the hour will come when they *must cross* the flood of death, and may be eternally *lost*, for want of the *Word*. *Christ* is the *Word*. In the *beginning* he was the *Word*. "Take heed, lest ye perish." A Mason, before he can be lawfully recognized as such, must *prove* himself. When the Queen of Sheba heard of the fame of Solomon concerning the name of the Lord, she visited him to *prove* him with hard questions. She communed with him, and he answered all her questions. "Examine me, 0 Lord, and *prove me*," said the Psalmist, in the integrity of his heart. *Try me* and *prove me*; try my worth and piety. Look into my soul; examine all

---

[326] Clarke's Com.; 2 Chronicles 4:16.

my feelings, thoughts and affections. I am no hypocrite— no impostor. O Lord, *examine* and *prove* me.

Masons are viewed as men *fraternizing* and *working* together. Each one must work, too, for himself, though we must bear one another's burdens, and so fulfill the law. But everyone must prove his own work.[327] While it is the duty of Christians and the members of our fraternity to sympathize with the distressed, and love one another, and do unto all men as they would they should do unto them, they must not forget that they have other work to do, and that the work must be *inspected* and *proved* by One who is both able and willing to inspect and prove every living stone which may be taken thither. All must be *tried*, and found worthy of the Lamb which was slain. Jesus died that sinners might live. The Entered Apprentice and the Fellow Craft have an interest in the blood which was shed. We are all of one blood and one flesh. Being justified by blood, we can be saved from the wrath to come, and pass the road of death with a glorious assurance of a resurrection. Peace was made through the blood of Jesus; and through his *death, resurrection*, and *ascension*, a bright in heritance *substituted* in the place of our *lost* innocence. Our garments are made white through the blood of the Lamb.[328] Michael and his angels overcame the dragon by the *blood* of the Lamb, and by the *Word* of their testimony. The *life* of the flesh is in the *blood*, and I have given it to you upon the altar to make an *atonement* for the soul.[329] And, says the apostle, almost all things are by the law purged with blood; and without shedding of blood is no remission.[330]

Let each craftsman seriously reflect how and in what way he was made a Master, or became entitled to have the

---

[327] Galatians 6:2-4.

[328] Revelation 7:14.

[329] Leviticus 17:11.

[330] Hebrews 9:22.

third degree conferred upon him, and he must perceive the consistency and harmony of the several degrees with the sublime doctrines of Him who rules in mercy. The Entered Apprentice, advancing to the inner chamber, through which he must pass to find an entrance to the third apartment of the edifice, may learn a beautiful and instructive lesson. Let us look for a moment upon the emblems which are delineated on the Fellow Craft's tracing board,[331] just beyond the pillars representing those which stood at the porch of the temple. There is a flight of winding steps, and at the head of the stairway is represented a brother clad and jeweled, and standing, as it were, and waiting to receive the candidate, who is supposed to be advancing. The plate is faint, but the door appears not to be entirely closed. It seems to be represented as being partly open, while the keeper is ready to invite him in, if his learning be good, if he has improved his time and opportunities, and has kept his *white* apron unspotted from the world. He *proves* himself and *passes on*. He surveys the temple of the universe, and gazes upon its splendid architecture, and the wisdom, strength, and beauty of the whole. But beyond is another plate which represents another of the craft, *clothed* and *jeweled* also, and standing in the middle of an open door. The candidate we may suppose to have passed the first station, which may account, in some measure, for the second door being represented as open, and the sentinel waiting to receive him, as one who has a right to pass into the presence of him who stands before the altar, with the letter G[332] sus-

---

[331] The tracing board is a painting or engraving representing the emblems peculiar to a degree, arranged for the convenience of the lecturer. — Mack. Lex., p. 315.

[332] The letter G, which ornaments the lodge, is not only expressive of the name of the Grand Architect of the universe, but also denotes the science of geometry, so necessary to artists. The adoption of it by free masons implies no more than their respect for those inventions which demonstrate to the world the power, the wisdom, and beneficence of the Almighty Builder, in the works of creation. — Ahi. Rez., p. 149. The patriarchs held that it was the duty of man to fear God, to bless him for mercies received, and supplicate him with profound humility:

Analogy of Masonry

pended above him in a halo of glory.[333] These emblems appear to contain an allegory, or a part of a continued allegory. Their meaning is veiled. In rhetoric and belles-lettres, an allegory is defined as a continued metaphor, as it is the representation of something by another that resembles it, and that is made to stand for it.[334] There are many allegories in the holy writings. Dr. Blair has selected a fine example of one, which will be found in the 80th Psalm, and represents the people of God under the image of a vine: "Thou hast brought a vine out of Egypt: thou hast cast out the heathen and planted it. Thou preparedst room before it, and didst cause it to take deep root, and it filled the land. The hills were covered with the shadow of it, and the boughs thereof were like the goodly cedars. She sent out her boughs unto the sea and her branches unto the river. Why hast thou broken down her hedges, so that all they which pass by the way do pluck her? The boar out of the wood doth waste it, and the wild beast of the field doth devour it. Return, we beseech thee, 0 God of hosts: *Look* down from heaven, and *behold*, and *visit* this vine."

We remarked in our introductory lecture that the fraternity of Masons spoke a peculiar language, consisting of signs, emblems, figures, and universal words.[335] And, in

---

that the knowledge of God is to be promoted; vows made to him are to be performed; and that idolatry is to be renounced. — 1 Eccles. Dict., p. 515.

[333] There are three species or kinds of allegory, which, under the literal sense of the words, conceals a foreign or distant meaning: 1st. The allegory properly so called, which is a continued metaphor. 2nd. The parable or similitude; and 3rd. The mystical allegory, in which a double meaning is couched under the same words. — Horne's Intro., p. 364.

[334] Hugh Blair, *Lectures on Rhetoric,* New York, 1836, p. 168 (hereafter *Blair's Rhet.)* We read of a door opened in heaven. — Revelation 4:1. Christ opened the door of faith unto the Gentiles. — Acts 14:27.

[335] Language is now provincial, and the dialects of different nations could not be comprehensible to men ignorant and unlettered. Hence the necessity of using expressions cognizable by people of all nations. Masons are possessed of that universal expression, and of such remains of the original language that they can communicate their history, their wants,

their peculiar dialect, an allegory may be adjusted, which will veil and convey its meaning in a more pleasing and captivating style than any which could be originated by the most accomplished rhetorician, in his mother tongue. Take the fragment of the allegory to which we have referred, as forming a portion of the degree of Fellow Craft, and examine it carefully, and it will be found perfectly consistent with the rules of rhetoric. Its moral or unfigured meaning is purposely obscure. Its sense is neither too bare nor too open, and when viewed in connection with that which precedes it, it will be found an affair of great nicety. It is happily conceived and admirably executed. *It is only by and through the Son and Holy Ghost that the soul of man can gain an audience with the Father, or pass into his holy presence. And the light of eternity is around and about the throne. Christ is our mediator and the Spirit our comforter.* Through their blessed interposition we may all find our way to the grand lodge above. There the brethren may find everlasting *peace, unity,* and *plenty.* They who are acquainted with the Lord are at *peace.* And they who seek *peace* shall find it. The end of the perfect man is *peace.* God speaks peace unto his people and all his saints. They who obey his law will have great peace. The inspired poet spoke of Jesus, long before his coming, as the Mighty God, the Everlasting Father, *the Prince of Peace.* But there is *no peace* for the wicked. They may cry continually *peace, peace,* when there is *no peace.* But God will call the righteous to *peace.* The Lord of *love* and *peace* will be with them forever and ever. Then, there is *peace* in the *presence chamber of our Master in heaven.* There will be found *unity* and *plenty* also. All dwell there together in *unity,* and their souls are filled with *plenteous* joy. The Lord is *plenteous* in mercy, and with him is *plenteous* redemption. The harvest even in time is *plenteous,* but the *laborers* are few. If men would only learn and obey the *word,* it would conduct them to a land of *peace, unity,* and

---

and prayers to every brother Mason throughout the globe. — Ahi. Rez., p. 191. The universal language and universal laws are called the landmarks of our Order, which it is not in the power of any man or body of men to alter.

plenty. The *Word* has great power. It made the world. It was heard in the midst of the thunders of Sinai. The Word is the law, and the Word gave the law. It is a sure and heavenly guide. It led the Israelites out of the land of Egypt, and often went before them. The *Word* will call the souls of the righteous to glory. *It will go down with them into the grave, and will raise them at the final day. It is the true Word.* How precious is the *Word! It was made known through the blood of Christ.* Its power was witnessed in the resurrection of Jesus, though *it* availed him not upon the cross. His prayer to the Father was in vain. *There was no help for the Son of God.* Christ was in *deep distress* and *extreme agony* when he offered up this prayer. It was when he hung upon the cross and a few minutes before he yielded up the ghost that he prayed; for about the *ninth* hour he cried with a *loud* voice, and uttered these remarkable words, *with his hands uplifted* and nailed to the tree: Eli, Eli, lama sabachthani? That is to say, *my God, my God, why hast thou forsaken me?*[336] These words were heard in heaven. They fell upon the ear of the Eternal Father, and the vibrating voice of the dying Savior unstrung the harps of angels and silenced the minstrelsy of the skies. The charter of gospel liberty could only be written in the blood of the Lamb, and sealed with his precious life-drops. The words: "My God, my God, why hast thou forsaken me?"[337] Were uttered prophetically by David. Indeed, nearly the whole of the 22nd psalm was prophetical of the passion, sufferings, resurrection, and triumph of the Lord our Master, who underwent a spiritual desertion. This psalm, hav-

---

[336] Matthew 27:46.

[337] Bishop Horne, commenting on these words, says: That Christ, the beloved son of the Father, when hanging on the cross, complained in these words, that he was deprived for a time of the Divine presence and comforting influence, while he suffered for our sins. If the Master thus underwent the trial of a spiritual desertion, why doth the disciple think it strange unless the light of heaven shine continually upon his tabernacle? Let us comfort ourselves, in such circumstances, with the thought that we are thereby conformed to the image of our dying Lord—that sun which set in a cloud, to arise without one. — Horne on Psalms.

ing been composed before the erection of the first temple, Solomon, the Son of David, must have been made acquainted with its prophetical character; and hence a Master Mason may readily account for the very striking analogy to which we have hinted.

The lifting up of hands may be said to be a scriptural sign of intercession, as when one lifts up the hands in prayer for Divine succor and relief. Our Savior, says a learned commentator, often prayed for his people, and interceded for them with his hands lifted up toward heaven. When David prayed to be delivered from the hands of his enemies, he said: Hear the voice of my supplications, when I cry unto thee, when I lift up my hands toward thy holy oracle.[338] Again, in the sixty-third psalm, where he expresses his confidence of the destruction of his enemies and his own safety, he says, speaking of his manner of blessing God—"Then will I bless thee while I live: I will lift up my hands in thy name." In a time of deep distress, and when his soul was full of troubles, he prayed for help, and said, "Lord, I have called daily upon thee, I have stretched out my hands unto thee." The mind of the Fellow Craft (to recapitulate) has been taught to reflect upon both the moral and material universe. While an Entered Apprentice, he was reminded of the necessity of divesting his soul and conscience of all evil; he beheld, as it were, rays of light emanating from that radiant Star in the midst of the pavement; he wore then and continues to wear an emblem of innocence—a *lamb-skin*. He has seen and passed by the theological ladder. He has been impressed with the holiness of the holy Mount; the beauty and efficacy of prayer; the necessity of a humble and contrite spirit; his blindness by nature; the goodness and mercy of God, who alone can bring him to light; the checkered scenes of life; its wants and necessities; its cares and trials; its *lights* and *shades*. But he is surrounded by an all-wise and merciful Providence.

---

[338] Psalms 28:2.

His thoughts are directed to heaven, and the truth of the Scriptures. All the greater and lesser lights have been shining on him. The cardinal virtues have been elucidated, and Faith, Hope, and Charity. The lives, manners, and doctrines of our patron Saints have necessarily passed in review. The circle, its perfect point and double triangles, and the ground floor of our moral edifice, have been surveyed. He has contemplated the beauties of holiness. He has passed to the inner chamber, and dwelt with infinite delight on the universe of matter and the universe of mind. The Bible has enabled him to read more clearly the volume of nature. The arts and sciences have furnished him subjects for study and investigation. He has had an opportunity to contemplate the progress of mind, its vast and ever-enlarging empire. And all these would lead him to knowledge of God and immortality. They would introduce him to Jehovah, and teach him to bow before his ineffable name. Are we not ever in the presence of God? The immortal mind is conscious of a God. The external universe tells of a God. And will we not adore and praise him?

There is something exceedingly grand and fearful in the view which is taken in one of the Bridgewater Treatises of the elements: "What a strange chaos is this wide atmosphere we breathe! Every atom, impressed with good and with ill, retains at once the motions which philosophers and sages have imparted to it, mixed and combined in ten thousand ways with all that is worthless and base. The air itself is a vast library, on whose pages are for ever written all that man has ever said or ever whispered. There, in their mutable but unerring characters, mixed with the earliest as well as the latest sighs of mortality, stand for ever recorded vows unredeemed, promises unfulfilled, perpetuating in the united movements of each particle, the testimony of man's changeful will." Then, the air we breathe will condemn the wicked and testify for the righteous. All nature will cry out against ungrateful and guilty men, who at the judgment will appeal in vain to the rocks and mountains to fall on them and hide them from their Maker. If they seek shelter in the clefts of the rocks and the caverns of the earth, they will be forced from their hiding-places to face the Judge, confess their crimes, and hear their sentence.

The first two degrees contain beautiful illustrations of a good life. The Christian Fellow Craft puts faith in God, and can ask God to try him—that God who was known to our fathers by the name of *I Am. Is the Christian Mason about to die?* He may commune with God. *I Am—try me!* Try me, and tell me if my soul can safely pass the way of peril, or go through the dark valley of the shadow of death with *firmness* and *integrity?* I know that I will rise at the *last day*; but will it be to a glorious resurrection? Will my body be taken up in-to heaven? *I Am!* [339] The God of Abraham, the God of Isaac, and the God of Jacob—try me! Try me with the plumb, and try me with the square. [340]

---

[339] The words *I am* have been variously understood. "They seem," says Dr. Clarke, "to point out the eternity and self-existence of God"; and that eternity and self-existence are symbolized in Freemasonry.

[340] To try the works of every Mason, the square is presented as the proba-tion of his life—proving whether his manners are regular and uniform; for Masons should be of one principle and one rank, without distinc-tions of pride and pageantry: intimating that from high to low the minds of Masons should be inclined to good works, above which no man stands exalted by his fortune. — Ahi. Rez., p. 125, note.

LECTURE IX.
The Temple of Solomon

The crowning splendour of all was the central temple, the place of the sanctuary and of the holy of holies, covered with plates of gold, its roof planted with lofty spearheads of gold, the most precious marble and metals everywhere flashing back the day, till Mount Moriah stood forth to the eye of the stranger approaching Jerusalem, what it had been so often described by its bards and people, a "Mountain of snow studded with jewels." [341]

In reading the Bible, we always look, as it were, on the same landscape; the only difference being, as we take in more and more of its statements, that more and more of the mist is rolled away from the horizon, so that the eye includes a broader sweep of beauty. [342]

A creature which is to pass a small portion of its existence in one state, to be preparatory to another, ought, no doubt, to have its attention constantly fixed upon its ulterior and permanent destination. [343]

---

[341] Croly, *op. cit*, p. 27.

[342] 1 Mel. Ser., p. 396

[343] William Paley, *The Works of William Paley*, London, 1833, p. 486.

Though abstinence from sin cannot of itself take away the power of it, yet it will put the heart in a state of preparedness for grace to take it away.[344]—

David, before he was numbered with his fathers, charged Solomon his son to erect that magnificent structure, the first temple[345]. Although the Psalmist had prepared the costliest materials for the building, and the richest furniture for its courts, it was never intended by the Almighty that the warrior king should rear that sanctuary. God, however, permitted him and his loyal people to contribute to the great enterprise; and for this David thanked and praised God's glorious name. "Now, therefore," said he, "our God, we thank thee, and praise thy glorious name. But who am I, and what is my people, that we should be able to offer so willingly after this sort?" And well might his majesty ask, *"Who am I?"* He was going the way of all the earth. He was in view of dusty death. The grave would soon receive his body. The glitter of his earthly diadem could not light up his countenance, or throw a radiance over his tomb. Death knew not his royalty. That harp, whose strings had oft been swept with the sweetest notes of praise and harmony, was soon to be stilled forever. And when his end drew nigh, David said to Solomon: My son, as for me, it was in my mind to build a house unto the name of the Lord my God; but the word of the Lord came unto me saying, thou hast shed blood abundantly and hast made great wars: thou shall, not build a house unto my name, because thou hast shed much blood upon the earth

---

[344] Robert South, *Sermons Preached on Several Occasions,* Philadelphia, 1844, Vol. 4, p. 451.

[345] According to the opinions of some writers, there were three temples, viz. the first erected by Solomon; the second by Zerubbabel and Joshua, the high priest; and the third by Herod, a few years before the birth of Christ. But this opinion is very properly rejected by the Jews, who do not allow the third to be a new temple, but only the second temple rebuilt. — 2 Horne's Intro., p. 98.

in my sight[346]. So the blood of war was upon David, and God forbade him to erect the contemplated house of worship—a place for the Ark of the Covenant. The work was given in charge to his successor. David[347] slept with his fathers. Solomon ascended the throne, and in his reign the stately edifice was reared. Calling to his council Hiram, king of Tyre, and Hiram, the widow's son, the work progressed, and in about seven years and six months it was finished. "It was magnifical, of fame and glory, throughout all countries." It is difficult for us to form any adequate idea of its proportions[348]; but we know that it was a costly and splendid temple, and that there was "nothing in the whole world like it for riches and glory." There are many descriptions of it, but their authors lived long after it was destroyed, and therefore we cannot rely on their accuracy, except so far as they agree with the description contained in the Bible. There are also many extravagant accounts of its cost. It has been estimated that there was consumed in the building more gold and silver than at present exists upon the whole earth[349]. Much, however, which has been written upon this

---

[346] 1 Chronicles 22:7-8.

[347] David was born in the year of the world 2919; Solomon in 2971.

E. N.: These dates, of course, come from the feverish nonsense of Bishop James Ussher in *The Annals of the World*, iv (1658), and have long been debunked.

[348] Various attempts have been made to describe the proportions and several parts of this structure; but as no two writers agree on this subject, a minute description of it may be very properly omitted. It retained its pristine splendor only thirty-three or thirty-four years, when Shishak, king of Egypt, took Jerusalem and carried away the treasures of the temple; and after undergoing subsequent profanations and pillages, this stupendous building was finally plundered and burnt by the Chaldæans under Nebuchadnezzar, in the year of the world 3416, or before Christ, 584. — 2 Horne's Intro, p. 98.

[349] 2 Ol. Land., p. 273.

David and his princes, we know, contributed 108,000 talents of gold, 1,017,000 talents of silver, both which together amounted to about 942,719,750 pounds sterling, and in weight amounted to about 46,000 tons of gold and silver. — Bib. Dict. Temple.

subject is entirely too vague and uncertain to command our belief. But the cost of the temple can be of little importance in advancing the object we have in view. Its location, design, and manner of erection are the essential matters for our consideration, and which will serve to elucidate our subject.

The house, when it was in building, was built of stone, made ready before it was brought thither: so that there was neither hammer nor ax nor any tool of iron heard in the house, while it was in building[350].

> "In awful state,
> The temple reared its everlasting gate.
> No workman's steel, no ponderous axes rung!
> Like some tall palm the noiseless fabric sprung."

How skilful must have been all the craftsmen. Every stone had a place assigned to it before leaving the quarry. The timbers were also pre pared in the forests of Lebanon. Immense blocks of marble and large timbers were fitted for the builder's use, and the whole was put together with mathematical precision, and with the assistance, says Dr. Clarke, of wooden mallets. And the building was covered in with radiant plates and spearheads of gold. The magnificence of the structure was only surpassed by the grandeur of its worship. Freemasonry is connected with every apartment of Solomon's temple and its religious service. It is associated with that great building from its foundation to its last and crowning stone. It is a system of Jewish rites and ceremonies, "made compact together" by our ancient Masters; and as the Jewish religion was designed to be only preparatory to a future and better revelation, so before the advent of the Messiah our ancient brethren perceived in Freemasonry traces of a full and perfect dispensation. If the Jewish religion contained promises of better things[351], each

---

[350] 1 Kings 6:7.

[351] Christianity, after all, is but Judaism in a more advanced stage; and it must, therefore, be our wisdom to trace carefully the religion in its pro-

step in Masonry is an advance toward a greater light, and each degree preparatory to another and a higher. Among Christians, the Jewish rites and ceremonies have passed away. The temple of Solomon is no more. It fell beneath the hand of the spoiler. It long since became a heap of dust and ashes. But the Masonic edifice was constructed of imperishable materials. In some moral Lebanon, waving with the rich emblems of immortality, its ancient builders found the true *lignum vitæ*. Its blocks of thought are purer than Parian marble, and its pillars more majestic than Jachin and Boaz. Consecrated genius, the miner that ever searches for the richest, ore, struck the deepest veins of wisdom, and furnished plates of truth and spearheads of reason for its roof, upon which the Sun of Righteousness now shines in splendor, and flashes back the immortality of man.

The temple of Solomon arose in mysterious silence: *"There was neither hammer nor ax nor any tool of iron heard in the house, while it was in building."* Then, there was no noise made in its construction. That very *stillness* was a *type*. The temple was a type of the kingdom of God; and the souls of men are to be prepared here for that place of blessedness. The stones must be all squared and fitted *here* for their place in the New Jerusalem; and being *living* stones, must be built up a holy temple for a habitation of God through the Spirit[352].

> *O God, how beautiful and vast*
> *Men's minds and fancies grow,*
> *When, in thy mould of doctrine cast.*
> *Their warm ideas flow!*
> *When 'tis thy church inspires the thought,*
> *And forms the bold design,*
> *Till, from a sullen rock, is wrought*

---

gress toward perfection, if we hope to comprehend it when that perfection was reached. — Mel. Ser., p. 414. So it may be said that if we would understand the principles or mysteries of Masonry, we must trace them carefully through the several degrees, for they are gradually developed or brought to light.

[352] Clarke's Com., 1 Kings 6:9.

A symbol so divine!

Arthur Cleveland Coxe, *Christian Ballads.*

Truly was our mystic temple erected in silence. All its splendid materials were prepared and numbered before they were placed in the building. And the silent work which goes on in and about our lodges should continually remind us of the mysterious ways of Providence, and his secret operations. The *silence* which reigned at the building of Solomon's temple, and the *secrecy* of our moral work, teach that quietude of soul and rapturous joy which exist in heaven[353]. *Silence* might be said to be emblematical of a heart at *peace* with God. The silence which was preserved at the building of the temple, we have said was mysterious, and what is not mysterious? There is mystery in everything. There is mystery within us and mystery without us[354]. In the beautiful but complicated structure of man—a *tenement* of clay, a *temple* of flesh—there are many strange and wonderful things. In the person of Adam arose a magnificent structure, and it was erected by a great and *mysterious Being*—the Architect of the universe. Originally, it was a fit temple for the worship of the Almighty. *The house of clay* is still a strange but ruined structure. There are *secrets* in and about its every apartment. Veins, arteries, ligaments, and flesh, and bone, have their *secrets.* The blood, which animates the human frame, flows on in *silence.* And how quiet are the communings of the heart. There are feelings, and thoughts, and sympathies, which never emerge from their solitary retreats. And who has ever heard those mighty spirits, which walk so majesti-

---

[353] The silence which was observed in building Solomon's temple may remind us of the secret operations of God in the souls of men, and of the peace of heaven. — Brad. Ser., p. 21. This excellent discourse has suggested to our mind some of the thoughts contained in the above lecture.

[354] By a silent, unseen, mysterious process, the fairest flower of the garden springs from a small, insignificant seed; the majestic oak of the forest from an acorn; the strongest and wisest man from a wretched, helpless, and senseless infant: the holy and exalted soul from a miserable sinner. — Horne's Disc., p. 29.

cally in history, or those associated events and principles which have come down from the past? Time, with a *quiet* and *noiseless* hand, is continually drawing out the invisible wires which connect century with century, those mystic lines which enable us to commune with the remotest ages. Yes, there is mystery everywhere; mystery in the *present*, mystery in the *past*, and mystery in the *future*.

To number every mystery were to sum the sum of all things:
None can exhaust a theme, whereof God is example and similitude.
Nevertheless take a garland from the garden, a handful from the harvest,
Some scattered drops of spray from the ceaseless, mighty cataract.
Whence are we—whither do we tend—how do we feel and reason?
How strange a thing is man, a spirit saturating clay!
Where doth the soul make embryos immortal—how do they rank hereafter—
And will the unconscious idiot be quenched in death as nothing?

*   *   *   *   *   *   *   *   *   *   *   *   *   *

O mysteries, ye are all one: the mind of an inexplicable architect
Dwelleth alike in each, quickening and moving in them all.

2 Tupper.

We have noted the time it took to construct Solomon's temple. But there was great preparation for it. It was the work of years, labor, and skill. The workmen were diligent and untiring in their efforts to aid and assist each other in preparing the materials and putting them up. And there were many engaged in the great undertaking. No less than seventy thousand Entered Apprentices, eighty thousand Fellow Crafts, and thirty-three hundred overseers of the work, besides three Grand Masters, devoted more than seven years' labor on the building[355]. This is a very striking

---

[355] This construction of the grand edifice was attended with many remarkable circumstances. From Josephus we learn that although more than seven years were occupied in building it, yet during the whole term it rained not in the day time that the workmen might not be obstructed in their labor. This famous fabric was supported by 1453 columns, and

portion of the history of that enterprise, which was conceived by David and executed under the direction of Solomon. Let us reflect upon the preparations which were made; the vast number of workmen employed; the industry and ability of those workmen; and the time they were engaged. Hiram, king of Tyre, sent his servants unto Solomon; for he had heard that Solomon was anointed king in the room of his father: for Hiram was a lover of David, and he knew that Solomon purposed to build a house unto the name of the Lord his God[356]. And these servants *prepared* all the timbers and stones in the forests and quarries. The *cedars* were all *cut* and *squared*, and were conveyed "by sea in floats unto the place" that Solomon appointed. It will be observed that the Scriptures are *silent* as to the place to which they were conveyed by sea. Dr. Clarke says that they might be readily sent down the coast on rafts, and landed at Joppa or Jamnia, just opposite to Jerusalem, at the distance of twenty-five miles. The stones were hewed, squared, and numbered. The materials[357] then were all *prepared*, and had only to be put together when they arrived at Jerusalem. What beautiful and moral lessons are derived from the *preparation* of those materials. Noah *prepared* for the flood. Abraham *prepared* to offer up his son Isaac as a sacrifice. God *prepared* for the coming of the Messiah: he was announced through signs, symbols, types, ceremonies, and prophecies. The Lord *prepared* for the establishment of his church on earth, and is *preparing* materials for his church in

---

2906 pilasters, all hewn from the finest Parian marble. There were employed in its building three Grand Masters, three thousand and three hundred overseers of the work; eighty thousand Fellow Crafts, and seventy thousand Entered Apprentices. All these were classed and arranged in such a manner by the wisdom of Solomon, that universal peace and order prevailed. — Ahi. Rez., p. 186.

[356] 1 Kings 5:1-5.

[357] "The pieces of timber," says Calmet, "were conveyed from the high parts of the mountains to the river Adonis, or to the plains of Byblos; thence they were conveyed to the seaport, where they were placed on rafts, to be carried by sea to the port of Joppa, which was the nearest port to Jerusalem.

heaven. Their foundation stones were laid soon after the fall of man. The Israelites *prepared* to take possession of the Promised Land. By the command of Joshua, the officers of the people passed through the hosts and commanded them, saying: *Prepare* you victuals; for within *three* days ye shall pass over this Jordan, to go in to possess the land, which the Lord your God giveth you to possess it[358]. 0, *prepare* mercy and truth, sung David[359]. *Prepare* your hearts unto the Lord, and serve him only[360]. John the Baptist *prepared* for the way of the Lord. The *preparation* of the heart in man, and the answer of the tongue, is from the Lord[361]. Then preparation is very essential. Do we prepare for a journey? We must all travel the way our fathers have gone before us. We are even now on our journey to the city of the dead, many of us wholly *unprepared*. Hope is on *this side* of the grave, and faith comes *before* hope. We must have faith in God, and experience a living sense of our *lost* condition, *before* we can hope for salvation. Repent and believe, say the Scriptures. Hope *prepares* us to look for something good. Its beautiful light is ever before the Christian in time, and on his journey to the Holy Land. Then the *preparation* of the materials of the temple is replete with heavenly meaning. The gradual erection of the edifice tells us that the change of the heart is not always the *work* of a day. The new birth has its period of conception and gestation, which must *precede* the righteous Spirit coming down into a world of lovely and beautiful things.

And the preparation of which we have been speaking is beautifully elucidated in our Masonic degrees. The degree of the Entered Apprentice implies the necessity of preparation. The Entered Apprentice should *prepare* himself for the second degree, and be made ready to take it. He should

---

[358] Joshua 1:11.

[359] Psalms 61:7.

[360] 1 Samuel 7:3.

[361] Proverbs 16:1.

never go down to Jerusalem until he can carry with him a proper specimen of his work, *prepared* in pursuance of the designs laid down on the tracing-board. Then he may become a Fellow Craft, and be furnished with the necessary tools to *mark* and *adjust* his work. The art and science of Masonry must be learned *gradually*. It has several departments, various steps and degrees. We must place our feet on the first round of the Masonic or theological ladder, before we can ascend the second; and we must receive the degree of Entered Apprentice, before we can obtain the Fellow Craft, and the Fellow Craft before the degree of Master Mason. Then, how complete is the analogy between the work of speculative Masonry and the preparation of the materials for King Solomon's temple. And what does the argument by way of analogy demonstrate? Every moral truth which the preparation of the materials of the temple teaches, our Masonic preparation also illustrates. It would be wise in us to think often of the necessity of preparation to be advanced in light and knowledge. Let it be deeply impressed on our minds and strictly observed.

Again: "There was neither hammer nor ax nor any tool of iron heard in the house, while it was in building." The sound of hammers, axes, and other metal tools were doubtless heard in the forests and quarries, where the timbers and stones were being prepared. There are material agencies used in *preparing* the souls of men to think and consider of their immortal nature, and in making them *ready to repent* of their sins; but the Son of God, that gracious and unseen Being, is preparing a house not made with hands. Every stone is adjusted in silence, and no noise will ever be heard in that house while it is in building; though when the great day of dedication shall come, all the holy angels will bring forth its capstone with shouting and praise. The material universe may impress us with the belief of a First Cause, its Master Builder; the dew, the sunshine, and rain may tell us of his goodness and mercy; human instruments may be used to *prepare* us for worshipping God with a humble and contrite spirit; but the unseen God alone can give us saving grace. His great work of mercy goes on *silently* on earth and in heaven. And what sublime *stillness* should pervade the mind, when it thinks of the might, and majesty and dominion of Jehovah. Let the *silent* prayer ascend; let the pure incense go up *unseen* from off the altar of a repentant soul. Our hearts are all beating their silent and "funeral marches to the grave." Their muffled notes will become *silent* after death. The clods of the valley may fall on our coffins and give back mournful and hollow sounds; but there is an awful *stillness* in the tomb. There is but very little noise in building the cities of the dead. Here and there comes a pale visitor, and he takes a house already *built* and *prepared* to receive him. Oh! How *silent* are the tenantry of those narrow mansions! Even the reptiles come and go into them to their repast, and no man knows whence they come or whither they go. *They wake not the sleepers.* But there is an oncoming day, when all the earth shall give up its dead. There is One with whom dwells the resurrection and the life. *I am the resurrection and the life,* saith the Lord. But what was the object of building the temple of Solomon? One purpose, we are informed, was that it might be a house of prayer for all nations. But this was not its only purpose. God intended to make it the seat of his visible presence, or the place of his habitation[362]. It was not designed, thought an eminent commentator, to be a place of worship *in*, but a place of worship *at*, where God was known to have a *peculiar residence*[363]. This worship *at* the temple, and *peculiar residence in* the temple, may serve to illustrate the worship *at* the temple of a redeemed soul, and the *peculiar residence* of the Spirit in that temple. He dwells in the soul of a righteous man. The

---

[362] The temple of Solomon was not built for this single purpose, that it might be "a house of prayer for all nations." It was designed to be a habitation of God, the seat of his presence, and a monument to his name. — Brad. Ser., p. 32.

[363] The residence of glory, first in the tabernacle and then in the temple, was a figure of the residence of God by his Spirit in the Christian church, and his eternal residence in that church brought to perfection in heaven. — 1 Horne's Intro., p. 385.

Holy Spirit comes down into the soul and regenerates it, and makes it fit for his presence—*his peculiar residence*. The olden temple was *prepared* and *finished* before the Lord of glory descended into the holy of holies and dwelt beneath the outstretched wings of the cherubim, above the mercy-seat. So must the heart of the sinner be *prepared* and *made ready* for the holy presence of the Lord. Then his Spirit will abide in it, and his glory fill it.

The peculiar residence of the indwelling of the Spirit would seem to be taught in the principles of the craft. We celebrate the dedication of the temple. The ceremony of the most excellent Master's degree closes with the following passage of Scripture: Now when Solomon had made an end of praying, the fire came down from heaven, and consumed the burnt offering and the sacrifices; and the glory of the Lord filled the house. And the priest could not enter into the house of the Lord, because the glory of the Lord had filled the Lord's house. And when all the children of Israel saw how the fire came down and the glory of the Lord upon the house, they bowed themselves with their faces to the ground upon the pavement, and worshipped, and praised the Lord, saying, For he is good; for his mercy endureth for ever[364]. The King of glory had descended; and who was the King of glory? The Lord, strong and mighty. "The Lord of Hosts, he is the King of glory." And the following psalm is also read during the ceremony: I was glad when they said unto me; Let us go into the house of the Lord. Our feet shall stand within thy gates, O Jerusalem. Jerusalem is built as a city that is compact together: whither the tribes go up, the tribes of the Lord, unto the testimony of Israel, to give thanks unto the name of the Lord. For there are set thrones of judgment, the thrones of the house of David. Pray for the peace of Jerusalem: they shall prosper that love thee. Peace be within thy walls, and prosperity within thy palaces. For my brethren and companions'

---

[364] 2 Chronicles 7:1-3. Cross' Chart, p. 96.

sakes, I will now say, Peace be within thee[365]. And why is this Scripture read in our lodges or chapters? Let us remember that the Jews were taken captive into Babylon by Nebuchadnezzar at the destruction of Jerusalem. They had been seventy years in the land of their captivity, and they longed to return to their native city. Jerusalem was their own city. It had been built up by their hands and the hands of their fathers. Destruction had come upon it. The spoiler had been there and carried its inhabitants away in chains. Their hallowed temple was laid in ruins, and they were exiles. Dr. Clarke, in commenting on the above psalm, puts the following words in their mouth: "Our heart was in Jerusalem, but our feet are in Chaldea. Now, God has turned our captivity, and our feet shall shortly stand within the gates of Jerusalem!" The whole of this psalm is a finished and sublime picture of the beauty and prosperity of Jerusalem, after the restoration of the Jews. The city was to be rebuilt. Its gorgeous towers and temples were to be built "compact together," and there were to be set thrones of judgment, the thrones of the house of David. Thither were "the tribes to go up, the tribes of the Lord."[366] And what for? "To give thanks unto the name of the Lord." Why pray for the peace of Jerusalem, why for the brethren and companions' sake did David sing: "Peace be unto thee?" Because he loved his brethren, and "because of the house

---

[365] Psalms 122:8; Cross' Chart, p. 91.

Bishop Horne supposes that the subject of this psalm is that joy which the people were wont to express, upon their going up in companies, to keep a feast at Jerusalem, when the Divine services were regulated, and that city was appointed to be the place of public worship. Dr. Clarke seems to think it had some reference to the captivity and the restoration of the Jews. We know its beautiful application in the most excellent Master's degree.

[366] The true Israelite, amidst the dangers of his earthly pilgrimage and warfare, looketh continually toward the heavenly city, whither he is travelling. Faith showeth him afar off the everlasting hills from whence cometh the help which must bring him in safety to them. He lifteth up his eyes in prayer to the Almighty, whose temple and habitation are thereon. — Bp. Horne.

of the Lord our God." Let us impress on our minds the beautiful Masonic lesson which is contained in the sentiments of David. It embraces, in a few words, the principles upon which our sublime edifice is founded, and by which it was built and remains compact together. David loved his brethren and his God. *"Peace be within thee!"* Jerusalem was the home of his brethren. "Peace be within thee. Because of the house of the Lord our God I will seek thy good."

But why do we read so much of the Scriptures in our lodges and chapters? And such significant portions of the Scriptures? What does the usage mean? It surely means something. There must be some reason for it. Freemasonry, we have repeatedly stated, was founded on the truths of the Bible, which it endeavors to enforce by scenic representations and ceremonies. Can any rational or well-informed Mason deny this? Before he does so, let him destroy the landmarks of the Order, and the temple also, before he would carry its worshippers into a strange land; for they would long to return to their native hills, the rites and traditions of their fathers, and the sublime and soul-touching associations of Moriah. It was when Solomon had made an end of praying, that the fire came down from heaven; but it was before the fire came down, that the cloud of God's glory descended, and that the Almighty was made manifest in the sanctum sanctorum. It was on the day of dedication[367], and the year of dedication was a jubilee. The silver trumpets had ushered it in amidst the rejoicing of all the people. The elders of Israel had been assembled in the devoted city of Jerusalem. Solomon had summoned them to meet together for a holy purpose. The stately temple was completed. It towered in all its grandeur. It was the wonder and admiration of the world. The craftsmen were all present at the dedication.

---

[367] When a Masonic hall has been erected, it is dedicated with certain well-known and impressive ceremonies, to Masonry, virtue, and universal benevolence. — Mack. Lex., p. 65. Corn, wine, and oil are Masonic elements used at the dedication.

"They had no more occasion for level or plumb-line,
For trowel or gavel, for compass or square."

Their work was all finished, and the Ark of the Covenant was about to be brought up "out of the city of David, which is Zion." How sublime and surpassingly grand were the ceremonies of dedication![368] "And all the elders of Israel came, and the priests took up the ark." And the tabernacle was carried up also, and all the holy vessels that were in it. Then the sacrifices commenced. All the congregation of Israel took part in the ceremonies. The sheep and the oxen to be sacrificed were numberless. When the ark[369] was borne into "the oracle of the house, to the most holy place," the cherubim spread forth their wings over the place, and covered the ark and the staves thereof. And when it was safely seated, Almighty Jehovah descended and filled the house with his glory. Yes, the Lord was visible there; and well might the wisest of men in the presence of all the congregation of Israel pour out a fervent and most eloquent prayer to Him for his multiplied blessings. What a mighty assembly had gathered together! The Lord of heaven and earth was there. And never before had such eloquence fallen from the lips of Solomon. His prayer is a specimen of true devotion, and of what a wise man can do

---

[368] When a Masonic edifice is erected, according to ancient custom, it must be dedicated. A portion of the ceremonies of dedication may be performed in public.

[369] The most striking analogy between the Ark of the Covenant and the sacred chests of other nations is exhibited in one of the South Sea islands, discovered by Captain Cook. It is described as a kind of chest, or ark, the lid of which was nicely sewed on and thatched very neatly with palm-nut leaves. It was fixed upon two poles, and supported upon little arches of wood, very neatly covered. In one end of it was a square hole, in the middle of which was a ring touching the sides, and leaving the angles open, so as to form a round hole within, or square one without. The general resemblance between this repository and the ark of the Jews is remarkable; but it is still more remarkable that upon inquiring of a boy what it was called, he said *Ewharre* or *Etaw*—the house of God.
— 2 Ol. Land., p. 298, note 23.

and say, "When out of the abundance of the heart the mouth speaketh."

That ever memorable occasion is celebrated in our lodges. It is the ground-work of one of its most beautiful degrees. It has been celebrated for thousands of generations, and is hallowed in the memory of the craft. And may we not with propriety say, that the splendid and eloquent prayer of our Grand Master, although it is not expressly incorporated into the regular body of Masonry, constitutes, by implication, a portion of our institution? If we are correct in the opinion that our Order was perfected at the completion of the temple, or even established after that period, but associated with the progress of that building and dedication, then we may very reasonably contend that every rite or event connected with it affords a subject for Masonic study and investigation.

The Shekinah was the sitting or dwelling of God, between the cherubim, on the mercy-seat or cover of the ark, whence he delivered his answers in an articulate voice[370]. The Divine Shekinah reappeared in human form in the second temple, after it, was repaired by Herod, and was the antitype of Isaac. The Shekinah among the Hebrews was a symbol of the present Deity. The Rabbis believed that it resided first in the tabernacle built by Moses, and that it descended at the consecration of the tabernacle, as it did at the dedication of the first temple[371]. It disappeared at the destruction of Jerusalem, but reappeared at the transfiguration of Christ, and also at his baptism. Its appearance in the tabernacle and Solomon's temple is generally supposed to

---

[370] 2 Horne's Intro., p. 255.

[371] The Rabbis affirm that the Shekinah first resided in the tabernacle prepared by Moses in the wilderness, into which it descended on the day of its consecration, in the figure of a cloud. It passed from thence into the sanctuary of Solomon's temple on the day of its dedication. It appeared at the baptism and transfiguration of Christ. — 2 Pict. Dict., p. 1230.

have been typical of the Messiah[372]. If so, does not Freemasonry recognize the type? Where is the type spoken of particularly? The bright cloud descended into the most holy place of the ancient temple, which was constructed by the express injunction, of the Almighty, which was a house of prayer, a place of worship solemnly dedicated to the Lord. Do we believe these things? What is the guide of our faith? The Holy Bible. Then all the types, shadows, rites and ceremonies of the Jews, as contained in the Old Testament, have been adopted expressly or impliedly into our system, and form a part of its mysteries.

---

[372] Josephus regarded the tabernacle and its furniture as being typical. — Jewish Antiq. Book 3, ch. 7.

Charles Scott

LECTURE X.
Symbolism and Mysteries in Masonry

All things being are in mystery; we expound mysteries by myster-
ies;
And yet the secret of them all is one in simple grandeur! [373]

Be content; thine eye cannot see all the sides of a cube at one view,
Nor thy mind in the self-same moment follow two ideas. [374]

What master of reason or subtilty is able to unriddle the gos-
pel? [375]

Man was originally the temple of Jehovah; an earthly, but yet a
magnificent structure, designed to show forth the power and wisdom
which could raise a fabric so glorious from materials so poor. [376]

And they shall bring the glory and honor of the nations into it. [377]

---

[373] Tupper, p. 48.

[374] Ibid., 76.

[375] Robert South, *Sermons Preached upon Several Occasions*, London, 1744, Vol. VIII., p. 380.

[376] Brad. Ser., p. 74.

[377] Revelation 21:26.

Masons speak of the mysteries[378] of their Order. A mystery may be defined to be something which is secret, hidden, or revealed but in part. The term is applied both to doctrines and facts[379]. The doctrines of the Trinity, and the incarnation of Jesus Christ, are great mysteries. As facts, they are mysteries. We read of outward and visible signs of secret or hidden truth. Christ, it is said, "instituted and ordained holy mysteries, as pledges of his love, and for a continual remembrance of his death." Christians are exhorted to prepare themselves to partake of these holy mysteries. Types, allegories, and parables contain mysteries; for they have a secret or hidden meaning[380]. The typical sense of the Scriptures is when, under external objects or prophetic vision, secret things, whether present or future, are represented; especially when certain transactions recorded in the Old Testament presignify or adumbrate those related in the New Testament[381]. The allegorical sense is, when the Holy Scriptures, besides the literal sense, signify anything belonging to faith or spiritual doctrine; and the parabolical sense is, when, besides the plain and obvious meaning of the thing related, an occult or spiritual sense is intended[382]. This spiritual sense is a mystical sense. The mysteries of Freemasonry exist in its signs, words, symbols, rites, and ceremonies, which have an allegorical, hidden, secret, spiritual, mystical meaning. They contain deep doctrines as well as

---

[378] That which is mystical in the Word is nothing else but what is spiritual and celestial; thus, what treats of the Lord, of his kingdom, and of the church. — Heav. Arc., p. 4923, n.

[379] That the term mystery is so applied, see Dict. of the Church, p. 345 [E. N.: William Staunton, A *Dictionary of the Church*, New York, 1844, p. 345]

[380] That which has a hidden, allegorical, or secret meaning, is termed mystical. — Dict. of the Church, p. 346. The term mysteries is applied to all those religious ceremonies which were conducted in secret by the ancients. — Mack Lex., p. 207.

[381] 1 Horne's Intro., p. 323.

[382] Ibid.

strange facts, which we have partly shown; doctrines which are holy mysteries, and facts which have left an indelible impression upon all time, and produced the mightiest results; doctrines and facts, whose mystical sense will never be revealed until we are raised to a higher state of existence.

The analogy which exists between the types and symbols of Masonry and those of the Bible, is of a very striking character, as the attentive reader must have perceived. They partake alike of a spiritual or mystical sense. Masonry generally speaks in symbols, or symbolical language, the expounding of which is closely connected with the interpretation of types. By symbols is meant "certain representative marks, rather than express pictures; or if pictures, such as were at the time characters; and besides representing to the eye the resemblance of a particular object, suggested a general idea to the mind." It has been doubted by theologians whether symbolical language should be referred to figurative or spiritual interpretation[383]. The better opinion seems to be, that it is most nearly allied to spiritual interpretation. A symbol, properly speaking, refers to something present or past; while a type refers to something future. But there are both types and symbols in Masonry, as in the Scriptures. A Masonic symbol often refers to a type associated with it. For example, the Masonic ladder is a symbol in its true sense, because it refers to or represents something past, the ladder which Jacob saw in his dream. But Jacob's ladder, which is emblematized in Masonry, was a type. So the blazing star is an emblem in the eye of a Christian brother, because to him it represents something past, which long since appeared; but if Freemasonry existed before the birth of Christ, then the star in the centre of the Mosaic pavement was emblematical of the prophetic star of which Balaam spoke; which star, in the eye of our ancient brethren, was a spiritual type of the one which really appeared. But there are types which are conveyed or signified by

---

[383] 1 Horne's Intro., p. 387.

means of external symbols, as is the case with prophetical types.

But there are Masonic symbols which are disconnected with types. For instance, there is the all-seeing eye[384], which represents the omnipresence of God, with whom there is a perpetual now. It is strictly a symbol. Various other examples might be given, were it conceived necessary. The Bible is full of symbolical language; and if we will diligently compare it with the symbolical language of Masonry, the most accurate analogy will be observed. It is a very ancient mode of conveying information. The symbolical language of the prophets, says an eminent bishop, is almost a science in itself. None can fully comprehend the depth, sublimity, and force of their writings, who are not thoroughly acquainted with the peculiar and appropriate imagery they were accustomed to use. This is the main key to many of the prophecies; and, without knowing how to apply it, the interpreter will often in vain essay to discover their hidden treasures[385]. Then there is a beauty and force in Masonic symbols. There is great necessity for us to be familiar with symbolical language, if we would perceive the secret meaning of prophecy, or discover the force, depth, and sublimity of the prophetical Scriptures; and in this will also be observed an-

---

[384] Eyes as applied to the Almighty denote, 1. His infinite knowledge, (Proverbs 15:3, Psalms 2:4); 2. His watchful providence, (Psalms 33:8; 34:15); 3. The omnipresence of Jesus Christ (Revelation 2:23; Hebrews 4:13.) As applied to man they denote: 1. The understanding, the eyes of the mind, (Psalms 119:18, Ephesians 1:18); 2. A friendly counselor (Job 29:15); 3. The whole man (Revelation 1:7); 4. Human designs (Deuteronomy 28:54-56.) — *Horne's Index to Symbolical Language of the Bible.*

Here we perceive that eyes as applied to God denote three things; as applied to man four things; which correspond with the two perfect figures, the triangle and the square. And three and four added together make *seven.*

[385] Bp. Vanmildert's Lec., p. 240. E. N.: William Van Mildert, *The Theological Works,* abundantly referenced by Thomas Hartwell Horne, specifically in *An Introduction to the Critical Study and Knowledge of the Holy Scriptures,* Philadelphia, 1825, p. 83, giving the exact quote used by Scott.

other beautiful relation, which our Order sustains to the sacred writings[386].

There are historical types in the Old Testament. So there are historical types in Masonry. The historical types in the Old Testament were exact prefigurations of the characters, actions, and fortunes of future persons who should arise under the gospel dispensation[387]. For example, Moses and Isaac were types of the Messiah. If the old Scriptures contained such types, it is very easy to see whence our ancient Masters derived knowledge of them, and why they would incorporate something similar into the Order. The founders of Masonry were acquainted with the historical types, and knew that they prefigured future events; for they had great faith in God, who had declared them to be typical. The historical types of Masonry may be termed inferred types, as divines make a distinction between express or innate and inferred types. The distinction is this: Those persons whom God declared to be typical, have been called innate, or natural historical types[388]; while all others are regarded as implied, or inferred historical types. Now, if, as we contend, there are any historical types embodied in Masonry, they cannot be called, in a scriptural sense, innate types, because they are not of Divine origin. The historical characters, as mentioned and delineated in the Bible, may be termed innate types; but as represented in our ceremonies or lectures can only be said to be inferred historical or

---

[386] The symbolical language of the Scriptures is of a very forcible and striking character. A king or kingdom is symbolized by a great eagle, with great wings full of feathers, which had divers colors. To be borne on eagles' wings, signifies divine miraculous deliverance. "Who can pursue the eagle through the air, and take from him what is committed to his charge?" A multitude of other examples might be enumerated.

[387] 1 Horne's Intro., p. 386.

[388] In some instances, the persons whose characters and actions prefigured future events, were declared by Jehovah himself to be typical, long before the events which they prefigured came to pass: these have been termed innate or natural historical types; and, these may be safely admitted. — 1 Horne's Intro., p. 380.

traditional types. The principal characteristic of an inferred, or implied type, is that in which the typical person is not known to be such until after the thing typified had actually occurred[389]. Now, our ancient brethren most probably knew their historical characters to be typical, because the founders of Masonry so regarded them, and they had been made acquainted with the innate historical types of the Old Testament. This knowledge of our ancient brethren has been lost in the lapse of centuries. At all events, it has not been transmitted to us, and consequently, the historical or traditional types of our institution can only be known as such by tracing out the analogies between the persons or things typified and the types themselves. The legal types[390] of the Old Testament may be said to have been introduced into the Masonic ritual as they existed in the "ritual law." Masonry, in its perfected state, is doubtless of Jewish origin; and as the book of the law is the source of much Masonic light,—as it was deposited by Moses in the ark of the covenant, and that ark, with all its precious treasures, was carried up and deposited in the holy of holies of the first temple, and the book was once lost and afterwards restored through the instrumentality of the Fraternity,— whatever that book contained of a typical nature was necessarily typical in Masonry; for our ancient brethren recognized the Divine authority of the five books of Moses. Then, if there are any legal types of the Messiah, they form a part of the body of Masonry. In Hebrews, Christ, we are told, was called of God a High Priest after the order of Melchisedek[391]. The ninth chapter of Hebrews points out

---

[389] 1 Horne's Intro., p. 386.

[390] The entire constitution and offerings of the Levitical priesthood typically prefigured Christ, the great high priest, and especially the ceremonies observed on the great Day of Atonement. So the Passover and paschal lamb typified the sacrifice of Jesus Christ: so the feast of Pentecost, which commemorated the giving of the law on Mount Sinai prefigured the effusion of the Holy Spirit. — 1 Horne's Intro., p. 385.

[391] Hebrews 5:10.

the typical meaning of the tabernacle, and its furniture, together with the ordinances observed at the tabernacle. Then, verily, the first covenant had also ordinances of divine service, and a worldly sanctuary. For there was a tabernacle made; the first, wherein was the candlestick, and the table, and the shewbread; which is called the sanctuary. And after the second veil, the tabernacle, which is called the holiest of all; which had the golden censer, and the ark of the covenant overlaid roundabout with gold, wherein was the golden pot that had manna, and Aaron's rod that budded, and the tables of the covenant; and over it the cherubim of glory shadowing the mercy-seat; of which we cannot now speak particularly[392]. In the 11th verse of the same chapter, Christ is called a High Priest: But Christ being come a high priest of good things to come, by a greater and more perfect tabernacle, not made with hands. "So," says Horne, "the Passover and the paschal lamb typified the sacrifice of Jesus Christ; so, the toast of Pentecost, which commemorated the giving of the law on Mount Sinai, prefigured the effusion of the Holy Spirit on the apostles, who were thus enabled to promulgate the gospel throughout the then known world. And it has been conjectured that the feast of the tabernacles typified the final restoration of the Jews." The very privileges of the Jews are regarded as types of those enjoyed by Christians.

There are mysteries in Freemasonry; and many consider that they furnish sufficient ground to repudiate or condemn the institution. Now, the Scriptures are liable to the very same objection; and if Masonry be rejected or condemned on account of its mysteries, then for the very same reason we might reject or condemn the Scriptures. And there have been infidels, and there are infidels now, who object to the Bible on the ground that it contains mysteries. "Some of the doctrines," say they, "of the Bible are not entitled to our belief, because they are mysterious; and where

---

392 Hebrews 9:1-5.

mystery begins religion ends." Horne, in his Introduction to the Holy Scriptures, has given a triumphant answer to this objection; and that answer may be regarded as a vindication of our Order. "Nothing is so mysterious," says he, "as the eternity and self-existence of God: yet to believe that God exists is the foundation of all religion. Above our reason the attributes of Deity unquestionably are; for who can conceive what eternity is? Duration without beginning, or succession of parts of time! Who can so much as imagine or frame any idea of a Being neither made by itself or by any other? Of omnipotence, of omniscience, and of immensity! How, indeed, can a finite capacity like ours comprehend an Infinite Being, which heaven and the heaven of heavens cannot contain! Vain mortal! Dost thou presume to scrutinize the nature and comprehend all the ways of the incomprehensible God?"

The body of a redeemed sinner has been called a temple of God. What! Know ye not that your body is the temple of the Holy Ghost which is in you, which ye have of God, and ye are not your own? For ye are bought with a price: therefore glorify God in your body, and in your spirit, which are God's[393]. This is a most remarkable saying, and contains a figure evidently drawn from the temple of Solomon, into whose holy of holies the glory of God descended and was made visible. As truly, says Adam Clarke, as the living God dwelt in the Mosaic tabernacle and in the temple of Solomon, so truly does the Holy Ghost dwell in the souls of genuine Christians[394]. When the soul is re-

---

[393] 1 Corinthians 6:19-20.

[394] All Christians were denominated Theophori, "temples of God," and sometimes Christophori, "temples of Christ." When Ignatius stood in the presence of the Emperor Trajan, the emperor demanded of him: "Who art thou, unhappy and deluded man, who art so active in transgressing our commands; and besides, persuadest others to their own destruction?" Ignatius replied: "No one ought to call (one who is properly styled) Theophorus unhappy and deluded; for the evil spirits (which deluded men) are departed far from the servants of God. But if you so call me because I am a trouble to those evil spirits and an enemy

deemed from sin, it is ready to be dedicated to the Lord, who will make it his habitation, and will write his name there forever, and it will be a "new name, which no man knoweth saving he that receiveth it."

In the United States, the Fellow Craft's degree is conferred in a blue lodge, and the Mark Master's in a chapter. We have always thought that there existed art evident connection between these degrees. When an Entered Apprentice is advanced to the degree of Fellow Craft, he is advanced to a new state or quality, and is then considered capable of adjusting his work. But his work or wrought stone should be marked and numbered before being adjusted, or laid in a building. A white stone, with a new name written in it, imports a new quality or state. When God made his covenant with Abraham, he gave him a new name[395]. So Sarai and Simon were called by new names, when they were placed in new circumstances[396]. "The white stone," says Dean Woodhouse, "presented to the conquering Christian, may be supposed to signify the approving sentence of God." On the stone there was to be a new name written. From the earliest ages it was customary to invest a person raised to dignity with a new name or title, expressive of his merits[397].

The church of God has also been called the temple of God[398]: He shall build the temple of the Lord, even he shall

---

to their delusions, I confess the justice of the appellation; for having (within me) Christ, the heavenly King! Loosen all their snares." Trajan replied: "And who is Theophorus?" Ignatius answered: "He that hath Christ in his heart." Then answered Trajan: "Carriest thou, then, within thee him who was crucified?" "Yea," replied Ignatius, "for it is written, I will dwell in them and walk in them." — Clem. Epistles, p. 55, note a.

[395] Genesis 17:5.

[396] D'Oyly and Mant's Com., Revelation 2:17.

[397] Ibidem.

[398] In the Bible, this title generally refers to that house of prayer which Solomon built for the honor and worship of God. The name of temple is now properly used for any church or place of worship set apart for the

build the temple of the Lord, and he shall bear the glory[399]. All the commentators agree in affirming that this passage contains a prophecy of the Messiah[400]. He was to build his temple on earth; even he should build the temple of the Lord and should bear the glory. And when the Messiah himself came, he spoke of his body: Jesus answered and said unto them: Destroy this temple, and in three days I will raise it up[401]. He spoke of the temple of his body. And who is the builder of God's temple—the church? Christ is its glorious architect[402]. He planned it. He drew its inimitable designs, laid off its vast dimensions, prepared all its materials, which are imperishable; and founded it on an eternal rock. And the glory of God has descended upon it, and the glory of the Lord shall fill it. The temple of Solomon, we have shown, was a type of the church; and Hiram, that man of wisdom, and understanding, and cunning in all works of brass, was its architect. In Masonic language, he was the builder. He drew its plan and superintended the work. Was not Hiram, then, a type of Jesus? If the temple was a type of the church, and Christ is the builder of the church, was not the builder of the temple intended to typify that mighty builder, Christ, who was to come after him?

The materials of the Masonic temple were brought from afar. And there is a house being erected, of materials gathered from all countries and all ages[403]. It will tower on

---

service of Almighty God. — Dict. of the Church, p. 449.

[399] Zechariah 6:12-13.

[400] 2 Brad. Ser., p. 263; D'Oyly and Mant's Com., Zechariah 6:12.

[401] John 2:19.

[402] The whole spiritual edifice above has been from eternity in the Divine mind. Every part of it has been thought over and determined on in that mind; nothing has been overlooked. All clearly was formed on a predetermined plan. There is design visible everywhere throughout it. It is one great whole. — 2 Brad. Ser., p. 264.

[403] The heavenly city, in the days of its pilgrimage on earth, enlists citizens out of all nations, and assembles a company of pilgrims out of all tongues; not caring for difference of manners, laws, and customs, but

some hill in eternity; and the banner of the cross will float in triumph above its dome, stained with the purest and costliest blood. And shall we ever behold that temple?[404] We must pass through a spiritual process and the road of peril, before we can hope to reach the summit of that hill, or even stand at its everlasting base. "This is the law of the house. From the top of the mountain, the whole limit thereof round about shall be most holy: behold! This is the law of the house." May we all reach that better land, the holy mount and holy temple, where a holier one than Ezekiel will sweep the heavenly lyre and a purer one than David will sing, to a harp of more than a thousand strings, the song of Moses and the Lamb forever and ever. And when the great work of redemption is finished, when the day shall come for the completion of the holy church—that grand lodge above—all the spirits of the just will sing, "Grace, grace unto it."[405]

---

rather seeking to preserve them for the sake of earthly peace, if only they hinder not the religion which teaches the only Most High and True. — St. Augustine's *City of God*, b. 19; 1 Brad. Ser., p. 18. Ages have been employed in building the temple in heaven. All the perfections of the Godhead have been called forth to raise and adorn it. It is the perfection of his workmanship. — 2 Brad. Ser., p. 266.

[404] The author has compared the soul of a righteous man to a polished stone, marked and numbered for the heavenly temple. Here that temple is regarded as an object which the redeemed may behold. Divines frequently indulge in the same kind of speech. For example, the Rev. Charles Bradley, in one of his sermons, asks the following questions. "Brethren, shall you and I ever see this temple? Shall we ever form a part of it? Is there a place for us in heaven? Is Christ making us ready for it?

[405] That must have been an hour of wonderful joy to the Savior, when, bowing his head on the cross, he said, "It is finished;" but think of the hour when he shall bring into heaven the last of his redeemed, and say, "It is finished," when he shall pass through the hosts of his angels, and stand on the summit of his glorious temple, and put on the last stone of it, and say, "I have done." There will be shoutings of "Grace, grace." — 2 Brad. Ser., p. 272.

Charles Scott

LECTURE XI.
The Temple and the Lodge

The sacrifice of Abraham, which consecrated Mount Moriah, is, to me, one of the most touching events in human history. I can never read over the unostentatious, brief account given in the Bible, without the profoundest emotions.[406]

Glory and brightness are on that hill-top, and shall be to the end of time; but there was a morning when gloom and terror crowned it, and heaven itself, all but God the Father, gazed on it in wonder, if not in consternation.[407]

Thus, in different periods of time, did God vouchsafe to give men a demonstrative proof of the reality of a future state.[408]

---

[406] Joel Tyler Headley, *The Sacred Mountains*, New York, 1847, p. 29. Hereafter Head. Sec. Mount.

[407] Idem, p. 157.

[408] Sears Bible Biog., p. 30

The temple of Solomon was situated due east and west on Mount Moriah, the most hallowed eminence in the memory of a Mason. The model of this august edifice was formed after that of the tabernacle, but of much larger dimensions. Moriah was also called Zion. This hill was cultivated before the temple was erected. There had been the threshing-floor of Araunah the Jebusite, on which David reared an altar unto the Lord[409], and on that very spot the temple was built.[410] And there, too, the father of all the

---

[409] 2 Samuel 24:18.

[410] Lamartine, in his Pilgrimage to the Holy Land, has preserved an oriental legend, invented and transmitted by the Arabs, detailing the circumstances which dictated Solomon's selection of a site for the temple. It is as follows: "Jerusalem was a ploughed field, and the ground on which the temple now stands the joint inheritance of two brothers; one of whom was married and had several children; the other lived a bachelor. They cultivated in common the field, which had devolved on them in the right of their mother; at harvest time, the two brothers bound up their sheaves, and made of them two equal stacks, which they left upon the field. During the night a thought was presented to the younger: 'My brother,' said he to himself, 'has a wife and children to maintain; it is not just that our shares should be equal; let me, then, take a few sheaves from my stack and secretly add them to his; he will not perceive it, and, therefore, cannot refuse them.' This project the young man immediately executed. That night the elder awoke, and said to his wife: 'My brother is young and lives alone, without a companion to assist him in his labours and console him under his fatigues; it is not just that we should take from the field as many sheaves as he does; let us get up and secretly go and carry a certain number of sheaves to his stack: he will not find it out tomorrow, and, therefore, cannot refuse them;' and they did so accordingly. The next day both brothers went to the field, and each was much surprised to find the two stacks alike; neither being able, in his own mind, to account for the prodigy. They pursued the same course for several successive nights, but as each carried to his brother's stack the same number of sheaves, the stacks still remained equal, till one night both determined to stand sentinel, to elucidate the mystery; they met, each bearing the sheaves for his other's stack." Now, the spot where so beautiful a thought at once occurred, and was so perseveringly acted upon by two men, must be a place agreeable to God; and men blessed it, and chose it whereon to build a house to his name. — 1 Lam. Pil., p. 283. E. N.: Alphonse de Lamartine, *A Pilgrimage to the Holy Land*, Philadelphia, 1836, Vol. 1, pp. 330-331.

faithful offered his son, his only son, Isaac, as a sacrifice, which is one of the most touching events which transpired on that holy hill. Take now thy son, thine only son Isaac, whom thou lovest, and get thee into the land of Moriah, and offer him there for a burnt-offering upon one of the mountains which I will tell thee of. Abraham, the patriarch and founder of the Israelite nation, had the most steadfast and unwavering confidence in the promises of the Almighty. He cheerfully obeyed the command of God. It requires no brilliant imagination to tell something of those feelings and affections which pervade a parent's bosom. Abraham was in his old age; the weight of years was pressing him down toward the tomb. Sarah had blessed him in his and her old age with a pledge of love, an only son, through whom the inheritance was to descend. The patriarch loved him, and Sarah did also. She laughed when he was born, and all that heard of the birth of Isaac laughed also. And God made Sarah laugh. Isaac,[411] the joy of all the household, had grown up and waxed strong, when his father "rose up early in the morning" and made all the necessary preparations, and "went out unto the place of which God had told him." "Like his great antitype," says Headley, "who bore his own cross up Calvary, Isaac carried the wood for the burnt-offering on his shoulders, while Abraham took the fire and knife in his hand." Isaac was an illustrious type of the Messiah; and God, there is great reason to believe, intimated to Abraham, through the typical event, the redemption of the world from sin and ruin. There were shinings of a glorious day which was to dawn in the future. The Sun of Righteousness shone afar off. The Mount was radiant with a holy light. Isaac carried the wood: Christ bore his own cross to the Mount. With slow and measured steps he ascended the hill of crucifixion. Multitudes followed on. A vast assembly moved in procession to the con-

---

[411] Isaac signifies laughter. — Heav. Arc., p. 2072, n. He was born in the year of the world 2109—died 2289. Abraham died in the year of the world 2184, aged 175.

secrated place, there to behold the awful scene. And what an event of awfulness and grandeur was enacted there. Who can think of it but with profound amazement! God, in his human and divine nature, hung upon the cross, in full view of the upturned faces of the great multitude. Before he had been taken thither, he had been stricken with rude hands. He had been mocked and reviled, before he was nailed to that cross which trembled in its socket when the victim was raised upon it. But who can describe that day and scene—the immense congregation—Moriah and its amphitheatre of mountains—the Son of God—His only begotten Son, in the agonies of death, with his arms out stretched to embrace a ruined world?

There was silence, as we have before remarked, during the building of the ancient house of the Lord, from the moment its corner-stone was laid until its completion. But a greater silence pervaded that large assembly which stood up before the cross of our Savior. The stillness was vaster than the people. Silence reigned in Jerusalem. Neither hammer nor ax nor any tool was used in the city on that eventful day. All had gone out to witness the tremendous tragedy which was to be enacted in the holy mountain. Jesus had been made ready for the sacrifice. The great work of his mission was about to be accomplished, and the plan of redemption consummated, for which all time had been preparing. The Grand Master of all the earth was about to die. The strokes had already fallen upon him heavy and fast. There had been often silence on that Mount before, (and moaning too,) but never so awfully sublime as now.

The wonderful and striking coincidences in the life and character of our Savior constitute a body of circumstantial evidence which seems difficult for the craft to resist. The force of the testimony cannot be repelled. It presses on the mind of the doubtful and devout with the weight of eternal truth. The testimony is sustained by all the external evidences of Christianity; while time, instead of weakening its strength, has imparted to it accumulated power. The holy mountains, like some twelve firm and unflinching apostles, lift up their heads as eternal witnesses of the truth. Moriah is associated with Ararat, and Sinai, and Hor, and Pisgah, and Horeb, and Carmel, and Lebanon, and Tabor, and Zion, and Calvary, and Olivet. They are all competent witnesses, and all their testimony is relevant. The events which transpired on those holy hills and the scenes which were there displayed of old, were parts of one and the same transaction. All generations preceding the crucifixion were accessory to the death of Christ. All mankind may be said to have participated in the deed. The death of our Savior was a great event, for which all ages had been preparing the way. There was a wonderful complication of circumstances, so intimately interwoven as to be hardly separable from each other[412]. And they are all connected with the principal fact, and constitute those surrounding circumstances which throw a flood of light and knowledge upon that mightiest of all transactions, the death of our Lord and Savior Jesus Christ. Then, how beautiful, how grand, and how sublime must be that view of ancient craft Masonry, which connects it with all time, all ages, all generations, and the redemption of the world! To sustain this view, it is not at all necessary that the Order should have existed from the creation of man. We need not make any fruitless attempts to show that Adam or any of the patriarchs belonged to the craft. Not at all. The present generation is connected with the first, and the last man born on the earth will 'be related to our great progenitor. The relation which all men in all ages bear to each other will never cease to exist. The Holy Land is full of the most sublime associations. A land of the prophets, of inspiration and sacred song. A land of wonders and prodigies. There walked Divinity incarnate; there lived, died, and rose again the perfect man, who displayed the most stupendous exhibitions of his love and mercy. Land of the Savior's tomb, which, says Lamartine, is the boundary of two worlds, the ancient and the modern. From this

---

[412] 1 Green Ev., p. 20.

point issued a truth that has renewed the universe—a civilization that has transformed all things—a word which has echoed over the whole world.[413] While time endures, the holy mountains will stand, and those material ties and moral associations which bind them together will never be severed. Ararat[414] once submerged with the deluge and on whose summit rested the ark of Noah is continually increasing in magnitude. Its snowy and frozen brow is daily approaching nearer and nearer to the heavens. Mount Sinai is a mass of eternal granite, which nothing but the consuming fires of the judgment can ever destroy. Horeb is a kindred summit, which will forever look down upon rich gardens and fertile valleys. Hor is consecrated by the tomb of Aaron. Pisgah overlooked the Promised Land, and was a holy mountain. Lebanon remains sublime as the metaphors which the sacred writers derived from that celebrated mountain. Lebanon shall only fall by a Mighty One. On the top of Carmel the faithful Elijah offered sacrifice: "The excellency of Carmel" will endure forever. Tabor is a mountain apart by itself, and the scene of the transfiguration. On the east of Moriah stands the Mount of Olives, fronting the temple hill. From this mount the Lord ascended, in view of Calvary and that sacred hill where stood that august type of his church, Mount Moriah![415] On thy eternal summit the holy lodge was held. Our fathers worshipped there, illumined by the light of other days. An ascending Savior threw upon it a blaze of immortality. The transactions of that Mount, its beautiful and sublime associations, their connection with events which transpired on the fraternity

---

[413] 1 Lam. Pil., p. 277.

[414] There is a tradition among the Armenians, that since the days of Noah no one has been able to climb this mountain, because it is perpetually covered with snow, which never melts but to make room for some newly fallen. — Calmet; D'Oyly and Mant's Com. Genesis 8:4.

[415] Mount Moriah is now crowned with the mosque of St. Omar, whose entrance has long been forbidden to the Christians, and kept sacred for the followers of Mahomet. — Head. Sec. Mount., p. 29.

of hills which had witnessed signs, tokens, and ceremonies, and heard the worshippers of the true God chanting the inspired songs of the prophet king, all belong to our Masonic lore.

The temple of Solomon was destroyed by fire. On its ruins arose another more glorious than the first, because of the entering into it of the Son of man. This world will be wrapped in flames and consumed to ashes; but out of its ashes will arise the new heavens and new earth. Christianity is Judaism advanced and consummated. The sacrifices of the Israelites were merged in the atoning sacrifice of Jesus. The old temple and the new were both destroyed. Not one stone was left upon another. But we know there is another temple on earth and another building above. There are many mansions of flesh which have rotted down into dust; but they will all be reconstructed when doomsday comes. The glorified bodies of the righteous will become beautiful temples, and a Mighty Master will preside over their mysteries and evolve the true worship. They shall resemble those temples which were caught up into glory. And they were types. Elijah never tasted death. Enoch[416] walked with God, and was not; for God took him[417]. Some of our Masonic antiquaries have asserted that Enoch was a Mason. They have been led to think so, perhaps, on account of some traditions of the Order which have a reference to his life and conduct. Masonry furnishes us with an account of some strange visions which the patriarch had, and which afforded some brilliant illustrations of the truth. Certain it is, that the memory of this antediluvian father is cherished by the fraternity and hallowed in the traditions of the Order; and whatever is illustrative in his life has been adopted into Masonry. The name of Enoch is intimately associated

---

[416] The translation of Enoch, which took place in the three hundred and sixty-fifth year of his age, afforded, at one and the same time, an evidence of the immortality of the soul and the resurrection of the body. — 1 Pict. Dict., p. 431.

[417] Genesis 5:24.

with the events of Moriah and the building of the first temple. And there is reason to believe that the patriarch, to whom the Almighty had manifested himself, was favored with a vision of the Urim and Thummim, the true meaning of which all the commentators on the Bible say has never been discovered. It is thought that nothing material was designed, and that they were not the work of man. The literal signification of the words are lights and perfections.[418] They were peculiar manifestations of Deity, or illuminations of truth. Rabbi Solomon says that the holy name of Jehovah, written on a plate of gold, and added to the pectoral, was the Urim and Thummim.[419] The traditions of Masonry, if we were permitted to make them public, would probably throw some light upon the true meaning of these words. God was never consulted by Urim and Thummim, from the consecration of Solomon's temple to the time of its destruction; and after its destruction, it is never once mentioned.[420] Masonic tradition informs us that Enoch stood in his day on the very ground on which that famous house was built; and that he had been entertained there with some remarkable visions, and was wonderfully favored on that holy spot with manifestations of the Shekinah. And although he may not have been, strictly speaking, a Mason, the founders of our institution deemed it wise to introduce into the regular lectures some very interesting facts of his history, which have been effectually preserved to the Masonic world. These traditions are not only curious, but valuable to the craft, as they serve to illustrate the principles of the Order. Enoch was at the head of the patriarchal dispen-

---

[418] Clarke's Com. and D'Oyly and Mant's, Exodus 28:30.

[419] The pectoral was placed on the high priest's bosom. Christ was in the bosom of the Father. The Urim and Thummim were a lighting guide to the Israelites. Christ is the same to his people; and with much greater propriety. The light of Urim, though a type of the gospel of Christ, was imperfect, because the latter light is more resplendent than the sun, more glorious than the arch of heaven, with all its glittering panoply. — 2 Ol. Land., p. 532, note 83.

[420] Clarke's Com. Exodus 28:30.

sation; Moses, of the law; Elijah, of the prophets; and our Savior, of the gospel[421]. Enoch was a "mysterious man of the longest immortality." He had been made acquainted with the ineffable name of the Almighty. He knew the Lord, for he had walked with him. He never knew corruption, for God took him when he walked with him. Here, then, is an ancient proof of another world, and immortality. If Enoch was not a Mason, he possessed knowledge which was after his day made a part of our mystic lore. His name is enrolled in the ancient archives of the Order. His memory has a niche in our temple; and we can never pass it by, without being reminded of the judgment to come. We may look beyond the flood, and in the eye of imagination behold the ascending patriarch. A bright cloud is beneath his feet—a glorious canopy above him. His eye of faith was even then fixed on that beautiful star which afterwards shone in the east. On and on he went—higher and higher he ascended—until he reached the land of life and light eternal. And the mysterious cloud which bore him thither threw its golden shadow upon the earth and covered all ages. But we cannot go the way Enoch did. With us, the dust of the sepulcher before the resurrection—darkness before light—death before the life to come—the night of the grave before an eternal day. But a Christian fraternity may gaze on the shining heavens which the patriarch mounted, and ponder upon that which was adumbrated when he set his feet on the battlements of the upper world—redemption and immortality.

The ascension of Enoch was typical of the ascension of Christ; and what place did he reach in glory? The Son of man ascended up where he was before[422]. St. Paul was caught up to the third heavens. Christ passed through the heavens[423]. He was higher than the heavens[424]. And he as-

---

[421] Pict. Dict., p. 450.

[422] John 6:62.

[423] Hebrews 4:14.

cended up far above all heavens[425]. Whither, then, did the patriarch go? Through the heavens—higher than the heavens—far above all heavens. He passed the "white-robed multitude" and the glittering hosts. He beheld joy smiling on the "fair brows of cherubim," and glistening in the "flowing locks of seraphim." He passed on to the most holy place—to the presence-chamber of Deity. There, anterior to the flood, and when this world was young, he stood before the throne, bone of our bone, and flesh of our flesh.

We are aware that many of the brethren may doubt, if they do not entirely differ with us in the views presented. In regard to the landmarks of our institution, there can be but little room for disputation. Nothing can be added to or taken from them, according to the constitutions of Masonry. They are permanent. But in regard to what these landmarks mean, it cannot be expected that we will all agree, any more than the commentators on the Bible should. The Jew has a right to one opinion, and the Christian to another; the Unitarian may entertain his own view, and the Trinitarian his; but their different creeds or beliefs can in no manner change the word of revelation. No man can add unto the words of the book, or take away from the words of the book of prophecy[426].

It is conceded that the obligations of Masonry will never conflict with our political or religious creeds; but the principles of the institution do certainly teach us both our social and religious duties. We are instructed to be good men and true[427], and to strictly obey the moral law; to be peaceable citizens, and to conform to the civil law of the land in which we live; to cultivate the social virtues, pro-

---

[424] Hebrews 7:26.

[425] Ephesians 4:10.

[426] Revelation 22:18.

[427] Gude menne and true, kennynge eidher odher to be soche, doe always love the more as they be more gude. — Ancient MSS. Bodleian Library; and Mas. Lib., p. 66.

mote the general welfare, avoid all quarrels, and hold in veneration our ancient patrons[428]. A Mason is obliged, by his tenure, to obey the moral law; and if he rightly understand the art, he will never be a stupid atheist, nor an irreligious libertine; and will never act against the great inward light of his own conscience[429]. Before any man can be initiated into the Order, he must not only acknowledge the existence of God, but he must put his trust in him. To trust in God, is something more than a mere belief in God. It is to rely upon him in all time of trouble and prosperity, to repose confidence in his promises, and to have faith in him. If we trust in him, our faith is well founded. By faith come hope and charity; and by faith only can we be made acquainted with things not seen[430]. *We walk by faith, not by sight.*—In the name of God shall the Gentiles trust; that is, they shall put their faith in him, and full belief in his declarations, expressed or implied, of future good. The Israelites put their trust in God, when they passed through the Red Sea. We are told in the Scriptures that fear came upon them when they ceased to put their trust in the Almighty[431]. And to trust in God implies something more than a bare act of faith. It implies an addition of hope, love, and affiance[432]. It

---

[428] Cross' Chart, p. 62.

We are charged to be lovers of peace, and obedient to the civil powers which yield us protection and are set over us, wherever we reside or work. No mason can be countenanced in his crimes or rebellion against the state. — Old Constitutions, sec. 2. It is the duty of every Mason to practice the social virtues; to avoid all manner of intemperance; to be industrious and just; to be patient, meek, self-denying, and forbearing; to govern his family with affection, dignity, and prudence; to succor the distressed and assist the poor; to abstain from all malice, slander, and evil speaking, and from all ungodly language—keeping always a tongue of good report. — Ibid. sec. 3. How few of the craft perform their duties!

[429] Old Constitutions, sec. 1.

[430] Hebrews 11:1.

[431] Numbers 14:11.

[432] John Pearson, *Exposition on the Creed*, Oxford, 1797, p. 23.

implies that our hope is centered in God; our affections are fixed upon him; that we are affianced to him, and pledged to a faithful performance of our duties. When we say, then, that our trust is in God, the declaration is as strong "as words can make up vows."

But let us present another view of the matter. We will suppose that to declare our trust in God, masonically means nothing more than an acknowledgment of our belief in the existence of a Supreme Being. Now, no atheist can be admitted to knowledge of the mysteries, according to the fundamental rule[433]. A belief in God is a part of the Christian's creed. It is the first article of his faith; and it is the first declaration of a candidate for initiation. It is the foundation of the Christian's creed, or the corner-stone upon which he builds. It is the first and necessary article of a Mason's creed. An atheist is in a hopeless condition, while there is great hope of improvement in one who believes in an overruling Providence. The latter may be instructed, and may be brought gradually to light and knowledge. The whole truth cannot shine upon him at once. He may be advanced in wisdom. He is furnished with the Holy Bible, to study and investigate. He believes in God, and God is the author of the Bible. Masonry does not tell him so in express words; but he is informed that the Bible is the first great light. Without that light, there would be moral darkness, and "chaos would come again." Then, it is the duty of a Mason to investigate the Bible and examine into its truth. He can never be bright, unless he studies that heavenly volume. His mind is directed to the serious consideration of its doctrines; and if he will only obey the instruction, by and by he will perceive that its truths are sub-

---

[433] The first, the essential qualification of a candidate is faith in God. — Mack. Lex., p. 101. There are three general heads of duty which Masons ought always to inculcate, viz.: to God, our neighbor, and ourselves: to God, in never mentioning his name but with that reverential awe which a creature ought to bear to his Creator; to our neighbor, in acting on the square, or doing as we would be done by; and to ourselves, in avoiding intemperance or excess. — Mas. Lib., p. 157.

limely enforced in the solemn ceremonies through which he has passed. As he advances in study, more light will become visible. Belief is not the result of a moment. It grows like the mustard seed. The initiate started out with a mere belief in God; now he relies upon his goodness and mercy. That God he now truly trusts. He argues with himself:— God inhabits eternity; and, like the circle, has neither beginning nor end. He is alpha and omega—the first and the last—the beginning and the ending. I put my trust in the Almighty; I believe in his omnipotence, which hath no bounds; I rely upon his goodness and mercy, for they have no limits; I acknowledge his overruling providence, which is infinite. God liveth forever. There must be a great future. Man is fearfully and wonderfully made. His soul is a thinking and sentient principle. It is immaterial. Is it not indestructible? Is the earth its home? The dust its final resting place? It cannot perish. It has an eternal destination. But where? It is polluted. It must be cleansed. The soul is immortal. It will survive the rubbish of the world. Material nature will expire—the cathedral of the universe will be burnt up—but the soul will rise above the funereal fires. Eternity is its destination. It will there grow in grace, or grow in crime. It will receive higher and higher degrees of wisdom in the spirit land of peace, or sink deeper and deeper in the world of the lost. Shall I be saved? I believe in God—my trust is in him. But I must fear, reverence, worship, love, and obey him: I must fear him, for he is a terrible God; I must reverence him, for he is a great God; I must worship him, for he is holy; love him, for he is good; obey him, for he is mighty, and hath power to kill, and will cast the disobedient soul into hell. I will endeavor to walk before the Almighty God and be perfect. If he visits me with adversity, I will humble my soul beneath the pressing and strong hand of my God, that he may exalt me in due time. I will drink of the bitter waters, and hope that every drop will increase my thirst, which nothing can slake but the Fountain of eternal joy. The road of my life may be rugged, but it leads to the city and the temple. The Christian will reach the sanctuary, for there is a sojourner who will travel with him through time; and when the great proclamation shall be issued from the throne, the soul of the good man will go up to the new Jerusalem, to aid and assist in rebuilding the house of the Lord, beneath whose living arches the mysteries of redemption will be revealed.

But it may be urged, that if a belief in God is the only article of faith which a worthy man is required to subscribe in order to entitle him to become a Mason, then the Jew, or any other person who believes in the existence of God, may partake of the mysteries. Does this militate against our views? It rather fortifies them. The Jew may never be brought to the light, or confess Christ crucified. He may believe in the fact of our lost innocence, and look forward to the means of its restoration: he may receive all the degrees, and still cling to the delusion of his fathers: he may only perceive in the signs, types, and symbols of our institution something to remind him of that Savior, who he believes is yet to come. But there is hope that the Jew may be made acquainted with the Word, which is Christ. The Jews were taken captive when their city was destroyed. Did they not return from Babylon to rebuild their city and their temple? They are now dispersed among all nations, but they will one day take up their march to their native land. They have lost the word, but they shall find it. God has said so; and they believe in their God. He has never violated his promises. Paradise was lost on earth—it will be regained in heaven. The garden which was eastward in Eden has been long a heap of ruins; but there is a lovelier Paradise beyond the stream of death.

The Jews have been looking for ages for their great King and Deliverer; while Christian Masons, with the aid of the light of the new dispensation, behold the types and prophecies fulfilled. And can we not call the Jew our brother? We can sympathize with him. "The sorrows of more than eighteen centuries are gathered on his brow." The finger of prophecy has pointed out the way of his mysterious being. We know the destiny of his race. We admire his ancient lineage and noble birth. Our Savior was a Jew. The blood of a Jew flowed to save a world. The Jews possess great power, if it were concentrated. The sinews of peace and war lie in the palms of their hands; and the day will surely come when their power will be seen and felt. Brighter days await them. They will all be brought to light, for they will travel to the East. The prophets have foretold their return to the land of Judea, the dear home of their fathers[434]. The veil will be removed from the face of Israel, and "the chain of their spirit broken;" when, like an army of redeemed free men, they will march to the Holy Land, and make the hills of Judea resound with the praises of the Lord our Redeemer. Very few of the race will, perhaps, ever become converted to Christianity, until the time for the fulfillment of prophecy shall roll round. Till then, their lives will continue to hang in doubt before them. According to the constitutions of the Order, every Mason must believe in the eternal existence of God, and pay that worship which is due to him; and the brethren are to be charged to adhere to the essentials of religion, leaving each brother to his own judgment as to the particular forms[435]. Every brother has a right to entertain any opinion which he may deem best as to the manner of worshipping God, and may place such construction upon the tenets of the Order as his judgment may dictate. Of course nothing can be engrafted upon the regular lectures, nor can the ancient landmarks be in any wise changed.

It is a remarkable fact, that the Jews substituted the word Adonai[436] for the incommunicable name of God.

---

[434] See D'Oyly and Mant's Com. Ezekiel 37:9; 1 Mel. Ser., pp. 210-302.

[435] Old Constitutions, sec. 1.

[436] They contend that the true pronunciation of the word signifying God or Jehovah has been lost, and that whosoever possesses it could reveal secrets or mysteries. — 1 Pict. Dict., p. 35. The Mohammedans have a tradition, that when Noah was in the ark, it moved or remained stationary at his pleasure, by the pronunciation of the sacred word.

They were averse to writing the name of Jehovah, except on very particular occasions[437].They acknowledge that the true pronunciation of the incommunicable name of God is lost. Jesus, when he hung upon the cross, and during his last agonies, pronounced it, but the Jews knew it not: Eli, Eli, lama sabachthani?—that is to say, My God, my God, why hast thou forsaken me? And some of them which stood there, when they heard that, said: This man calleth for Elias. And straightway one of them ran, and took a sponge, and filled it with vinegar, and put it on a reed, and gave him to drink. The rest said, Let be, let us see whether Elias will come to save him[438]. Justin Martyr, in his Apology for the Christians to Antoninus Pius, says, that all the Jews taught that God, who cannot be named, spoke to Moses. Whence the prophetic spirit reproached them by Isaiah thus, saying: "The ox knoweth his owner, and the ass his master's crib; but Israel doth not know, my people doth not consider." And, in like manner, Jesus Christ himself also said, upbraiding the Jews for that they knew not what the Father is and what the Son is: "No one knoweth the Father but the Son; neither knoweth any one the Son but the Father, and they to whomsoever the Son shall reveal it." And the Word of God is his Son[439].

---

[437] Eccl. Dict. We have heard with our ears and our fathers have declared to us, that in their time and in times of old, it was not lawful for anyone to mention the sacred and mysterious name of the Most High, except the high-priest, once a year, when he entered into the holy of holies alone, and, before the ark of the covenant, made propitiation for the sins of Israel. — 3 Ol. Land., p. 543, n. 17. In the persecution which took place after the death of Antoninus Pius, Attalus, in the midst of his torments, while being roasted in an iron chair by a slow fire, was asked what was the name of God. His reply was, "God is not like man, he hath no name."

[438] Matthew 27:46-49.

[439] Justin Martyr's Apology, p. 82. E. N.: It is impossible to ascertain the actual source used by Scott, but there are abundant editions of the Apologies of Apologies of Justin, Tertullian and Minutius Felix. The quote can be found in any edition of the *Apologies of Justin Martyr*, Chapter 43: How God appeared to Moses.

Masonry, we have much reason to hope, will go far toward furnishing the word of God to the nations which are now wandering in darkness. Some of the craft may be found in every land, and the Order will yet accomplish much under the providence of the Almighty, for it is the pioneer of Christianity. It can penetrate places, with little difficulty, where the light of the gospel has never been shed; and it is calculated to prepare the minds of men for the reception of the Holy Scriptures. Even the fact that there are Masons among all nations and tongues, invites the mind to the contemplation of that glorious time when light and knowledge will penetrate the darkest corners of the earth, and the deserts and waste places shall rejoice and blossom as the rose; when every tribe, and kindred, and nation, and tongue, will be brought to a knowledge of the Lord; when the Jew and Gentile will meet and mingle together, without any jar or discord, to worship one God and obey one Master.

Charles Scott

A Free Mason

LECTURE XII.
The Master Mason

And we say, that this Christian resurrection of life is the vesting and setting of the souls of good men in their glorious, spiritual, heavenly, and immortal bodies.[440]

And are you sure that old age will come with all these circumstances inviting to repentance? It may be, and it is very likely to be, to life, what the winter is to the year, a time of chillness and numbness, and of deadness of the faculties for repentance.[441]

Who but the Father of spirits, possessed of perfect prescience, even of the knowledge of the will, and of the actions of free, intelligent, and moral agents, could have revealed their unbounded and yet unceasing

---

[440] Ralph Cudworth, *The True Intellectual System of the Universe*, New York, 1838, Vol. 2, p. 235.

[441] Zachary Pearce, *Sermons on Several Subjects*, London, 1778, Vol. III, Sermon 16.

wanderings, unveiled their destiny, and unmasked the minds of the Jews and of their enemies in every age and in every clime?[442]

*From its base
Ev'n to yon turret's trim and taper spires,
All is of the choicest masonry.*[443]

The third degree of the Order of Masons is called the Sublime degree of a Master Mason[444]. Before the completion of the first temple, it is said that there were only three Master Masons[445], and each one doubtless possessed an equal know ledge of the mysteries appertaining to the third degree. The Savior of mankind is often spoken of in Scripture as our Master. And ye shall say unto the good man of the house, The Master saith unto thee, Where is the guest-chamber, where I shall eat the Passover with my disciples?[446] When Christ foretold the destruction of Jerusalem, it was asked: Master, but when shall these things be? And what sign will there be when these things shall come to pass?[447] Some of the Sadducees denied the doctrine of the resurrection, and put certain questions to Jesus, and ad-

---

[442] Alexander Keith, *Evidence of the Truth of Christian Religion, Edinburgh*, 1830, p. 29.

[443] William Mason, *Elfrida*.

[444] In this degree, which is the perfection of symbolic or ancient craft Masonry, the purest of truths are unveiled amid the most awful ceremonies. None but he who has visited the holy of holies and travelled the road of peril, can have any conception of the mysteries unfolded in this degree. — Mack. Lex., p. 192.

[445] *To the praiseworthy three
Who founded this degree,
May all their virtues be
Deep in our hearts.*

Old Song.

[446] Luke 22:11.

[447] Luke 21:7.

dressed him under the title of Master[448]. The father of a lunatic, desiring to have his son healed and the unseen spirit rebuked which possessed his child, cried out from the midst of a large company, and said: Master, I beseech thee to look upon my son; for he is mine only child[449]. Even Judas Iscariot called our Savior Master: He saith unto him, Master, Master; and kissed him[450]. All the disciples called him Master. The title was applied to him as a ruler and instructor. But be ye not called Rabbi: for one is your *Master, even Christ; and all ye are brethren*[451]. The disciple is not above his Master: but every one that is perfect shall be as his Master[452]. And what is the duty of a Master? It is to teach and instruct, particularly in regard to Divine things. Jesus imparted Divine instruction, and came down from heaven on a Divine mission. He was the Ruler of the universe. He was and is Master of all things; and he will raise us all at the judgment. It is only through the power and merits of the Lion of the tribe of Judah that we can ever hope to be raised to a blessed immortality.

The word *raised* [453] is a Masonic term. It is also a Scriptural one: How are the dead *raised* up?[454] There is one glory of the sun, and another glory of the moon, and another glory of the stars; for one star differeth from another star in

---

[448] Luke 20:28.

[449] Luke 9:38.

[450] Mark 14:45.

[451] Mathew 23:8.

[452] Luke 6:40.

[453] This term is used to designate the reception of a candidate into the third degree of Masonry. It alludes to a portion of the ceremony, which is fully understood by a Master. — Mack. Lex., p. 193. The third degree is the summit of ancient craft Masonry. — Ibidem. The enlightened Hutchinson said the Master Mason represented a man under the Christian doctrine, saved from the grave of iniquity, and raised to the faith of salvation. — Ahi. Rez., p. 182.

[454] 1 Corinthians 25:35.

glory. So also is the resurrection of the dead. It is sown in corruption; it is raked in incorruption. It is sown in dishonor; it is raised in glory: it is sown in weakness; it is raised in power. It is sown a natural body; it is raised a spiritual body. Behold, I show you a mystery: We shall not all sleep, but we shall all be changed, in a moment, in the twinkling of an eye, at the last trump: for the trumpet shall sound, and the dead shall be raised incorruptible, and we shall be changed[455].

The doctrine of the resurrection[456] is a sublime doctrine, and is powerfully enforced in our Masonic bodies. Our ancient Masters believed and taught the truth of the resurrection. Immortality, we know, was brought to light through the gospel; for our Savior said of himself: I am the resurrection and the life. But there is nothing to be found in the Old Testament or the New which proves that our brethren, who lived anterior to the Christian era, had no idea of the doctrine of the resurrection. It was one of the articles of the Jewish religion when Christ appeared upon the earth[457]. Then, from this fact alone, we might lawfully infer that the doctrine was known before the coming of the Messiah, though the Sadducees disputed the doctrine. Christ proved the truth of the doctrine, in his own person or resurrection. Job, or the author of the book of Job, ages before, it seems, believed in it: Oh that my words were now written! Oh that they were written in a book! That they were graven with an iron pen and lead in the rock forever! For I know that my Redeemer liveth, and that he shall

---

[455] 1 Corinthians 15:52

[456] This doctrine is elucidated in the third degree, and sublimely evolved in the ceremonies. Our solemn observances, says brother Mackey, diffuse a sacred awe, and inculcate lessons of religious truth. The Master's degree testifies our faith in the resurrection of the body; and, while it inculcates a practical lesson of prudence and unshrinking fidelity, it inspires the most cheering hope of that final reward which belongs alone to the just made perfect.

[457] Matthew 22:23.

stand at the latter day upon the earth[458]. And though after my skin worms destroy this body, yet in my flesh shall I see God: whom I shall see for myself, and mine eyes shall behold, and not another; though my reins be consumed within me[459].

We are aware that this selection from Job has received the closest criticism, and that there are many who differ in opinion as to the proper construction which ought to be given to it. Some have contended that it has a direct and unequivocal reference to the doctrine of the resurrection and our Redeemer; while others endeavor to maintain the position that it alludes only to the restoration of Job to health, family comforts, and general prosperity[460]. But if the passage is construed upon the one principle, which Dr. Clarke has laid down, the interpretation seems clear and distinct. This is the principle: "Job was now under the especial inspiration of the Holy Spirit, and spoke prophetically." How it can be reasonably argued that Job, who was in-

---

[458] Bishops Hall, Patrick, Pearson, Sherlock, Home, Dr. S. Clarke, Peters, Scott, and others, all agree that the passage quoted in the text referred to our gracious Redeemer, then to come. See D'Oyly and Mant's Com., where these interpreters are cited. Scott says that the prophecy of Enoch (Jude 14, 15) revealed a future judgment. The murder of Abel suggested the idea of a reward for the righteous in another world; and Enoch's translation, the belief that good men will enjoy the felicity in that better world in an embodied state.

[459] Job 19:23-27.

The following is the version of Dr. Hale of this passage:

> "I know that my Redeemer (is) living,
> And that at the last (day)
> He will arise (in judgment) upon dust (mankind).
> And after my skin be mangled thus,
> Yet ever from my flesh shall I see God :
> Whom I shall see for me (on my side)
> And mine eyes shall behold him not estranged ;
> (Though) my reins be (now) consumed with me."

2 Horne's Intro., p. 237

[460] Clarke s Com., Job 19:23.

spired and spoke prophetically, referred to the restoration of his health and prosperity, we are at a loss to determine. Did not the Spirit of inspiration have a higher design in view? When those gifted ones of old spoke prophetically, did they only anticipate an event which was to happen on the morrow? The most of the prophecies were to be accomplished after the lapse of many centuries. If Job was inspired when he uttered these sublime words, and he spoke prophetically, can we doubt that he referred to the resurrection of his body, which he knew and felt was soon to return to the dust, and that Redeemer, through whose almighty grasp his body would be raised at the judgment? "And though after my skin worms destroy this body, yet in my flesh shall I see God." And how does he reason the matter? "For I know," says he, "that my Redeemer liveth, and that he shall stand at the latter day upon the earth." And can it be that he had no conception of the resurrection, of the judgment, of our Savior? Was he not speaking of death, corruption, and incorruption? Does he not, in express words declare that after his body should be destroyed by worms, he would see God? How? "In my flesh" shall I see him. When? "In the latter day." And why then? Because he knew that his Redeemer should stand upon the earth then; he knew that his Redeemer liveth, and would come to judge the world, when all then in the grave should hear his voice and come forth, "they that have done good unto the resurrection of life, and they that have done evil unto the resurrection of damnation." And how did he know this? By inspiration. Job did not expect to be restored to health. He was, in fact, contemplating death. His prophetic vision was fixed beyond the tomb. The eye of his gifted soul was looking forward to that mighty day when he should be raised with the bodies of the congregation of the dead—when bone should come to its bone—sinew to sinew—flesh to flesh. Job had a personal interest in the resurrection. It consoled him to feel that interest. I shall see God for myself, said he. And we shall all see him in our flesh, when he

comes to judge the quick and the dead. How deep and solemn will be the transactions of that day!

> *"Each waiting soul must claim his own, when the*
> *archangel soundeth,*
> *And all the fields and all the hills shall move a mass*
> *of life;*
> *Bodies numberless, crowding on the land, and covering*
> *the trampled sea,*
> *Darkening the air precipitate, and gathered scathless*
> *from the fire;*
> *The Himalayan peaks shall yield their charge, and the*
> *desolate steppes of Siberia,*
> *The Maelstrom disengulf its spoil, and the iceberg*
> *manumit its captive:*
> *All shall teem with life, the converging fragments of*
> *humanity,*
> *Till every conscious essence greet his individual frame;*
> *For in some dignified similitude, alike, yet different in*
> *glory,*
> *This body shall be shaped anew, fit dwelling for the*
> *soul:*
> *The hovel hath grown to a palace, the bulb hath burst*
> *into the flower,*
> *Matter hath put on incorruption, and is at peace with*
> *spirit."*

It is supposed by many able critics that the poem or
book of Job was composed about the time of the Jewish
captivity. If this supposition be correct, and that book asserts the doctrine of the resurrection, we must believe that
the doctrine was at that time known to the Jewish nation.
But it is altogether probable that Job was his own biog-
rapher. If so, then the doctrines of the resurrection and future judgment were known at a very early period of the
world; for Job was a contemporary with Eliphaz, the
Temanite. But whether he was the writer of the book or
not, there is much reason to suppose that its author lived
anterior to the days of Moses, though some of the most

learned commentators have thought it not improbable that Moses dictated the inspired poem.

But we need not rely altogether on the book of Job to prove the knowledge or belief of the Jews upon the subject. The books of Moses and the writings of the prophets were received by the Israelites as divine; and certainly there is much to be found in those writings and prophecies which should lead us to think that these favored people had some knowledge of a resurrection. Did they not look forward to a Redeemer, to the coming of Jesus Christ? They believed the soul was immortal. Did they not also believe in the resurrection of the body? The great truth, we doubt not, was communicated in the earliest ages of the world. The translation of Enoch and Elijah must have afforded the strongest proof of a future world of rewards and punishments, and of an existence in that world of embodied but purified nature. The fact of Enoch's translation and the belief consequent to it, were transmitted through the family of Abraham, and handed down from century to century. No Mason, who has studied our land marks and the moral machinery of our institution, can hesitate to believe that our three most ancient Masters were acquainted with the doctrine of the resurrection of the body, as well as the soul's future state of existence.

The theology of the patriarchs taught the doctrine of pardoning mercy. If thou doest well, shalt thou not be accepted? And if thou doest not well, sin lieth at the door[461]. The patriarchs had a divine assurance of a Savior. The promised seed is spoken of in the third chapter of Genesis: And I will put enmity between thee and the woman, and between thy seed and her seed: it shall bruise thy head, and thou shalt bruise his heel. God called Abraham and blessed him with the promise of Christ: And I will bless them that bless thee, and curse him that curseth thee: and in thee shall

---

[461] Genesis 4:7.

all the families of the earth be blessed[462]. In the renewal of God's covenant with Abraham, God said, Sarah thy wife shall bear thee a son indeed; and thou shalt call his name Isaac: and I will establish my covenant with him for an everlasting covenant, and with his seed after him[463]. And the Lord blessed Isaac and said: I will make thy seed to multiply as the stars of heaven, and will give unto thy seed all these countries; and in thy seed shall all the nations of the earth be blessed[464]. Jacob blessed Judah, and declared that "the scepter shall not depart from Judah, nor a law giver from beneath his feet, until Shiloh come; and unto him shall the gathering of the people be[465]. The patriarchal religion was signally exemplified in Abraham, who was illustrious for his faith, piety, and righteousness, and whom God was pleased to favor with special discoveries of his will. From him descended many great nations, among whom this religion, in its main principles, seems to have been preserved in the book of Job. There were also remarkable vestiges of it, for a long time, among several other nations; and, indeed, the belief of one Supreme God, of a Providence, of a hope of pardoning mercy, a sense of the obligations of piety and virtue, and of the acceptance and reward of sincere obedience, and the expectation of a future state, were never entirely extinguished[466]. This belief in another state of being was handed down to the Israelites. Hear the words of Jesus Christ, addressed to the Sadducees: But as touching the resurrection of the dead, have ye not read that which was spoken unto you by God, saying, I am the God of Abraham, and the God of Isaac, and the God of Jacob?

---

[462] Genesis 12:3. "In thee," that is, in thy seed, ch. xxii. 18. "And that seed is Christ." — Galatians 3:16; Acts 3:25.

[463] Genesis 17:19.

[464] Genesis 26:4.

[465] Genesis 49:10.

[466] 1 Horne's Intro., p. 140.

God is not the God of the dead, but of the living[467], David and Solomon both were acquainted with the doctrine of a future existence, and also of the resurrection, as we have reason to think. And moreover, said Solomon, I saw under the sun the place of judgment, that wickedness was there; and the place of righteousness that iniquity was there. I said in my heart, God shall judge the righteous and the wicked: for there is a time there for every purpose and for every work[468]. The existence of a future state of rewards and punishments, and the resurrection, were more clearly made known in the progress of ages, and were powerfully established in the life and character of the Messiah. "Behold, I show you a mystery!" And what was that mystery? The truth of the resurrection of the body. It shall be raised again. Our ancient craftsmen evolved this mystery. It was shadowed forth in their scenic representations. The doctrine of the resurrection is a cardinal doctrine in Masonry. It is believed by the fraternity throughout the world, wherever pure free Masonry exists and is practiced.

The resurrection from the dead, then, is a fundamental truth, taught in the old Scriptures, and powerfully verified in the New Testament. Jesus raised the dead three times. He raised himself, through his own strength, which was the power of the Godhead. "I lay down my life," said the Lord Jesus, "that I might take it again. No man taketh it from me, but I lay it down of myself. I have power to lay it down, and I have power to take it up again." But it was through the infinite power of the Godhead that Christ was raised from the dead. The divinity resided in humanity. Christ was God in the flesh. He is the Son of God, and co-equal with the Father. God is a unit. There are three persons and one God. The Father, Son, and Holy Ghost raised Jesus from the tomb. None but the Mighty Master can raise the dead. The efficient cause of the resurrection of Christ is

---

[467] Matthew 22:31-32.

[468] Ecclesiastes 3:16-17.

to be considered, says Bishop Pearson, either as principal or instrumental. The principal cause was God himself; for no other power but that which is omnipotent can raise the dead. It is an act beyond the acting of any creature, and disproportionate to the power of any finite agent[469]. But the energies of omnipotence resided in the Lion of the tribe of Judah. He awoke from the sleep of death, and sprang from the tomb with divine majesty; and was afterwards raised to that sublime world, where he now sits at the right hand of the Father Almighty. The great Father of all, said the enlightened Hutchinson, in his lecture on the third degree, commiserating the miseries of the world, sent his only Son, who was innocence itself, to teach the doctrine of salvation; by whom man was raised from the death of sin unto the life of righteousness; from the tomb of corruption unto the chambers of hope; from the darkness of despair to the celestial beams of faith; and not only working for us this redemption, but making with us the covenant of regeneration; whence we are become the children of divinity and inheritors of the realms of glory[470].

The resurrection of Jesus Christ lies at the foundation of Christianity. And it is through him we shall be raised. We have endeavored to show that the preparatory degrees of the Order shadowed forth the resurrection, or certain prophetic types of an event illustrative of it. And Christ made prophetic declaration concerning his own resurrection. He foretold his death, and that he would rise on the third day. The very day preceding his crucifixion, he instituted a memorial of his death. His predicted resurrection caused the soldiers to guard his tomb, and the stone which covered it to be sealed. After three days I will rise again. Command therefore that the sepulcher be made sure until the third day, lest his disciples come by night, and steal him away, and say unto the people, he is risen from the dead: so

---

[469] Pearson on the Creed, p. 386.

[470] Ahi. Rez., p. 181.

the last error shall be worse than the first. Pilate said unto them: Ye have a watch: go your way, make it as sure as you can. So they went, and made the sepulcher sure, sealing the stone, and netting a watch[471]. Masons describe the state of religion under the Jewish law in the following style: Her tomb was in the rubbish and the filth cast forth from the temple, and acacia wove her branches over her monument[472]. But, through power of the atonement, religion came forth, like the damsel which was not dead but slept, to a glorious resurrection.

The ceremony of the Master's degree is truly sublime, and never fails to make a deep impression on every reflecting brother. The following selection from Ecclesiastes is usually introduced during the ceremony: Remember now thy Creator[473] in the days of thy youth, while the evil days come not, nor the years draw nigh, when thou shalt say, I have no pleasure in them; while the sun, or the light, or the moon, or the stars, be not darkened, nor the clouds return after the rain: in the day when the keepers of the house shall tremble, and the strong men shall bow themselves, and the grinders cease because they are few, and those that look out of the windows be darkened, and the doors shall be shut in the streets, when the sound of the grinding is low, and he shall rise up at the voice of the bird, and all the daughters of music shall be brought low; also when they shall be afraid of that which is high, and fears shall be in the way, and the almond tree shall flourish, and the grasshopper shall be a burden, and desire shall fail: because man goeth to his long home, and the mourners go about the streets: or ever the silver cord be loosed, or the golden

---

[471] Matthew 27:63-66.

[472] Ahi. Rez., p. 181.

[473] The Hebrew is "thy Creators," in the plural. The plural is employed to show the plurality of persons in the unity of essence, namely, Father, Son, and Holy Ghost. For these three Divine persons consulted together concerning the creation of man. — Genesis 1:26; Jones of Nayland, D'Oyly and Mant's Com., Ecclesiastes 12.

bowl be broken, or the pitcher be broken at the fountain, or the wheel broken at the cistern. Then shall the dust return to the earth as it was: and the spirit shall return unto God who gave it[474]. How beautiful and appropriate is the selection to be used on the occasion of conferring the third degree. It contains a thrilling picture of old age and the terrors of death. The three steps delineated on the Master's carpet are the open emblems of the principal stages of human life, namely, youth, manhood, and old age. In youth, as Entered Apprentices, we ought to be industrious in the attainment of useful knowledge; in man hood, as Fellow Crafts, we should apply our know ledge to the discharge of our respective duties to God, our neighbor, and ourselves; that in age, as Master Masons, we may enjoy the happy reflections consequent on a well spent life, and die in the hope of a glorious immortality[475]. Let us present another view: From youth to old age, things recent and things confirmed are denoted, as one of the purest and wisest of men believed. Old age, then, may be compared to a period of fullness: Thou shalt come to thy grave in a full age, like as a shock of corn cometh in his season[476]. Old age is a time for putting off what is human; and while it denotes a new principle of representation, it also denotes an end of representation. Anciently, the third degree of Masonry closed the elucidation of the mysteries. The Christian dispensation, which is the third and last, is the end of Divine representation. There is fullness in the gospel, and all things are confirmed.

---

[474] Ecclesiastes 12:1-7; Cross' Chart, p. 34. This is, perhaps, one of the finest allegories in the Old Testament: the inconveniences of increasing years, the debility of mind and body, the torpor of the senses, are expressed most learnedly and eloquently indeed, but with some degree of obscurity, by different images derived from nature and common life; for, by this enigmatical composition, Solomon, after the manner of the oriental sages, intended to put to trial the acuteness of his readers. — 1 Horne's Intro., p. 365.

[475] Cross's Chart, p. 38.

[476] Job 5:26.

The reading of the above selection from Ecclesiastes is as the rehearsal of some sublime eulogy on the character of our ancient institution. It sustains, too, the views which we have expressed, while it contains a powerful and eloquent vindication of the moral tendencies of the Order. It bids the young to remember their Creator in the days of their youth; which injunction, masonically applied, bids us to remember our Creator in the days of our apprenticeship. It is the duty of every Entered Apprentice to adore and worship God, while the evil days come not, nor the years draw nigh when he shall say, I have no pleasure in them. Here is a reason assigned why he should remember his Creator. There are evil days ahead. In the Master's degree the third step is taken, and that step represents old age, when death must needs be near at hand; when the evil days will come; when everyone who has not remembered his Creator, will say, I have no pleasure in them. But there is pleasure to be found in the snows of wintry life. Age may come, and with it evil days, decrepitude, penury, and death; but the Christian Mason will experience much pleasure in the contemplation of a glorious hereafter. He knows that although he must descend into the grave, he will be raised again; and while the body, for a season, shall return to the earth as it was, his spirit shall return unto God who gave it[477].

---

[477] If anyone considered the matter well, would this appear more incredible than it would if we were not in the body, and any one should assert that it was possible for bones and tendons and flesh to be formed, as we see in the human body, out of a mere drop of seminal matter! For let us suppose an imaginary case. If ye were not such as ye are, nor of such an origin, and any one should show you the generating substance and a painted representation, (of the human form,) and should persist in affirming that the one could be produced from the other, would ye believe him before ye saw the effect produced? No one would be bold enough to assert that ye would. In the same manner ye now disbelieve, because ye never saw a dead man raised to life. But, even if ye would not at first have believed, that from a little drop of seminal matter such bodies could be formed, which yet ye see are formed; so consider, that it is not impossible for human bodies, decomposed, and, like seed, resolved into earth, to arise in due season, at the command of God, and to put on incorruption. — Justin Martyr's Apol., sect. 25.

If the first step in Masonry is emblematical of youth, (which step is cautiously taken in the degree of Entered Apprentice,) then the Entered Apprentice should be reminded of his duty to God. The Entered Apprentice is led to anticipate age, is taught to prepare for it and its evil days. Die he must. The silver cord must be loosed, or the golden bowl broken, or the pitcher broken at the fountain, or the wheel broken at the cistern. And is there not wisdom in Masonry? The preacher mentioned in Ecclesiastes was called wise, because he taught the people knowledge. He gave good heed and sought out and set in order many proverbs. The preacher sought to find acceptable words: and that which was written was upright, even words of truth[478]. The words of the wise are as nails fastened by the masters of assemblies.

All things in the Masonic lectures are carefully arranged, collected, and set in order. They contain the most acceptable words, for they are all upright, words of truth. They are the words of the wise, used in times long since passed away; and the words of the wise, in a scriptural sense, are, says Dr. Clarke, doctrines of faith illustrated by suitable language. But let us hear the conclusion of the whole matter: fear God and keep his commandments: for this is the whole duty of man. In youth, manhood, and old age, we should fear God and keep his commandments; for God shall bring every work into judgment, with every secret thing, whether it be good or whether it be evil[479].

Old age is not the most favorable season in which to commence the service of God. Youth is the best time. Manhood should wax strong or grow in faith. The Master Mason should be a good man, wise unto salvation. He represents one, as it were, in the last stage of existence. The step he has taken is emblematical of old age, when death, in the course of nature, will soon overtake him, and, perhaps,

---

[478] Ecclesiastes 12:10.

[479] Ecclesiastes 12:14.

in a moment when he least expects it. Old men often come to their end by accident and violence. Let us take good heed, therefore, how we estimate the moral lessons which are embraced in the several degrees. Our emblems, figures, and ceremonies are replete with the most momentous significations. The symbolical representations are full of meaning, a meaning which is partly open and partly concealed in the depths of our mystic philosophy. There are solemn and mysterious intimations in every sign, and word, and emblem, and device. Many of our mysteries repose in parabolic language; like the mysteries of redemption. Such is the remarkable correspondence between the principles of Masonry and Christianity; and yet it seems easily accounted for according to our view. Masonry is chiefly founded upon the truths of the Old Testament, and the correspondence between the law and the gospel is perfect; which affords a most potent argument in behalf of the Divine authority of the Christian dispensation.

But, to return to the consideration of the Masonic allusions in that sublime passage selected from Ecclesiastes. In the third verse of the chapter, the human body is compared to a house. There is aptitude in the metaphor. Oh! How solemn and sublime is the picture of old age! The splendid mansion of the soul has become old. It was once the paragon of all earthly houses. The human body was once a temple in which first innocence resided. But evil drove away the beautiful tenant, and has ever since retained possession of our nature. Nothing short of a mysterious law can dispossess sin and restore innocence to its original estate. But no one should wait until the house is old and seemingly worthless, when it is about to fall all to pieces, to commence the action. It may be barred by time. Death may interpose and abate the suit. Death is always near old age. He haunts the house. There are many strange noises heard in and about it; particularly at night, when there is no sleep. Death for a while may step about the outer courts, but he soon enters the inner chamber, and finds his way to the place where the keeper of the house is. The shadow of his dark wing will cover the apartment, and there will be no light there. And the soul of the wicked shall be afraid of that which is high, and fears shall be in the way. The keeper of the house will flee away and go in search of a long home. And when the keeper is gone, the house must needs be neglected and tumble into ruins. It will fall down and rot. But reptiles only for a while shall dwell in it. How melancholy would those ruins be, if there was no assurance that the mansion would be reconstructed in the latter day. "Blessed be the God and Father of our Lord Jesus Christ, which, according to his abundant mercy, hath begotten us again into a lively hope, by the resurrection of Jesus Christ from the dead." Oh! May peace and harmony dwell with us all in old age! Let all the brethren obtain wisdom and the Master's faith fullness. Let us put our houses in order, for we know not when our souls will be called hence.

> *"Gird up thy mind to contemplation, trembling inhabitant of earth;*
> *Tenant of a hovel for a day—thou art heir of the universe forever!*
> *For neither congealing of the grave, nor gulfing waters of the firmament,*
> *Nor expansive airs of heaven, nor dissipative fires of Gehenna,*
> *Nor rust of rest, nor wear, nor waste, nor loss, nor chance, nor change,*
> *Shall avail to quench or overwhelm the spark of soul within thee!*
> *Thou art an imperishable leaf on the evergreen bay-tree of existence;*
> *A word from wisdom's mouth, that cannot be unspoken;*
> *A ray of love's own light; a drop in mercy's sea;*
> *A creature marvellous and fearful, begotten by the fiat of omnipotence.*
> *I that speak in weakness, and ye that hear in charity,*
> *Shall not cease to live and feel, though flesh must see corruption;*

For the prison-gates of matter shall be broken, and the
*   shackled soul go free,*
Free for good or ill, to satisfy its appetence forever:
Forever—dreadful doom, to be hurried on eternally to
*   evil!*
Forever—happy fate, to ripen into perfectness forever!"

The following verses in the 37[480]th chapter of Ezekiel have been recommended to be solemnly recited by the Master of a lodge during the ceremony of the third degree: The hand of the Lord was upon me, and carried me out in the Spirit of the Lord, and set me down in the midst of the valley which was full of bones, and caused me to pass by them round about: and, behold, there were very many in the open valley; and lo, they were dry. And he said unto me, Son of man, can these bones live? And I answered, 0 Lord God, thou knowest. Again he said unto me, prophesy upon these bones, and say unto them, 0 ye dry bones, hear the word of the Lord. Thus saith the Lord God unto these bones; behold, I will cause breath to enter into you, and ye shall live: And I will lay sinews upon you, and will bring up flesh upon you, and cover you with skin, and put breath into you, and ye shall live; and ye shall know that I am the Lord. So I prophesied as I was commanded: and as I prophesied there was a noise, and, behold a shaking, and the bones came together, bone to his bone. And when I beheld, lo, the sinews and the flesh came up upon them, and the skin covered them above; but there was no breath in them. Then said he unto me, prophesy unto the wind, prophesy, son of man, and say to the wind, thus saith the Lord God; come from the four winds, 0 breath, and

---

[480] The chief design of Ezekiel's prophecies is to comfort his brethren in captivity, who deplored their having too lightly credited the promises of Jeremiah, who had exhorted them speedily to submit to the Chaldees, on account of the approaching ruin of Jerusalem. As these captives saw no appearance of the fulfillment of Jeremiah's predictions, God raised up Ezekiel to confirm them in the faith, and to support, by new prophecies, those which Jeremiah had long before published, and even then continued to announce in Judea. — 2 Horne's Intro., p. 284.

breathe upon these slain, that they may live. So I prophesied as he commanded me, and the breath came into them, and they lived, and stood upon their feet[481].

We refer to the prophecy of Ezekiel chiefly to show the opinion which Brother Cole and others entertained of the sublime doctrines illustrated in the Master's degree. The name of Ezekiel imports the strength of God[482]. His death is nowhere mentioned in the Bible. So there are other personages of whose death there is no account to be found in the Scriptures. Some say that the prophet was put to death while he was a prisoner in Babylon that he had the foregoing vision, which had an immediate reference to the dispersion and restoration of the Jews[483]. The tribes of Israel are scattered over the earth: they have no particular habitation, no government of their own, no country, and no home which they can call their own. They are scattered, lost, and have been for ages. Millions of the race have gone down to the valley of death, and their bones are very dry. But those bones shall live. All in the grave and out of it shall have a part in the restoration. And how vast will be the army of the Israelites, when they shall march to the land of the holy sepulcher! All the dry bones shall then live. Bone will crawl to its bone; sinew and flesh will come upon them and skin cover them above[484]. And upon the wings of the four winds will be borne living souls, to abide again in their houses. Then how exceeding great will be the hosts, which will take up their march out of the valley of death, to join

---

[481] The reader is referred to the powerful and eloquent discourse of the Rev. Henry Melvill on the prophetic character of this vision. — 1 Mel. Ser., p. 302.

[482] 2 Horne's Intro., p. 283.

[483] Clarke's Com., Ezekiel 27.

[484] Everywhere shall the process be rapidly carried on of the bones being combined into the skeleton, and covered with the flesh, and animated by the Spirit, till the whole earth shall ring with the tread of "an exceeding great army." This will be a perfect accomplishment of the prophetic vision. — 1 Mel. Ser., p. 312.

the ranks of the living Israel! They will bear a more noble standard than the Roman eagle. Behold the cross and its blood-stained banner waving over them. Marvelously have they confessed Christ crucified. On they march, keeping time to the music of Moses and the Lamb. One thought, one feeling, one hope, one faith, one great heart, animate the vast assembly. And when they shall move in sight of their ancient home, and catch the first glimpse of their native hills, and behold the sacred mountains, lifting up their hoary heads to bid them welcome, what a universal shout will go up and echo throughout all the land of Judea! It will sound in the valleys and the concave rocks. The will of God has been obeyed. The prophecies are fulfilled. His ancient and chosen people have owned and confessed the Lord Jesus Christ. Their city will be rebuilt, and rest firmly on its triple hills—the "metropolis of the regenerated earth."[485]

But the doctrine of the resurrection is taught also in this vision of Ezekiel. That valley of vision was strewn with the relics of departed Israelites. Those bones are the whole house of Israel. Before the prophetic eye of Ezekiel, the dead came up out of their graves. The vision was designed, first, as an emblem of the wretched state of the Jews; secondly, of the general resurrection of the body[486]. It was certainly typical of the latter event, when all the dry bones of humanity would come together and be reunited. They shall all live. They shall hear the word of the Lord. Shall they all live? O Lord God, thou knowest. They shall know that Jesus is the Lord our Savior. They will know him, even in the midst of the noise: their spirits will know him, when the bones are shaking and coming together.

The hope of Israel is now lost, but it will be found again. The word was lost in the beginning, but it will be restored. We have all lost our first estate, but we may hereaf-

---

[485] 1 Mel. Ser., p. 219-307; D'Oyly and Mant's Com. on Ezekiel 37: 9.

[486] Clarke s Com., Ezekiel.

ter find it. The dispersion of the Jews reminds us of Paradise lost: their predicted restoration bids us look forward to Paradise regained.

Three degrees or processes have been remarked in the mystic vision. While the prophet foretold, on the authority of God, that there should be a restoration to their own land, there was first a noise, which was followed by a general shaking, during which the bones became arranged. Second, the flesh and skin came upon them, so that the dry bones were no longer seen. Third, the spirit or soul came into them, and they stood up perfectly vivified[487]. And thus will we all be raised, when the Lord comes in his power and glory. Suddenly we shall hear a noise, and there will be a gathering together of the dust of all centuries, and all the dead shall stand up perfectly vivified before the Mighty Master.

In the third degree of Masonry, we have abundant reason to contemplate death. We must all taste of it. The blows of the destroyer will, sooner or later, fall heavy and fast, and must prove fatal. And into the grave we must go. The earth will be heaped in upon us. Dust will be cast upon our heads. We shall sleep in the dust[488]. Dust we are, and unto dust we shall return[489]. Our earthly house of this tabernacle must be dissolved[490]. Rafter after rafter must come down—beam after beam shall fall. The dust shall return to the earth as it was[491]. It is appointed unto all men once to die, but after this the judgment[492]. Let us remember the words of the Master's inimitable prayer, selected from Job: Man that is born of a woman is of few days and full of

---

[487] Clarke's Com. on Ezekiel

[488] Job 7:21.

[489] Genesis 3:19.

[490] 2 Corinthians 5:1.

[491] Ecclesiastes 12:7.

[492] Hebrews 9:27.

trouble. He cometh forth like a flower and is cut down: he fleeth also as a shadow, and continueth not[493]. Confidence shall be rooted out of our tabernacle, and we shall be brought to the king of terrors[494]. But death is a peaceful messenger, sent to the good man. Old Simeon took up the child Jesus in his arms, blessed God, and said: Lord, now lettest thou thy servant depart in peace, according to thy word: for my eyes have seen thy salvation[495]. The Lord will never leave the righteous, nor forsake them[496]. Jesus will be their very present help in the trying hour; for it is written that death shall then be swallowed up in victory. And who giveth the victory? Thanks be to God, who giveth us the victory through our Lord Jesus Christ[497].

Need arguments be multiplied? What means our funeral service? Why do Masons administer such solemn rites at the burial of a brother? Why are none but Master Masons entitled to receive Masonic burial?[498] Our funeral ceremony recognizes the truth of the Christian religion. A Master in good standing may be interred with all the formalities and solemnities of the Order. Before any funeral obsequies are performed, the fraternity, being summoned by the order of the Master, assemble at the lodge room, where the lodge is opened in the third degree[499]. The Master begins the service by saying: "What man is he that liveth and shall not see

---

[493] Job 14:1-2.

[494] Job 18:14.

[495] Luke 2:28-30.

[496] Hebrews 13:5.

[497] 1 Corinthians 15:54-57.

[498] No Mason can be interred with the formalities of the Order, unless it be by his own special request whilst living, communicated to the Master of the lodge of which he died a member; nor unless he has been advanced to the third degree of Masonry; foreigners, sojourners, and particular officers excepted, and those at the discretion of the Grand Master. — Ahi. Rez., p. 106.

[499] Cross' Chart, p. 80.

death? Shall he deliver his soul from the hand of the grave?" The brethren respond: "Man walketh in a vain shadow; he heapeth up riches, and cannot tell who shall gather them." The service is characterized with a unity of sentiment and feeling. "When he dieth he shall carry nothing away; his glory shall not descend after him. Naked he came into the world, and naked he must return. The Lord gave, and the Lord taketh away; blessed be the name of the Lord."

Why are the public grand honors given at the grave? Let the enlightened Mason answer. With slow and measured step, the fraternity proceed in a body to the new-made tomb. They gather around the narrow home of the departed brother. The coffin is lowered silently to its vault. A requiem is sung, while the brethren generally march three times around the grave. Each one deposits with the remains a sprig of evergreen. The Master deposits a lamb skin, which is an emblem of innocence. "How important," continues the service, "for us to know that our Redeemer liveth, and that he shall stand at the latter day upon the earth." We are aware that the form of our funeral service is a modern production, however ancient the rite of Masonic burial may be. But the service proves the view of Masons in a Christian land in regard to Masonic truth. There is not a denomination of Christians in the world who has not a funeral service, or who does not perform some ceremony on funeral occasions.

> *Our mother, the church, hath never a child*
> *To honor before the rest,*
> *But she singeth the same for mighty kings*
> *And the veriest babe on her breast;*
> *And the bishop goes down to his narrow bed,*
> *As the ploughman's child is laid;*
> *And alike she blesseth the dark-brown'd serf*
> *And the chief in his robe array'd.*
> *She sprinkles the drops of the bright new birth*
> *The same, on the low and high,*

And christens their bodies with dust to dust,
When earth with its earth must lie.
Oh, the poor man's friend is the Church of Christ,
From birth to his funeral day;
She makes him the Lord's, in her surpliced arms,
And singeth his burial lay.

Arthur Cleveland Coxe, *Christian Ballads*

The rites of sepulture are of ancient origin. Jacob, before he was gathered unto his people, charged his sons about his burial: Bury me with my fathers in the cave that is in the field of Ephron the Hittite: in the cave that is in the field of Machpelah, which is before Mamre, in the land of Canaan, which Abraham bought with the field of Ephron the Hittite for a possession of a burying-place. There they buried Abraham and Sarah his wife; there they buried Isaac and Rebekah his wife; and there I buried Leah[500]. Funeral processions were then also common. Jacob's funeral was attended by a very large company. When Joseph went up to bury his father, there went up with him the servants of Pharaoh, the elders of his house, the elders of the land of Egypt, all the house of Joseph, and his father's house, and there went also with him chariots and horsemen[501].

There is not a Mason who has investigated the traditions of our Order, and reflected upon our ancient ceremonies, who can for a moment doubt that our ancient craftsmen observed funeral rites and paid funeral honors to the dead. Although our burial service is the production of modern times, still it was, we believe, founded upon a well authenticated tradition, and in conformity to the ancient usages of our institution. In saying that our present funeral service is a modern production, it is by no means intended that the ceremonies at the grave—such as the grand public honors, circumambulating the grave, depositing the sprig of

---

[500] Genesis 49:29-31.

[501] Genesis 50:7-9.

evergreen or acacia, the lamb skin, &c.—are modern. The secret history of the Order proves these ceremonies to be ancient, or that they were coeval with the origin of Freemasonry. Brethren in all ages have loved to meet at the tomb of a departed worthy brother, and join hands and renew in silence the tokens of their friendship. The present form of service announces the fact, that from time immemorial it has been the custom among the fraternity of free and accepted Masons, when requested by a brother, to accompany his corpse to the place of interment, and there to deposit his remains with the usual formalities. The lamb skin, we have shown, was an ancient badge and emblem; the grand honors, public and private, are certainly ancient; and the custom of depositing in the grave a sprig of acacia had an ancient emblematical meaning. The acacia is the name of a plant, most of whose species are ever green. The acacia of Freemasonry was a shrub, which grew in great abundance in the neighborhood of Jerusalem, and was used to mark the place where a dead body was interred[502]. Brother Mackey remarks that much of the Masonic history of the acacia is incommunicable; but he states, that its evergreen nature, united to other circumstances, is intended to remind us of the immortality of the soul. Another learned Mason has said that the acacia of Freemasonry implies, "that the sins and corruptions of the old law, and devotees of the Jewish altar, had hid religion from those who sought her; and she was only to be found where innocence survived, and under the banner of the Divine Lamb."

Our funeral ceremony resembles very much that of the Jews. If a distinguished member of our fraternity should die, an oration suitable to the occasion should be delivered at his grave. So, if a person of distinction die among the Jews, when the funeral reaches the burying-ground, a funeral eulogy is pronounced, and the mourners walk around the grave and recite a set form of prayer. The dead body is

---

[502] Mack. Lex., p. 11.

lowered into its resting-place, with the face toward heaven; and they say unto the departed: "Go in peace." We would say: "Friend of our hearts, there rest in peace." The Master of the lodge first throws earth upon the body, saying: "Earth to earth, ashes to ashes, dust to dust;" and after him it is proper for all the brethren to do likewise. Among the Jews, the nearest relative first casts earth on the body; then all present do the same[503]. The Jews, before they leave the burying-place, pluck bits of grass three times and cast them behind their backs, saying: "They shall flourish like grass of the earth." Masons give at the grave, the grand public honors three times; and when the Master says, "Almighty Father, into thy hands we commend the soul of our loving brother," the brethren respond three times: "The will of God is accomplished. So be it."

Monuments were common also. The simplest tombs were hillocks of earth, heaped up over the grave. The earliest sepulchers were probably caverns. In order to honor the memory of the dead, their sepulchers were distinguished by monuments[504]. The burial place of a Master Mason is said to be beneath the holy of holies. And there is a representation of a most interesting monument on our Masonic charts; and there is a beautiful inscription[505], which might be delineated on the tomb of a departed Master.

Sepulchers, anciently, were sometimes hewn in rocks: "What hast thou here, and whom hast thou here, that thou hast hewed thee out a sepulcher here, as he that heweth

---

[503] Bible Dict., p. 100.

[504] 2 Horne's Intro., p. 201.

[505] In ancient times, inscriptions appear to have been placed on tombstones, denoting the persons that were there interred. Such was the title or inscription discovered by Josiah, which proved to be the burial place of the prophet, who was sent from Judah to denounce the Divine judgments against the altar which Jeroboam had erected more than three centuries before. Simon Maccabaeus built a splendid monument at Modin, in honor of his father and his brethren. — 2 Horne's Intro., p. 202.

himself out a sepulcher on high, and that graveth a habitation for himself in a rock?" Hezekiah slept with his fathers, and they buried him in the chiefest of the sepulchers of the sons of David[506]. Jacob set a pillar upon Rachel's grave[507]. Jesus was laid in Joseph's own new tomb, hewn out of a rock. Memory often erects a monument to the dear departed. She may be compared to some beautiful virgin weeping over a broken column, with her sibylline book open before her, holding in her right hand a sprig of acacia, and in her left an urn, while Time is playing with her beautiful and flowing locks; and, as she weeps over her untimely loss, she records the virtues of the deceased, treasures the glowing ashes in the urn, and points aloft to immortality.

---

[506] 2 Chronicles 32:33.

[507] Genesis 35:20. This is the earliest monument mentioned in the Scriptures. It is evident it was standing when Moses wrote; and its site seems to have been known in the time of Samuel and Saul. — 1 Samuel 10:2. The monument now shown in the vicinity of Bethlehem as Rachel's tomb is a modern and Turkish structure, which may, perhaps, be the true place of her interment. — 2 Horne's Intro., p. 202.

LECTURE XIII.
Symbols of the Master Mason

The plants of the garden, the animals of the wood, the minerals of the earth, and meteors of the sky, should all concur to store his mind with inexhaustible variety; for any idea is useful for the enforcement or decoration of moral and religious truth; and he who knows most will have most power of diversifying his scenes, and of gratifying his reader with remote allusions and unexpected instruction.[508]

There is no kind of knowledge, which, in the hands of the diligent and skilful, will not turn to account. Honey exudes from all flowers, the bitter not excepted; and the bee knows how to extract it.[509]

Natural good is so intimately connected with moral good, and natural evil with moral evil, that I am certain, as if I heard a voice from heaven proclaim it, that God is on the side of virtue.[510]

---

[508] Rasselas [sic] E. N.: Scott seems to have taken this quote from Bp. Horne, but it refers to Samuel Johnson, *Rasselas, Prince of Abyssinia, a Tale,* Boston, 1831, p. 29.

[509] Bp. Horne. E. N.: See George Horne, *Essays and Thoughts on Various Subjects,* London, 1808, Preface, p. x.

[510] Lacon [sic] E. N.: refers to Caleb Charles Colton, *Lacon, or Many Things in few Words,* London, 1837, p. 145, CCC

Things breed thoughts; therefore, at Thebes and Heliopolis,
In hieroglyphic sculpture are the priestly secrets written.[511]

Things teach with double force; through the animal eye and
through the mind,
And the eye catcheth in an instant what the ear shall not learn
within one hour.[512]

The third section of the Master's degree illustrates certain hieroglyphical emblems, and inculcates many useful lessons to extend knowledge and promote virtue[513]. While design is manifested in all our Masonic work, it possesses the highest credentials, and carries with it the most demonstrative evidence of its beauty and power.

There is the pot of incense, which is an emblem of a pure heart[514]. The incense which was offered on the altar of incense and before the ark, was a mixture of sweet spices, and was made under the particular direction of the Almighty. He commanded Moses to take sweet spices, stacte, onycha, and galbanum, these sweet spices with pure frankincense: and thou shalt make it a perfume, a confection after the art of the apothecary, tempered together, pure and holy[515]. Incense is sometimes used in Scripture as a symbol

---

[511] Tupper, p. 241.

[512] Tupper, p. 206.

[513] Ahi. Rez., p. 185.

[514] Masonry, like Christianity, instructs us that the most pleasing incense that can be offered to the great I Am, is the incense of a grateful and pious heart. — Mack. Lex., p. 242. Emanuel Swedenborg, in his Heavenly Arcana, says that incense denotes three things of worship which are gratefully perceived, as well as spiritual worship, which is effected by confessions, adorations, and prayers. — Heav. Area., n. 9475 and 10298. The pot of incense is an emblem of a pure heart, which is always an acceptable sacrifice to the Deity; and, as this glows with fervent heat, so should our hearts continually glow with gratitude to the great and beneficent Author of our existence for the manifold blessings and comforts we enjoy. — Ahi. Rez., p. 186.

[515] Exodus 30:34-35.

of prayer[516]. David sung: Let my prayer be set before thee as incense, and the lifting up of my hands as the evening sacrifice[517]. Aaron burned sweet incense upon an altar of shittim wood every morning and evening; when he dressed the lamps in the morning and lighted them at even[518].

It was an ancient Hebrew custom for the priest to burn incense when he went into the temple of the Lord. Incense was offered morning and evening by the officiating priest upon an altar of gold; but on the great day of expiation, the high priest himself took fire from the great altar in a golden censer; and on descending thence, he received incense from one of the priests, which he offered on the golden altar. During such offering, the people prayed silently without; and to this most solemn silence St. John alludes in Revelation, when he says, that there was silence in heaven for about the space of half an hour. As the smoke and odor of this offering was wafted into the holy place, close by the veil of which stood the altar of incense, so do the prayers of the faithful ascend upward and find admission to the highest heaven[519]. The prayer of faith is always acceptable to the Deity; and as the pot of incense glows upon our altars with fervent heat, so should our hearts continually glow with gratitude to God. The prophet Malachi predicted that the offering of incense should be observed throughout all ages and countries: From the rising of the sun even unto the going down of the same my name shall be great among the Gentiles; and in every place incense shall be offered unto my name, and a pure offering: for my name shall be great among the heathen, saith the Lord of hosts[520]. Then, the pot of incense is a scriptural emblem, and should ever remind us of our duty to offer every morning and evening

---

[516] Luke 1:10.

[517] Psalms 140:1-2.

[518] Exodus 30:7-8.

[519] Horne's Intro., p. 191.

[520] Malachi 1:11.

acceptable prayer and a pure offering unto the throne of the Heavenly Grace.

The beehive[521] is also a significant emblem, and inculcates a beautiful moral. It is an emblem of industry. Labor has been imposed upon all. We must earn our bread by the sweat of our brows. It also teaches us to be faithful and diligent members of society; the necessity and advantages of regular government; and our dependence on each other. The bee is known to be a very busy insect. The beehive is an elegant building. Its cells are all nicely and beautifully arranged. A swarm of bees may be compared to a nation—a fraternity of laborers, working and dwelling together in unity. Honey, which is the product of their labor and skill, is frequently mentioned in the Bible. We read of a good land, a land flowing with milk and honey. The brethren of Joseph carried down to him in Egypt a little balm and a little honey. John the Baptist lived in the deserts on locusts and wild honey. Honey was common food in olden times. The judgments of the Lord, says the Psalmist, are sweeter than honey and the honey-comb[522]. Whatever is sweet and medicinal, is likened to honey. My son, eat thou honey, because it is good; and the honey-comb, which is sweet to thy taste: So shall the knowledge of wisdom be unto thy soul[523]. Thy lips, 0 my spouse, drop as the honey-comb: honey and milk are under thy tongue[524].

There is an omnipresent and All-Seeing Eye which beholds our every thought and deed, whether they be good or evil. How powerful is the language of that eye! If we would

---

[521] The beehive is an emblem of industry, and recommends the practice of that virtue. It teaches us that, as we came into the world rational and intelligent beings, so should we ever be industrious ones, never sitting down contented, while our fellow-creatures are around us in want, when it is in our power to relieve them. — Ahi. Rez., p. 186.

[522] Psalms 19:10.

[523] Proverbs 24:13-14.

[524] Song of Solomon 4:11.

only look unto our gracious God, he would always guide us with his eye, which sparkles in every star and glows in every sun. His eye is ever upon us, and we cannot fly from his presence: "If I ascend," said the Psalmist, "up into heaven, thou art there: If I make my bed in hell, behold, thou art there: If I take the wings of the morning, and dwell in the uttermost parts of the sea; even there shall thy hand lead me; and thy right hand shall hold me. If I say: Surely the darkness shall cover me: even the night shall be light about me. Yea, the darkness hideth not from thee; but the night shineth as the day; the darkness and the light are both alike to thee." The universe was made in the presence of the Almighty, for he is its Creator. He is as near to us now as he was to Adam, the first reasonable creature on earth of his handiwork. The law was given to Moses by a present Deity. On Sinai was his throne. His lightning was there, and his thunder also. And our God is everywhere. He is with us in our lodges. He sees all our secret work. He knows what we do, and the spirit in which we act. God is a spirit, and we can only look upon him through the eye of the soul. God's providence is ever watchful, for his eye is in every place. Then, the All-Seeing Eye is an emblem of one of the attributes of Deity. How boundless is his knowledge: how universal his presence! His eye surveys all time and all eternity. It searches the heart and penetrates the most secret places. It searcheth the reins and the heart[525]. Thou God seest me, said Hagar. God is present when every evil design is conceived, and every good resolution is formed. And in his light we see light[526]. The heaven is his throne, the earth his footstool[527]. Such is the majesty, such the grandeur of the Almighty, whose All-Seeing Eye is emblematized in our lodges. Let us not forget that he has said that he would guide us with his eye. May it guide us all in the way of truth;

---

[525] Revelation 2:23.

[526] Psalms 36:9.

[527] Isaiah 66:1.

and may it light up that hour in which we shall pass the gates of death, carrying with us all our work for the inspection of our Lord and Master. His eye sees every sand .in the hour glass[528], and every sweep of the scythe[529]. Oh, he is with us always: in life and in death, in the coffin and the grave. Had he not made us immortal, the sprig of evergreen would not have been emblematical. He is the glory of the universe, which is a great temple. He is with the rising, southing, and setting of the sun. He opens and adorns the day. He is with the sun in his coming. He stands upon a height which no mortal foot can reach, the summit of eternal grandeur, and beholds the sun rise above the mountains of the east. He closes the day, and is both its beauty and glory. Christ is the beauty and glory of his church. He is the beauty and glory of earth, for he is our Redeemer. He is the beauty and glory of heaven, for he sits at the right hand of the Father, to call his disciples from labor to refreshment. And there is one in heaven who will pay our wages, if any be due. The wages of sin, we know, is death; but the wages of righteousness is eternal salvation. All the servants of the Lord will be paid fair wages. But woe unto him that buildeth his house by unrighteousness and his chambers by wrong[530]. The righteous shall always have a pass word, which will enable them to travel to that spirit-land, where they will ever increase their wages in the labor of love. They will forever grow in knowledge, virtue, and goodness.

We have spoken of the sun. God made it to rule the day, and the moon to govern the night. The sun has a symbolical meaning in Scripture: The sun shall be turned into

---

[528] The hour-glass is an emblem of human life. Behold! How swiftly the sands run, and how rapidly our lives are drawing to a close. — Brad. Ser., p. 40; Ahi. Rez., p. 188.

[529] The scythe is an emblem of time, which cuts the brittle thread of life and launches us into eternity. — Brad. Ser., p. 40; Ahi. Rez., p. 188.

[530] Jeremiah 22:13.

darkness and the moon into blood[531]. Jesus Christ is spoken of under the figure of the "Sun of Righteousness." Joseph dreamed a dream, and behold, the sun, the moon, and the eleven stars made obeisance to him[532]. The sun signified his father, the moon his mother, and the stars his brethren. Dr. Clarke thought that the stars represented not only the brothers of Joseph, but alluded also to the zodiac—his eleven brethren answering to the eleven stars, and himself to the twelfth. A good ruler over men, ruling in the fear of the Lord, is compared to the light of the morning without clouds[533]. *A good ruler, then, may be appropriately seated in the East.*

Bishop Horne, commenting on the fifth verse of the 19th Psalm, says: In the centre of the heavens there is a tent pitched by the Creator for the residence of that most glorious of inanimate substances, the solar light; from thence it issues with the beauty of a bridegroom and the vigor of a champion, to run its course and perform its operations. And as the material light is always ready to run its heavenly race, daily issuing forth with renewed vigor, like an invincible champion, still fresh to labor; so likewise did he who saith of himself, "I am the light of the world," rejoice to run his glorious race. He excelled in strength, and his works were great and marvelous; he triumphed over the powers of darkness; he shed abroad on all sides his bright beams upon the church; he became her deliverer, her protector and support; and showed himself able, in every respect, to accomplish for her the mighty task he had undertaken. What a marvelous instrument of the Most High is the sun at his rising, considered in this view![534] We leave the brethren to make the application; for the sun is an emblem or symbol in our lodges. The motion of the sun is progressive,

---

[531] Acts 2:20.

[532] Genesis 37:9.

[533] 2 Samuel 23:4.

[534] Bp. Horne on Psalms, p. 203.

and directed from west to east. The moon, with respect to the stars, has a progressive circular movement from west to east. The planets revolve about the sun from west to east. The earth rotates from west to east. So the satellites circulate from west to east around their primaries[535].

While the Bible often speaks in figurative or symbolical language, we have seen that there are many passages which are susceptible of both a literal and spiritual sense. And in what does Masonic work consist, in a speculative sense? A lodge may be said to be at labor, in the transaction of all necessary business, but more particularly when engaged in conferring degrees. The terms of operative masonry are symbolically applied to speculative; for as our operative ancestors, when congregated in lodges, were engaged in the building of king Solomon's temple and many other edifices, so free and accepted Masons are supposed to be employed in the erection of a superstructure of virtue and morality, upon the foundation of Masonic principles, which they were taught at their admission into the Order[536]. It is highly important to consider whether we have served our most Worshipful Grand Master with freedom, fervency, and zeal, in our probationary state. We must serve a proper time in learning and practicing the principles of truth and the elements of virtue. To perform good work and true work, laborers in time must be made acquainted with the moral instruments, and apply them to their natural and depraved condition, that the works of wisdom may be manifested. It is our solemn duty to forsake evil and learn to do well; leave off all evil practices, evil desires, and evil passions. It is our duty to go diligently to work and get out all the unclean things within us. We must gauge our time, lay off our work, and execute it faithfully. We must divest, if possible, our souls from every evil clinging to them; and *throw sin over*

---

[535] William Augustus Norton, *An Elementary Treatise on Astronomy*, Philadelphia 1839, p. 5. Hereafter Nor. Astron.

[536] Mack. Lex. E. N. p. 437 on the 1872 edition.

our shoulders, and leave it in the rubbish of time. A great day is coming, and evil will be unfit for that day. The flinty heart is almost incapable of being made ready. It may, perhaps, be necessary to break it into atoms and construct it anew, before it will receive a polish. We can only learn to do well by ceasing to do evil. The mere practice of rites and ceremonies will not do. Forms and ceremonies are all proper and just, but the soul must be prepared and internally qualified to enjoy those rites and perform those ceremonies. The heart must be engaged in them. Faith may be cultivated. It is a good work. Hope and charity are good works. By walking in the light of the law and the gospel, we will reach the end of our work; we will be enabled to finish it, so that, when we die, our souls will be raised to a glorious fellowship, the fellowship of saints and angels. Such is Masonic fellowship, in its highest signification. In the first great light, we may learn something of this fellowship—true fellowship. God is faithful, and it is through him that we are called unto the fellowship of his Son Jesus Christ our Lord[537].And what a glorious privilege, what a great mystery, to be raised to a fellowship with our God to mansions of light, where we may both see and hear our sublime destiny. Such fellowship implies knowledge of virtue and goodness, mercy and truth, the will and perfections of Deity. If we know God, we shall be at peace: Thereby good shall come unto us[538]. And this is life eternal, that they might know thee, the only true God, and Jesus Christ, whom thou hast sent[539]. Lord, lift up the light of thy countenance upon us. That which was from the beginning, which we have heard, which we have seen with our eyes, which we have looked upon, and our hands have handled, of the Word of life; for the life was manifested, and we have seen it, and bear witness, and show unto you that eternal life, which was with

---

[537] 1 Corinthians 1:9.

[538] Job 22:21.

[539] John 17:3.

the Father, and with his Son Jesus Christ[540]. Concerning spiritual gifts, then, we should not be ignorant. The Evangelist, our patron Saint, beheld a great multitude, which no man could number, of all nations, and kindred, and people, and tongues, which stood before the throne, and before the Lamb, clothed with white robes[541]. Their investiture is symbolical of innocence and purity. White is an emblematical color, which may be observed in the Masonic apron and gloves. King Solomon recognized the emblem[542]: Let thy garments be always white[543]. St. John the Evangelist was acquainted with the emblem: Thou hast a few names in Sardis which have not defiled their garments; and they shall walk with me in white: for they are worthy. He that overcometh, the same shall be clothed with white raiment[544]. The sublimest of the prophets said: Though your sins be as scarlet, they shall be as white as snow; though they be red like crimson, they shall be as wool[545]. White, then, is an emblem of innocence. There were twelve innocent disciples, whose garments have been made white with the blood of the Lamb; and who, long since, appeared before the throne and testified that they had no part nor lot in the death of our Savior. All who are in heaven are arrayed in white, for they are innocent of the blood which was shed upon the hill of crucifixion.

But how was he punished through whom Jesus was betrayed into the hands of his enemies? There were others who participated in the unlawful act, but Judas Iscariot was the chief offender. If they were guilty, he was thrice guilty. He hailed him as Master. He betrayed the innocent blood,

---

[540] 1 John 1:1-3.

[541] Revelation 7:9.

[542] The temple of Solomon was built of white stone. — Josephus, b. 8, ch. 3, p. 166.

[543] Ecclesiastes 9:8.

[544] Revelation 3:4-5.

[545] Isaiah 1:18.

and hanged himself; and his bowels gushed out *in the midst.* Such was the earthly penalty of his crime.

Twelve is a symbolical number[546]. There were twelve tribes. The signs in the zodiac are twelve. There were twelve precious stones in the breast plate of the high priest. There are twelve sacred mountains. When St. John the Divine was carried away in the Spirit, he beheld the wall of the heavenly Jerusalem, and it had twelve gates, and at the gates twelve angels, and names written thereon of the twelve tribes of the children of Israel. The wall had twelve foundations, and in them the names of the twelve apostles of the Lamb. And here we may perceive the consistency of Masonic analogy. The apostles were messengers, and were sent out in search of the lost sheep of the house of Israel. The command was, Go ye into all the world and preach the gospel: go north, go south, go east, and go west[547], and bring them to a knowledge of the word; and, if possible, to that Word which was in the beginning: that the nations may be restored to that which was lost, to their first estate, a true knowledge of God.

The number fifteen[548] is referred to twice in ancient craft Masonry. If it be emblematical, we are left to indulge in speculation as to its probable meaning. The numbers three, five, and seven are frequently alluded to in the three first degrees. They are also scriptural numbers. Add them together, and the sum will make fifteen. There is a Masonic

---

[546] There stood round about the brazen sea twelve oxen which looked to the four winds of heaven, three to each wind. — Josephus, b. 8, ch. 3, p. 166. See Revelation 7:4-8.

[547] The form of the camp of the Israelites during their sojourning in the wilderness was quadrangular, having three tribes placed on each side. The four grand divisions in their encampment formed a square; three tribes encamped on the north, three on the south, three on the east, and three on the west.

[548] The brazen bases made for the quadrangular lavers were five cubits in length, four in breadth, and six in height. Five, four, and six added together make fifteen.

propriety in setting apart or subtracting three from fifteen. If three be taken from fifteen, twelve remain; or, *e converso*, if twelve be subtracted from fifteen, three will remain. The patriarchal dispensation was the first dispensation; the Levitical the second; and the Christian the third. There is fullness in the latter. It was in the development of the third degree of religious truth, that the perfect Man was crucified or murdered. The knowledge of the mysteries of redemption resided originally with the adorable Trinity; for the plan of salvation was known from the beginning only to the God head. The Son of God came down from heaven to build his church on earth. Its broad foundations covered his own grave that it might tower with wisdom, strength, and beauty, above the ruins of sin and death. The Christian system was not completed until after the death of Christ; and it was not until after his death and resurrection, that the twelve apostles were commissioned to preach the gospel unto all nations. With the twelve commenced the propagation of the gospel light now shining in so many lands. The mysteries of ancient craft Masonry were known only to King Solomon, Hiram king of Tyre, and Hiram the widow's son, if these persons were, as we have contended, the founders of our Order. The mysteries of Masonry were planned, we think, before the foundation of the first temple was laid. They were not evolved or fully developed and made known until after the completion of the building, or about the time of its completion. The mysteries of redemption were not fully illustrated until the object of our Savior's mission was accomplished. The Son of God, the Sovereign Builder, prepared every material for the erection and completion of his spiritual temple, from all eternity; and yet that temple was not to be finished until after his death. If our traditions are to be relied on, we must believe that it was not until after the completion of Solomon's temple, that a plan was adopted for the propagation of Masonic truth. And twelve favored craftsmen were first invested with the sublime secrets of the Order, and that chosen band of brothers instructed the nations. These twelve, with the three Grand Masters, make fifteen, which number, anciently, denoted a new state. After the crucifixion of Christ, commenced the preaching of the gospel and the glorious kingdom of righteousness. The twelve craftsmen, like the apostles, were humble individuals. If the apostles were obscure by birth and illiterate by education, the craftsmen were no less humble, for they were elevated from among the laborers to the degree of Master. If the former delivered the truths of Christianity in simplicity of style, the latter taught the mysteries of Masonry in the same way. If the former preached Christ crucified, "not with the enticing words of man's wisdom, but in the demonstration of the Spirit," the latter taught the principles of our institution in the spirit of truth. The twelve apostles were chosen witnesses of God to testify to his resurrection. They were witnesses of all things which Christ did, both in the land of the Jews and in Jerusalem; and when he was raised up the third day, and shown openly, not to all the people, but unto his chosen witnesses, the apostles were commanded to preach unto the people, and to testify of Him who was ordained by God to be the judge of quick and dead[549]. The apostles had served their Master faithfully. They were with him on the sea and on the land, in the forests and amid the multitude. They saw the sepulcher in which he was buried, "wherein was man never yet laid." They beheld him dead and after he rose from the grave.

The Israelites commenced their journey from Egypt to the promised land of Canaan on the fifteen day of the month. Moses wrote their journeying by the express commandment of heaven. And they departed, says he, from Ramses in the first month, in the fifteenth day of the first month: On the morrow after the Passover, the children of Israel went out with a high hand in the sight of all the Egyptians[550]. On the fifteenth day of the second month

---

[549] Acts 10:39-42.

[550] Numbers 33:3.

they reached "the wilderness of Sin, which is between Elim and Sinai," where there was plenty of water and shade. The Passover was instituted on the fourteenth day of the first month in the evening[551]. And it was upon the fifteenth of the same month, at midnight, the first-born of Egypt were all slain. And on the first day of unleavened bread, when the Passover of the Jews was to be slain, in the evening, Jesus eat the Passover with his disciples, and instituted the holy Eucharist[552]. According to Moses, the first day of unleavened bread was the fifteenth[553]. But the first day of unleavened bread is called the fourteenth in Matthew, because they began to remove leavened bread from their houses on the fourteenth, before the lamb was killed[554]. On the same night (the fourteenth) Christ was betrayed. The next day he was condemned by Pilate and crucified. This was the fifteenth day of the month[555]. Well may it be said, that with the fifteenth day of that eventful month commenced a new state of things. The Son of Man was crucified on that day; his blood was then shed, which was to wash away the sins of the world. The flood prevailed fifteen cubits above the highest mountains; and as the waters covered the whole earth, so shall the flood of gospel light prevail over all the nations. The fountains of the great deep of human thought and feeling will be broken up, and the windows of heaven shall be opened, and the Spirit of God will descend, and righteousness pervade the world.

Every event which transpired at the building of Solomon's temple is typical in Masonry. Everything about the tabernacle involved a mystery. We have shown that the temple itself was typical. The Shekinah appeared in the holy

---

[551] Exodus 12:6.

[552] Matthew 26; Mark 14; Luke 22.

[553] Exodus 12:17.

[554] D'Oyly and Mant's Com., Matthew 26:17.

[555] Matthew 27.

of holies of the tabernacle[556] and the temple. And why did God vouchsafe to abide there for a time? Ask the prophets of old. They answered the question long ago, and their response has been transmitted from age to age. That response is contained in the account of the first sacrifice which consecrated Moriah. The Jews heard it, in the voice of Him who spoke as never man spake; in the agonies of the garden; in the groans of our Lord's expiring nature; in the blood which trickled down his pierced side; and in the great drops which fell from his lofty brow; in the sound of the hammer which nailed him to the tree; in the fervent prayer which ascended from his lips: "Father, forgive them, for they know not what they do;" and, in the loud voice which cried out, "It is finished."

St. Paul spoke of the mystery of the tabernacle, and looked upon it as a type of the Messiah. The temple was far superior to the tabernacle; and in proportion as it surpassed the latter in splendor, so it was a more brilliant type of the church. There were carved on the walls of the temple, within and without, *open* flowers. In the tabernacle the flowers were represented in the *bud*. Figuratively, the *ground floor* of the temple may be considered the earth, the *inner chamber* the region of the stars, and the *holy of holies* the upper sky, where God for ever dwells in glory[557]. On the ground floor are assembled all the Entered Apprentices—the followers of the Lamb—the disciples of Jesus. They would throw off

---

[556] If anyone do but consider, says Josephus, the fabric of the tabernacle, and take a view of the garments of the High Priest, and of those vessels which we make use of in our sacred ministrations, he will find that our legislator was a divine man, and that we are unjustly reproached by others; for if anyone do without prejudice, and with judgment, look upon these things, he will find that they were everyone made in way of imitation and representation of the universe. — Jewish Antiq. b. 3, ch. 7.

[557] The Rabbis usually divide the whole frame of things into three worlds: the first, the inferior or the depressed and lowest world—that is, this world; the second is called the middle or inmost world—this is the world of the spheres, containing the aerial region and the starry heavens; the third is the superior world—this is the world of angels, of God, of souls, the spiritual world. — Sears, on the Creed, p. 75, note.

the robes of scarlet, .and put on garments of white. In their present checkered scene of existence, they perceive a mixture of light and darkness. In this life, the state of the Christian "is not altogether evil, nor completely blessed." He is to be "brought out of darkness into light." On the ground floor, his light is neither clear nor dark, but "it shall come to pass, that at *eventime* it shall be light." The Entered Apprentices should all work together for good, for they that be wise shall shine forth as the sun, when the *word* sinks down into their ears and dwells in them richly.

LECTURE XIV.
Three

Despise not, shrewd reckoner, the God of a good man's worship,
Neither let thy calculating folly gainsay the unity of three;
Nor scorn another's creed, although he cannot solve thy doubts;
Reason is the follower of faith, where he may not be precursor.[558]

Therefore, it were probable and just, even to a man's weak think-
ing,
To have one for God who always may be learnt, yet never fully
known,
Throned in his sublimity beyond the grovellings of lower intellect,
Should claim to be truer than man's truest, the boasted certainty
of numbers,
Should baffle his arithmetic, confound his demonstrations, and
paralyze the might of his necessity,

---

[558] Tupper, p. 68.

Standing supreme as the mystery of mysteries, everywhere, yet impersonate,
Essential one in three, essential three in one.[559]

What Bishop Horne says of the Mosaic types, may be aptly applied to the three degrees of ancient craft Masonry: "They are like triangular prisms, that must be set in a due light and posture, before they can represent that great variety of spiritual mysteries contained in them." The number three is a mystic number, and seems to be a favorite one in Freemasonry[560]. It pervades the whole body of the institution. It may be traced in its signs, angles, steps, and words. It is found in our ritual. Three discreet questions are put to the candidate for initiation, and each must be affirmatively answered before he can be received into the lodge. The candidate is prepared for admission in three different ways, and yet those ways of preparation are one. There were three ancient Grand Masters, as we are informed by tradition, namely: Solomon king of Israel, Hiram king of Tyre, and Hiram the widow's son. Every lodge has three principal officers: a Master, a Senior and Junior Warden. No lodge can be opened or governed without these officers. They aid and assist each other in Masonic work. No degree can be conferred without them. There are three principal Masonic stations, which may be said to represent, in one sense, the rising, southing, and setting of the sun. There is but one sun to us, and that sun which gains the meridian rises in the east and sets in the west. Every well governed or constitutional lodge is furnished with the Holy Bible, square, and compasses. We recognize a God, Master, and

---

[559] Tupper, p. 151.

[560] This number has particularly attracted the attention of Dr. Oliver, whose able and philosophic work, entitled the "Historical Landmarks of Freemasonry," I have recently examined. Without assuming too much, it may be proper to state, that the substance of the above lecture was prepared before the "Historical Landmarks of Freemasonry" was issued from the English press.

the craft. There are three ornaments, the Mosaic pavement, indented tessel, and blazing star. We have the rough ashlar, the perfect ashlar, and trestle board. Anciently, lodges were dedicated to King Solomon, now to two patron saints. Masonry has three social objects in view, Brotherly Love, Relief, and Truth. It has adopted and enforces the practice of the three theological virtues, Faith, Hope, and Charity. Jacob's ladder is represented as having three rounds. The most of the degrees have three sections, which are distinct, and yet they constitute portions of the lecture appertaining to the particular degree to which they belong. There are three symbolical degrees. Anciently there were only three degrees. We use the plumb, square, and level: the trowel, the gavel, and gauge. There are three principal orders of architecture—the Doric, Ionic, and Corinthian; which are represented particularly by three pillars, denominated Wisdom, Strength, and Beauty. Three of the cardinal points are well guarded, the east, south, and west. On our tracing board are represented two hills and a valley. There, too, may be seen the mount, ladder, and clouded canopy, and three burning tapers. There are three greater and three lesser lights. There is the circle, with its mystic triangles. The two pillars representing the pillars which were erected at the entrance of King Solomon's temple are ornamented with net work, lily work, and pomegranates. Unity, Peace, and Plenty, are also represented. The maul, spade, and coffin, are solemn emblems. Geometry, which is one of the sciences illustrated in the second degree, treats of the powers and properties of magnitudes in general, where length, breadth, and thickness are considered, from a point to a line, from a line to a superficies, and from a superficies to a solid. And a point is an indivisible part of space; a line is a continued point, namely length; a superficies has length and breadth. A solid is a figure of three dimensions, namely, length, breadth, and thickness[561]. If we add up the columns and pilasters of the temple, the number three will be the

---

[561] Ahi. Rez., p. 176; see also Euclid's *Elements*.

exact divisor of the sum. So if the number of Grand Masters, overseers, Fellow Crafts, and Apprentices, which wrought at the building, be summed up, the exact divisor of the whole number will be three. This mystic number is veiled in our Masonic words and syllables. It is shrined in the depths of the ritual. It may be seen in its angles, horizontals, and perpendiculars. We are reminded of it when we meet upon the level, act upon the plumb, and part upon the square. We may hear it in the raps of the gavel; see it in the signs; feel it in the grips; hear it aloud, and hear it in whispers. It may be observed by the Apprentice when he first enters a lodge; it meets him there always, at prayer as well as at work. It may be traced in every degree. It is an essential number, and is to be found in the ceremonies of the inner chamber, and in the august evolutions of the holy of holies. When the hour of danger or distress, penury or disease, comes upon any of us, it will, when masonically manifested, bring the faithful brother to our aid and "assistance, and the fraternal priest will linger about our beds of death, and pray for the admission of our souls into the celestial lodge. And this mystic number or emblem is displayed around the opened grave, in the funeral signs and ceremonies. The grand honors are given three times at the burial of a brother: when his departed soul is commended to God, the brethren repeat three times the following words: *The will of God is accomplished. So be it.*" Observe the number of invocations, and their structure. The Master standing at the head of the grave, says: *"May we be true and faithful; and may we live and die in love."* The brethren respond: *"So mote it be."* Again, the Master says: *"May we profess what is good, and may we always act agreeably to our profession."* The response is heard: *"So mote it be."* And again the Master says: *"May the Lord bless us and prosper us, and may all our good intentions be crowned with success."* Then the answer is heard: *"So mote it be."* A pause succeeds, and then the rolls are thrown into the grave with the usual forms, while the chaplain repeats in an audible voice: *"Glory be to God on high, on earth peace and good will toward men!"* The response is made: *"So *mote it be, now, from henceforth and for evermore."* The Master, while performing the rest of the ceremonies, throws into the grave first a lamb skin, then a sprig of evergreen, and lastly a few clods, pronouncing these solemn words: "Earth to earth—ashes to ashes—dust to dust."

We know of a lodge of the holy Saints John at Jerusalem, by which we learn its existence, the persons to whom dedicated, and its location. Every one deemed worthy to know its mysteries is entitled to its rites, lights, and benefits. Not only is the number three to be discovered in the structure of the Masonic ritual, but it is manifested in all our ceremonies. And is there no mark of design in this? We cannot suppose that such frequent references to this number are merely accidental. Such hypothesis would be repugnant to reason and experience. It has a significant meaning, and is intended to illustrate some truth. Many believe that it refers to the doctrine of the adorable Trinity[562]. Many enlightened craftsmen have stated that it is not only an emblem of the Trinity, but that it is so explained in our lectures. If this statement be true, then there would be no room for speculation. We doubt, however, whether Masonry affords any such explanation; for the doctrine of the Trinity is one of those great mysteries which can never be comprehended, and is so intimately associated with the incommunicable name of Jehovah, that our ancient brethren would hardly have done more than to teach it emblematically, or evolve it in their ceremonies. If our supposition be correct, that the Masonic lectures do not clearly explain the emblem, or contain any direct reference to its hidden meaning, it would seem to fortify the opinion that it referred to something connected with the incommunicable

---

[562] It is said that the Trinity in unity; the incarnation of the Deity; a vicarious atonement for sin; and the influence of the Divine Spirit on the mind of man, are held by the eastern nations, though in gross ignorance respecting the only living and true God. Brahma is the one God of the Hindus, and yet they represent him as subsisting in three persons. Their most ancient representation of the Deity is formed of one body and three faces. — Burnet on 39th Art.

name of Deity. We are not disposed to engraft anything into the regular body of Masonry, but greatly desire to see the landmarks remain pure and unaltered. We would not add a stone to the edifice, or take one from it. It would mar the beauty of the building. But we claim it as our right and privilege to express an opinion as to the probable meaning of any of the Masonic emblems, when they are not explained in our lectures so as to exclude all comment. The opinions of the fraternity cannot affect the landmarks, any more than the expositions of theologians can change the text of the Bible, which is immutable.

The number three, as a Masonic emblem, is coeval with the erection of the first temple. There were three eminent persons associated in that great work. There were three principal apartments in that edifice. Its stones were hewed, marked, and numbered. They were conveyed by floats to Joppa, and thence to Jerusalem. It is said that the sacred mountain of Moriah was circumambulated three times before the foundation of the temple was laid. "The temple of Solomon," said brother Davies of Shrewsbury, "has three foundations; the first of which contained seventy stones, five rows from north to south, and fourteen in each row running from east to west. The centre row corresponded with the upright of a cross, whose transverse was formed by two stones on each side of the eleventh stone, from the east end of the centre row of which the upright is formed, and the fourth stone from the west end of it. This stone, which hence occupied the place of the crossing of the beams, was under the centre of the sanctum sanctorum," where the Ark of the Covenant was situated and the Divine Presence was manifested. He contended that the design contained an evident reference to the cross of Christ; and that this cross was so placed, that the part where the heart of Christ would be at the time of his crucifixion was under the centre of the holy of holies[563].

---

[563] 2 Ol. Land., 263, n.

Cedar, olive[564], and fir were the only kinds of wood used in constructing Solomon's temple. We are informed by tradition that it was the custom of Hiram the builder to pray three times every day—to pray at the rising, southing, and setting of the sun. Such was the practice of King David, Daniel, and others. We read of three pieces of typical furniture in the holy place: the golden candlestick, the table of shewbread, and the golden altar. The inner court of Solomon's temple "was built with three rows of hewed stone, and a row of cedar beams." Adam Clarke significantly in quires: "Does not this passage intimate that there were three courses of stone and then one course of timber all through the wall? Three strata of stone, and one stratum of timber, and so on." Calmet thinks that to this mode of building the prophet alludes, when he says: "The stone shall cry out of the wall, and the beams out of the timber shall answer it."

In the world of nature, this emblem of the Almighty is also visible. There are three kingdoms, the animal, vegetable, and mineral. It is supposed there are three imponderable fluids: galvanism, magnetism, and electricity. The air we breathe is composed of three elements: nitrogen, oxygen, and hydrogen. And they are all essential to life. If any one of them be taken away, death must ensue. Nature has her triple associations. The thunder and lightning dwell among the clouds. We have rain, hail, and snow. The snows of the Polar Regions are full of treasures. Many of their configurations are triangular. In one of the plates of Sears's Bible Illustrations, representing the snow-crystals of the arctic regions may be seen figures of the double equilateral triangle. Captain Scoresby says, that "some of the general varieties in the figures of the crystals may be referred to the temper-

---

[564] I have visited, says Lamartine, every country of the globe where olive trees grow. They live for ages. I have seen, on the summit of Mount Lebanon, the cedars said to have been Solomon's: this is by no means impossible. Nature has given to certain of its vegetable productions more duration than to empires. — 1 Lam. Pil., p. 304.

ature of the air; but the particular and endless modification of similar classes of crystals, can only be referred to the will and pleasure of the First Great Cause, whose works, even the most minute and evanescent, and in regions the most remote from human observation, are altogether admirable."

It has been calculated that in the space of one hour, which is sixty minutes, the human heart beats thirty-six hundred times, and discharges seventy-two hundred ounces of blood; and in twenty-four hours the blood circulates through the body six hundred times[565]. There is a present, past, and future time. There are three brains or three departments of the brain in the human skull. There are three different kinds of time employed by astronomers in their calculations: sidereal, apparent or true solar and mean solar time. An eclipse of a heavenly body is occasioned by the interposition of some opaque body between it and the eye, or between it and the sun. For instance, an eclipse of the moon is occasioned by an interposition of the body of the earth between the sun and moon. With respect to the objects eclipsed, there are only three kinds of eclipses, namely: of the sun, of the moon, and of the satellites. The motions of the planets are regulated, or are in conformity to the three laws discovered by Kepler[566].

> *Matter, and breath, and instinct, unite in all the*
> *beasts of the field;*
> *Substance, coherence, and weight, fashion the fabrics of*
> *the earth;*
> *The will, the doing, and the deed, combine to frame a*
> *fact;*
> *The stem, the leaf, and flower; beginning, middle, and*
> *end;*
> *Cause, circumstance, and consequent; and every three*
> *is one.*

---

[565] $60/3=20$ $3600/3=1200$ $7200/3=2400$ $24/3=8$

$20/60$ $1200/3600$ $2400/7200$ $8/24$

[566] See Nor. Astron. p. 78.

*Yea, the very breath of man's life consisteth of a trinity
of vapours,*
*And the noonday light is a compound, the triune
shadow of Jehovah.*[567]

Then, our mystic number finds an analogy in nature[568].
It is also found in the Bible. In the Old Testament the attention is not particularly called to it. The reference to it is
not open, nor was it designed to be open. Nor was it so designed in Masonry. There were three angels who appeared
to Abraham in the plains of Mamre. On the third day's
journey, he came in sight of Moriah, where he was to build
an altar and offer his sacrifice. Moses, on Mount Sinai, beheld a cloud, and about it fire, and above the fire a Great
Being. The Ten Commandments were delivered from the
top of a mountain, in the presence of all the people, and
with the sound of a trumpet. The goodly child Moses was
hid for three months[569]. There are three different tabernacles mentioned in the Old Testament previously to the erection of Solomon's temple; namely, the tabernacle of the
congregation; then the one erected by Moses for Jehovah;
and lastly, the one erected by David in his own city, for the
reception of the ark[570]. If Pharaoh would not believe in two
signs, the Almighty directed that he should be spoken to in
the voice of the third sign[571]. Three often signifies, in the

---

[567] The rainbow, which is light analyzed, is but three colors, blue, yellow,
and red, with their intermediate shades. I think no one of these can be
mixed or made of others, and in their union they produce colorless
light. — Tupper, p. 158.

[568] Milton, in his *Paradise Lost*, describes the gates of hell in the following
manner:

> *Three folds were brass,*
> *Three iron, three of adamantine rock*
> *Impenetrable, impaled with circling fire,*
> *Yet unconsumed.*

[569] Exodus 2:2.

[570] 2 Horne's Intro., p. 96.

[571] Exodus 4.

Bible, greatness, excellence, and perfection[572]. We read in Isaiah: "In that day shall Israel be the third with Egypt and Assyria." Have I not written unto thee three things? Said Solomon. A sentiment thrice uttered implied earnestness and excellence. 0 earth, earth, earth, hear the word of the Lord[573]. Jonah was three days and nights in the fish's belly. Elijah, before he offered up his prayer to Jehovah on Mount Carmel, poured water in abundance three times over the sacrifice. In the Mount of God, which is Horeb, before the Shekinah was manifested to him, a mighty wind rent the mountains, then came an earthquake, and after that a fire. Moses requested of Pharaoh to go three days' journey into the desert, and sacrifice unto the Lord[574]. When they departed from the Mount of the Lord three days' journey, the Ark of the Covenant went before them in the three days' journey[575]. The Lord said unto Moses: Go unto the people to-day and to-morrow, and let them wash their clothes, and be ready against the third day: for the third day the Lord will come down in the sight of all the people upon Mount Sinai[576]. Dr. Lightfoot says that, anciently among the Jews, the Old Testament was divided into three parts. The first, beginning with the law, was called the Law; the second, beginning with the Psalms, was called the Psalms; the third, beginning with the prophecy of Jeremiah, which anciently stood first, was called Jeremiah, under which name all the quotations from the prophets were made.[577]

---

[572] 2 Horne's Intro., Gen. Index.

[573] Jeremiah 22:29.

[574] Exodus 5:3.

[575] Numbers 10:33.

[576] Exodus 19:10-11.

[577] Simon Greenleaf, *An Examination of the Testimony of the Four Evangelists*, Boston, 1846, p. 476.
There are many symbolical words in the Bible, and frequently applied in three different ways; as, for example:
Day means, 1. A year in prophetical language. 2. An appointed time or season. 3. A state of truth, hope, and knowledge.

How emphatic did Christ speak, when he told Peter that he would deny him thrice: "Verily, verily, I say unto you, before the cock crow thou shalt deny me thrice." Our Savior, in describing his church, clothes her with the sun, puts the moon under her feet, and on her head a crown of stars. St. John repeatedly refers to the number three, in Revelation. He tells us, that when the first angel sounded his trumpet, there followed hail and fire, mingled with blood, and a third part of the trees were burnt up; when the second angel sounded, a third part of the sun became blood, and a third part of the creatures in the sea that had life died, and a third part of the ships were destroyed; and when the third angel sounded, a great star from heaven fell upon a third part of the rivers, and a third part of the waters became wormwood; and then a third part of the sun was smitten, and a third part of the stars; the day shone for a third part of it, and the night likewise. And the Evangelist beheld an angel flying through the midst of heaven, saying, with a loud voice: Woe! Woe! Woe! To the inhabitants of the earth. Three times did Jesus inquire: "Simon, son of Jonas, lovest thou me?" Three favored persons beheld the transfiguration: Peter, James, and John. There appeared unto them Elias and Moses talking with Jesus; and Peter answered and said, Master, it is good for us to be here: and let us make three tabernacles; one for thee, and one for Moses,

---

Dragon, 1. A symbol of a king that is an enemy. 2. Satan acting and ruling by his visible ministers. 3. Any hurtful thing.

Eagle. 1. A king or kingdom. 2. The Roman army, whose ensigns or standards were eagles. 3. Emblem of renewed strength.

Eyes—as applied to God. 1. His knowledge and prescience. 2. His watchful providence. 3. Omnipresence of Jesus Christ.

Flesh. 1. Riches. 2. Mortal man. 3. Human virtues or religious privileges.

Head. 1. The understanding. 2. Chief of a people. 3. Metropolis of a country.

Horn. 1. Strength. 2. Divine protection. 3. Royal power.

Keys. 1. Power or authority. 2. Commission of the gospel ministry. 3. Means of scriptural knowledge.

Star. 1. A prince or ruler. 2. Eminent pastors of churches 3. Apostolical teachers. — See Horne's Index of Sym. Lan. of the Bible.

and one for Elias. Christ raised the dead only three times. Three persons hung upon the cross of Calvary. The accusation against Jesus was written above his head in three different languages. And Pilate wrote a title, and put it on the cross. And the writing was, Jesus of Nazareth the King of the Jews. This title then read many of the Jews: for the place where Jesus was crucified was nigh to the city: and it was written in Hebrew, and Greek, and Latin[578]. While he hung upon the tree, they bade him come down, saying: "Thou that destroyest and buildest the temple in three days." When he gave up the ghost and died, nature clad herself in mourning and wept for three hours. It was commanded that the sepulcher should be made sure for three days. He was in the grave three days. He rose on the third day. Our Lord crucified, dead, and buried, said Peter, James, and John. The Savior is our prophet, priest, and king. When the risen Lord appeared unto Mary Magdalene, she cried out *Rabboni*. Stephen, Paul, and John saw Jesus in his ascended state. The kingdom of God is righteousness, peace, and joy in the Holy Ghost. "Woman! Why weepest thou?" was the language of two angels, and of Jesus to Mary. Those about the throne rest not day nor night, saying, Holy, holy, holy, Lord God Almighty, that was, and is, and is to come[579]. There are three in heaven who wear the

---

[578] John 19:19-20.

[579] Nine, being the square of three, is called a perfect ternary. — 2 Ol. Land., p. 220. The figure nine is a mystic figure in Masonry However many nines may be added together, or by whatever number or numbers it may be multiplied, the line of figures for the sum or product may be added together, and it will consist of one or more nines. For instance, twice 9 are 18—the 1 and 8 are 9; 4 times 9 are 30, and 3 and 6 are 9. A learner finds some amusement in increasing the amount, as if he expected that some variation might be found; but when he gets to 11 times 9, he finds the product is only 99—two nines. And at the next step higher, viz. 12 times 9, he obtains only 108, or one 9. Then he may be shown the fact that nine digits, 1, 2, 3, 4, 5, 6, 7, 8, 9, amount to a large number of nines; namely, 5 nines are 45 ; and he may be taught that if, instead of adding a line up, he will multiply the middle figure by the last figure, namely, 5 times 9, he will find the value of the whole most readily; and this upon a principle of taking averages, to which he

will have occasion to resort in higher departments of the science. He may then be directed to notice the effect of adding together two lines formed of the nine digits, but in reversed order. For instance,

1	2	3	4	5	6	7	8	9
9	8	7	0	5	4	3	2	1
1	1	1	1	1	1	1	1	10

There is something striking to the eye in such a product, for the wonderful number recurs in nine ones; and it may serve to induce thinking. Or, let the one line be subtracted from the other, in this way:

$$987654321$$
$$123456789$$
$$864197532$$

In this result the odd and even numbers become curiously arranged; the whole of the nine digits are there, as in the upper line; there is no surplus or repetition; there is only one figure of a kind; of course they amount to five nines. Would the pupil wish to see a sum in multiplication, the product of which shall contain several figures alike? Tell him to set down all the digits except 8, and if he would like the product to be all ones, let the line be multiplied by one nine, thus:

$$12345679 \times 9 = 111111111$$

And here again is the faithful number, for the product presents nine ones. If the product of twos would please him, let him multiply the line with two nines or 18, and so on with 27, 36, &c, until, by multiplying by 9 or 81, he will have a product of all nines, and nine of them:

12345679	12345679	12345679
18 .	45 .	81 .
98765432	61728395	12345679
12345679	49382716	98765432
222222222	555555555	999999999

The pupil may try the intermediate numbers to produce threes, fours, sixes, sevens, and eights. There will be found nine of each, and the figures of each product added together will be of equal value to each respective multiplier. If the figure 9 be multiplied eight places in a line by two and the other digits, up to nine inclusive, the whole line of results will be ranged alike, from left to right, and from right to left; that is, from a to a, reading the figures in either direction, thus:

9	9	9	9	9	9	9	9
2	3	4	5	6	7	8	9

a 18 27 36 45 54 63 72 81 a

human form. There are three that bear record in earth, and three that bear record in heaven. And the Very first word of power in the first chapter of Genesis, which is God, implies plurality. The Hebrew word Elohim is a plural noun. Huramen corresponds with the Latin word inveni, which corresponds with eureka, which signifies I have found it. Simon Ben Joachi says: "Come and see the mystery of the word Elohim: there are three degrees, and each degree is by itself alone, and yet they are all one, and joined together in one, and are not divided from each other."

The same facts are often detailed by three of the gospel witnesses, and each of the three uses different language in their narration, but their language is substantially the same. For example, Matthew states: And behold, there came a leper and worshipped him, saying, Lord, if thou wilt, thou canst make me clean[580]. Mark says: And there came a leper to him, beseeching him, and kneeling down to him, and saying unto him, if thou wilt, thou canst make me clean[581]. In Luke the fact is thus related: And it came to pass, when he was in a certain city, behold a man full of leprosy: who seeing Jesus fell on his face, and besought him, saying, Lord, if thou wilt, thou canst make me clean[582]. Many similar examples might be cited. We will only refer to one more: Now from the sixth hour there was darkness over all the land until the ninth hour[583]. And when the sixth hour was come, there was darkness over the whole land until the ninth hour[584]. And it was about the sixth hour, and there

---

And the first figure in each couple, for either end, is in simple rotation from one to eight. — Boss's Menial Calculator.

[580] Matthew 8:2.

[581] Mark 1:40.

[582] Luke 5:12.

[583] Matthew 27:45.

[584] Mark 15:33.

was darkness over all the earth until the ninth hour[585]. Are not these things "marvelous in our eyes"? Such is "the mystery of God, and of the Father, and of Christ."

Mysterious truth! that the self-same should be
A Lamb, a Shepherd, and a Lion too!
Yet such was He
Whom first the shepherds knew,
When they themselves became
Sheep to the Shepherd-Lamb.
Shepherd of men and angels—Lamb of God—
Lion of Judah—by these titles keep
*   The wolf from thy endangered sheep.*
Bring all the world unto thy fold;
Let Jews and Gentiles hither come
In numbers great that can't be told;
And call thy lambs, that wander, home.
Glory be to God on high;
All glories be to the glorious Deity.

Bp. Jeremy Taylor.[586]

When we reflect upon the source of Masonic knowledge, we are forced to the conclusion that the founders of our institution borrowed our mystic number three from the holy writings, and not from the customs and rites of heathen worship. And though many heathen nations, it is said, had a high regard for the emblem[587], we would rather think that they also obtained it, either directly or indirectly, from the Scriptures, than to entertain the opinion that Masonry could have derived it from idolaters.

The power and majesty of the Deity are impressed on all his works. His Spirit breathes, lives, moves, and has its

---

[585] Luke 23:44.

[586] Jeremy Taylor, *The Whole Works of Right Reverend Jeremy Taylor, Lord Bishop of Down, Connor and Dromore,* London, 1835, Vol. III, p. 743.

[587] Three was considered among the pagan nations as the chief of the mystical numbers, because, as Aristotle remarks, it contains within itself a beginning, middle, and an end. — Mack. Lex., p. 313.

being in that volume which was dictated by the third person in the Trinity. God is manifested on every page of that immortal work. And, by the aid of its eternal light, we can perceive luminous traces of his goodness, mercy, and truth, in the external universe. Without the assistance of express revelation, we would be able to follow effect to cause; but with that revelation, we find a name for that cause—the Creator and Builder of the universe—an omnipotent, omniscient, and omnipresent God. And although we might survey, without that Great Light, the beautiful realms of nature, and adore an unknown Spirit, it is in the Bible that we are made familiar with his name, and obtain a sure knowledge of his power, wisdom, and mercy. It is there, and there only, that we have marked out that path which leads to the habitation of our heavenly Master, where the mysteries of the God head will be revealed to all his followers. And in heaven only will be brought to light the wonders of Revelation. While the soul inhabits the flesh—its earthly lodge—it can never fully embrace the mysteries of redemption or the incommunicable truth of the Trinity. We must enter the temple of the New Jerusalem, and be raised in its holy of holies, before the heavenly knowledge will be imparted. We may linger here on some Pisgah of Christian hope, and dream of the Promised Land, where the just made perfect dwell; but it is only from the summits of eternal glory that we can behold scenes of essential beauty and peace. And there are heights in the spirit-world to be scaled—holy mountains to be ascended. We may infer from the revelations of St. John the divine, that the Holy Land, with its rich and magnificent scenery, its mountains and ancient city, exists in a new and resplendent beauty, in that world of "harpers harping with their harps." Our patron Saint may not have seen in reality the glories of the upper kingdom, with its mountains gleaming in the light of eternity, or its city "with its walls of jasper, its gates of pearl, and its streets of pure gold." But there is a city above, and there is a mystic temple which towers on the celestial Moriah; and he either saw them as they are, or through the medium of types and figures, splendid illustrations, or brilliant imagery. His prophetic soul beheld the coming down of the New Jerusalem. He saw afar off the new heavens and new earth. And when will the King of Israel come? When will the King of Glory descend? When shall the Mighty Master approach? "The Lord our God is one Lord." Father, Son, and Holy Ghost are one. "Glory be to God in the highest, peace on earth, and good will toward men."

Charles Scott

LECTURE XV.
Conclusion

I am but one, and I always distrust myself. I only hint my thoughts. You'll please consider whether you will not think that it may seem to deserve your consideration.[588]

They listen'd; for unto their ear,
The word, which they had long'd to hear,
Had come at last—the lifeful word,—
Which they had often almost heard.[589]

Meditation here
May think down hours to moments. Here the heart
May give a useful lesson to the head,
And learning wiser grow without his books.[590]

---

[588] Asgill [sic] E. N.: Scott takes the quote from Robert Southey, *The Doctor &c.*, He cites Asgill in the contents, under the description of the Interchapter V., and is found in all editions.

[589] Trench. E. N.: R.C. Trench, quoted in Churton, *op. cit.*, p. 52.

Jesus Christ is the name given to the Savior of man-kind[591]. All Christians believe him to be the true Messiah,

---

[590] William Cowper, *The Works of Cowper and Thompson*, Philadelphia, 1853, p. 94.

[591] Josephus testifies to the person and even to the Divinity of Christ. He says: Now, about this time, Jesus, a wise man, if it be lawful to call him a man, for he was a doer of wonderful works, a teacher of such men as receive the truth with pleasure. He was the Christ. And when Pilate, at the suggestion of the principal men amongst us, had condemned him to the cross, those that loved him at first did not forsake him; for he appeared to them alive again the third day, as the divine prophets had foretold these and ten thousand other wonderful things concerning him. — Antiq. of the Jews, b. 17, ch. 3, p. 364.

E. N.: A long time since this quote it has been proven that Jesus was never mentioned by Josephus, at least not in a manner most people would recognize. In fact, two paragraphs doctored in the Middle Ages by some unknown monk are the only explicit references found in Josephus's entire body of work and are undoubtedly not in the original—including the one quoted above, not to mention those that we know were deleted! We cannot, however, blame Scott for this error, as in his time the quote was generally accepted to be correct, and the Greek Orthodox Church believed in it to the point of appending Josephus's work to the New Testament as sacred writ. Vide: William Wright Hardwicke, *The Evolution of Man*, London, 1899, p. 194:

"In the Antiquities of Josephus (xiii.3) an obvious interpolation has been made, as is shown by a purple patch in the original, different to the rest of the MS., between an account of a sedition by the Jews against Pontius Pilate and an account of Anubis and Pauline in the temple of Isis. This is brought forward as historical evidence in favour of the Messiah's actual existence; but it is a clear and distinct insertion, and possesses all the evidences of being a forgery, causing a break in the continuity of the narrative. Josephus —a Jew, be it observed—is made to say: 'Now there was about this time Jesus, a wise man, *if it be lawful to call him a man,* for he was a doer of wonderful works; a teacher of such men as receive *the truth* with pleasure.' Now, it is not likely that a Jew would show such a respect towards Jesus, who was known among his own people as a seditious person; and talk about his teaching 'the truth.' Further on he is made to say: '*He was the Christ,* and when Pilate had condemned him to the cross, those that loved him at the first did not forsake him; for he appeared to them alive again the third day, as the divine prophets had foretold these *and ten thousand other wonderful things* concerning him.' These are expressions, not of a *Jew,* but of a

---

through whose death, resurrection, and ascension was achieved the redemption of the world. He is the Great King and Deliverer, for whose advent all previous time had been preparing, and of whom the prophets spoke, and types also. He came in form and fashion as a man, to accomplish the profound mystery of his wisdom and love. He was God manifest in the flesh[592]. In Him dwelt all the fullness of the Godhead[593]. In his person resided the Divine and human nature. He was the perfect man and the perfect God, which two characters find an apt and sublime illustration in one of the emblems of our Order. If the circumference of the circle be divided into six equal parts, and lines be drawn from point to point through the circle, there will be obtained a double equilateral triangle, or two triangles interlacing each other, within the circle, the apex of one pointing upwards to Divinity, and the apex of the other downward to humanity[594]—the upper triangle representing the perfect God, and the lower triangle the perfect man.

Christian; and surely the writer could not have remained a Jew another hour!

Forgeries were easy in those days, when books were written on skins or papyrus, to which fresh pieces could be attached. Another interpolation, and the only other one which mentions Jesus, is also found (xx., ix. 1) where the words in italics are shown to have been surreptitiously inserted in the original: 'He assembled the Sanhedrim of Judges, and brought before them *the brother of Jesus, who was called the Christ, whose name was* James, and some others,' etc."

A good synopsis may also be found in Robert Eisenman, *James, the Brother of Jesus*; Penguin, 1998, pp. 26, 65-9, 401-2.

[592] 1 Timothy 3:16.

[593] Colossians 2 9.

[594] "If you take a very accurate pair of compasses," says the enlightened Willoughby of Birkenhead, "set to a certain radius, and describe a circle, then, without altering the radius, you divide the circumference, you obtain seven points, including the point within the centre, which is the number of perfection, and will give you the cube with seven stars and the double equilateral triangle, the latter being the emblem of Christ—the perfect God and perfect man. The apex pointing upwards, alluding to his Divinity, that pointing downwards to his humanity." — 1 Ol. Land., p. 174, n. 53.

The triangle was regarded by the ancients as a symbol or emblem of Deity. "It still retains that allusion," says Mackey, "as an emblem of Freemasonry." Among the Hebrews the ineffable name of God was expressed by a *yod* in the centre of an equilateral triangle[595]. Many have supposed that the triangle had a reference to the Trinity. Such seems to be the opinion of Dr. Oliver, Hutchinson, and other distinguished Masons. There certainly cannot be found a more remarkable emblem of the Divine and human nature of our Savior than the double equilateral triangle to which we have alluded. The circle[596], in which it is obtained, is itself a symbol of the Almighty, while the common centre of the circle is the point from which all perfect forms emanate. The equilateral triangles are found within the circle; they interlace each other, and are inseparable. The persons of the Trinity have a "mutual inexistence and permeation of one another." The Divine and human nature of Jesus Christ proceeded from God. The Divinity resided in humanity, and humanity was inseparable from the Divinity; and they were so blended as to excite our admiration and engage our love. The triangles are united. And mercy and truth met together in Christ, and righteousness and peace kissed each other[597]. It was requisite that the Divine and human nature should meet together in one person. It was essential that the Messiah should be both a perfect man and a perfect God. It was necessary that he should be perfect, for such a high priest became us, who is holy, harmless, undefiled,

---

[595] Mack. Lex.

[596] At sea, the visible horizon, or the line bounding the visible portion of the earth's surface, is everywhere a circle, of greater or less extent, according to the altitude of the point of observation. — Nor. Astron., p. 1. Navigators have sailed around the earth, and, steering their course in one direction, have arrived at the place from which they started. The polar star is not stationary, but describes a small circle. The diurnal motion of the stars is circular. The path of the sun is a circle.

[597] Psalms 85:10.

separate from sinners, and made higher than the heavens[598]. He offered himself through the Eternal Spirit, without spot to God[599].

The Almighty may be compared to the common centre of the universe. A circle may be described from any centre, at any distance from that centre. All straight lines drawn from the centre to the circumference are equal to one another[600]. The equilateral triangles which may be obtained in the circle may be viewed as emblems of infinity. Their equal sides commence in the circumference and end in it. How beautifully, then, does the circle and the perfect figures which may be obtained in it represent that harmony and order which pervade every part of God's universe. All that He has made is perfect from the centre to the circumference. "The circle of the universe has its centre everywhere and its circumference nowhere."

There is mention made, in our charts, of the Lion of the tribe of Judah; and who did the Lion of the tribe of Judah symbolize? The tribe of Judah had a lion embroidered on its ensigns, and the lion was adopted as a symbol of that tribe. Judah is a lion's whelp[601]. The lion hath roared, who will not fear?[602] The Lord also shall roar out of Zion[603]. Behold, says the Evangelist, the Lion of the tribe of Judah, the root of David, hath prevailed to open the book, and to loose the seven seals thereof[604]. Jesus Christ, then, is called

---

[598] Hebrews 7:26.

[599] Hebrews 9:14.

[600] Euclid's Elements.

[601] Genesis 49:9. Under the symbol of a lion, says Dean Woodhouse, it pleased the Holy Spirit, by the mouth of the patriarch, to foretell the victorious superiority of the tribe of Judah, which was seen to take place partially and typically in the person of David and his successors, but was to receive a more sublime and final completion in Christ.

[602] Amos 3:8.

[603] Joel 3:16.

[604] Revelation 5:5.

the Lion of the tribe of Judah. All our Masonic manuals speak of the Lion of the tribe of Judah, through whom the Christian Mason expects to be raised in the morn of the resurrection.

The power of Christ to raise the dead was triumphantly displayed while he tabernacled in the flesh. When he cried with a loud voice, Lazarus, come forth; he that was dead came forth, bound hand and foot in his grave clothes; and his face was bound about with a napkin[605]. But mark what the Lord did before he bade the dead arise. Jesus, groaning in himself, cometh to the grave. He was the while holding communion with the Father; for when the stone was rolled away from the tomb of Lazarus, he lifted up his eyes and said: Father, I thank thee that thou hast heard me[606]. The enlightened Mason is acquainted with the necessity of that holy prayer on that occasion, or of invoking the aid of the Supreme God, through whose energies alone could the dead be raised. Solomon knew that the power of resurrecting the dead resided in the Godhead. Jesus relied upon the Father. How mild and gentle are those words: "Father, I thank thee." How confident and majestic the command: "Lazarus, come forth." How awful was the summons! How quickly was it obeyed. He spake, and Lazarus came forth! If we would be raised in glory, we must pray for ourselves to the Father of all mercies. Jesus prayed to the Father for power to raise up Lazarus; and he groaned and wept for us, and cried with a loud voice, when he gave up the ghost. He has taught us how to pray, and the fervent prayer must go up to the throne from off the altar of the heart, to beget a lively hope of a glorious resurrection. It will be too late to pray when the Son of man comes to judge the earth. Doomsday will afford no time for meditation or prayer. It will be a day of awful transactions and strict settlement of accounts. The ear of mercy will then be deaf to the cries of

---

[605] John 11:43.

[606] John 11:41.

the wicked, and the mountains will not hide them from the face of the Judge.

There are three steps and three degrees in symbolical Masonry. Each step or degree is an advance toward light and knowledge. There is more revealed in the Fellow craft's degree than in the degree of Entered Apprentice, and there is a fullness of light and knowledge in the degree of Master. Mankind, before the appearance of the Messiah, had been partially instructed under the patriarchal and Levitical dispensations. But the world was then comparatively in darkness. More light was wanted, and the Messiah came to give more light, to teach and instruct the world in the mysteries of his kingdom. A bright Mason is one enlightened in the degrees, and illuminated with truth. Darkness is the reverse of light. It is symbolical of ignorance and sin. The testimony of the scriptural types from the beginning of the Mosaic dispensation was rendered more and more lucid, until their light was merged in the greater light of the antitype. The manifestations of our Redeemer were not sudden; but in the language of an eminent writer: "His rising upon the world resembled the rising of the natural sun: preceded by the dawn, the twilight and preparatory glories of the east, at length he himself appeared, clothed in radiant and serene majesty."

Now, Christ raised the dead only three times, and at each successive time a greater power was displayed. In the case of Jairus's daughter, the maid had been dead but a very short time. When Jesus went to the ruler's house, and saw the minstrels and people making a noise[607], he said unto them: Give place: for the maid is not dead, but sleepeth[608]. He took her by the hand, and the maid arose.

The son of the widow of Nain had been dead a longer time. He was being carried to his grave, when Christ came

---

[607] It was customary among the Jews to employ minstrels or pipers to play mournful tunes, &c. upon a funeral occasion.

[608] Matthew 9.

and touched the bier, and they that bore him stood still: and he said: Young man, I say unto thee, arise. And he that was dead sat up, and began to speak[609]. The third and last time that Christ exercised the power of raising the dead, was in the case of Lazarus. He was buried and had been dead about four days. Corruption had begun its work. His spirit was to be called back to its polluted tenement. By the omnipotent grasp of the Almighty, Lazarus was raised from decay and death. Jesus groaned, and prayed, and wept, on his way to the tomb of his friend. Yes! Jesus wept! He called his body a temple. He wept. Then there were sorrow- and mourning in that temple. But if Lazarus was lost in death, his life was found again. The Son of God had offered up his holy prayer.

> *He ceased,*
> *And for a minute's space there was a hush*
> *As if th' angelic watchers of the world*
> *Had stay'd the pulses of all breathing things*
> *To listen to that prayer. The face of Christ*
> *Shone as he stood, and over him there came*
> *Command, as 'twere the living face of God,*
> *And with a loud voice, he cried, "Lazarus!*
> *Come forth!"*[610]

There were witnesses to these three great events. And there were mourners too for the departed. The fame of these events went abroad throughout all the land. The occurrence of raising Lazarus was altogether unexpected. No one present could anticipate by what word or process the miracle was to be wrought.

Nain was situated about two miles south of Mount Tabor, on the brow of a hill[611]. It was at the gates of that city,

---

[609] Luke 7:14-15.

[610] Nathaniel Parker Willis, *Poems of Early and After Years*, Philadelphia, 1848, p. 81.

[611] Nain was a small city or town in Galilee, not far from Nazareth, at the gates of which our Savior raised to life a widow's only son. Eusebius

and while the funeral procession was at the declivity of the Mount, the miracle of restoring the widow's son was performed. Lazarus lived at Bethany, which was near the city of Jerusalem. He was buried in Bethany. This miraculous event throws a flood of light over our ancient lectures[612]. Bethany is situated on the eastern brow of Olivet. It is supposed that Lazarus was entombed in a rock hewn out on the side of the Mount. The tomb was so conveniently situated that several persons could encircle it. And several persons went to his grave and saw him raised from the dead.

We have frequently alluded to the innocence of our first parents in the Garden of Eden. Adam was made upright. He was tried by the rule of God's measurement, and was found upright. One of the first lessons impressed upon the mind of a Mason is, that he should be upright. Every Entered Apprentice and Fellow Craft engaged at the building of Solomon's temple were enjoined to be obedient to the will of their masters. God planted a garden eastward in Eden[613], and there he put the man whom he had formed, that he should dress and keep it; and the Lord commanded him, saying, Of every tree of the garden thou mayest freely eat; but of the tree of the knowledge of good and evil, thou shalt not eat of it: for the day thou eatest thereof thou shalt surely die[614]. The command of God was violated. Adam's desire for knowledge was too great. He became impatient. The tree was desirable to make one wise. He ate of its fruit; and what was the consequence? Its

---

places it about two miles to the south of Mount Tabor, situated on the declivity of a mountain. — 2 Pict. Dict., p. 917.

[612] Jesus Christ led his disciples out as far as Bethany, and he lifted up his eyes and blessed them. And it came to pass that while he blessed them, he was parted from them, and carried up into heaven. — Luke 24:50-51.

[613] The Garden of Eden, like the temple of Solomon, was an emblem of the church upon earth.

[614] Genesis 2:16-17.

"Mortal taste
Brought death into the world, and all our woe
With loss of Eden."

Death was the penalty of the crime: "Dust thou art, and unto dust shalt thou return." But there were other consequences. *Original purity was lost.* This was a universal calamity. It involved all posterity. Every human being on the earth—the ground-floor of God's temple, became tainted with the crime. Although the descendants of Adam had no actual part in the violation of the law, still they were mysteriously connected with that singular event. They must needs be involved. It could not be otherwise, and consistent with the integrity of heaven and steadfastness of .the Almighty. The whole was wisely agreed upon and determined in the council-chamber of eternity by the Triune God. The Lamb had been slain from the foundation of the world[615]. The death, resurrection, and ascension of our Savior were all necessary means of restoration, God provided a remedy for our ruined nature from all eternity: propitiation was made for sin the moment it was committed.

The church of God rests upon and rises up over the grave of Jesus. Its materials were being pre pared during his short ministry. The temple could not be built or completed until after his death. When Jesus was about to expire on the cross, he cried out, "It is finished." His work was done, his earthly agonies were over. He had been rejected; but have ye not read in the Scriptures, The stone which the builders rejected, the same is become the head of the corner?[616] These words were originally spoken by David, and they are quoted no less than six times in the New Testament. They referred to the Messiah. David saw afar off that precious

---

[615] The scheme of redemption by the death of the only begotten Son of God was determined from the beginning; that is, when God ordained the deliverance of man, he ordained the means. — D'Oyly and Mant's Com., Genesis 4:4.

[616] Luke 20:17.

cornerstone which was rejected, and knew it would become the head of the corner. He spoke of the event as having already happened. The stone which the builders refused is become the head stone of the corner[617]. Bishop Horne says that the 118th Psalm is a "triumphal hymn, sung by King Messiah, at the head of the Israel of God on the occasion of his resurrection and ascension." Our Savior, then, was compared to a corner stone, rejected of men, who were the chief priests and rulers of the Jews[618]. He was crucified and cast into the rubbish of the grave The expression rejected, says Dr. Clarke, is one borrowed from Masons, who, finding a stone, which being tried in a particular place, and appearing improper for it, is thrown aside, and another taken; however, at last, it may happen that the very stone which had been before rejected, may be found the most suitable as the head stone of the corner.[619]

Evil came into the world through disobedience and an inordinate desire for knowledge of the heavenly mysteries. The innocence of nature was lost, and it could only be restored in one way. Christ died for us, and through his merits only can we ever find that which was lost. His blood was shed for us. He died for all mankind. We believe that every Entered Apprentice who wrought at the building of Solomon's temple, would have been entitled, if found worthy, to enter upon the Master's carpet when that temple was completed. Three Master-Workmen, of one mind and one feeling, presided over the work. Three persons and one

---

[617] Psalms 118:22.

[618] Christ is sometimes spoken of as the foundation of the church. He is also called the chief corner stone of it. He is also called the great builder of it. This, says the Rev. Charles Bradley, is the ordinary way of the inspired writers. Christ they knew to be all in all. No one figure, they see, can set forth his importance. Therefore they apply figure after figure to him. — 2 Brad. Ser., p. 264.

[619] It is said that Adam Clarke was a Free Mason, and from the light which he has shed upon various passages in the Bible, there can be little room to doubt the statement. It is stated that Bishop Horne and Calmet were Free Masons.

God constructed the temple of the universe. The infinite goodness and benignity of the .Almighty, from his wonderful plans and designs, could only restore our fallen nature through the death, resurrection, and ascension of his only begotten Son, who esteemed it not robbery to be called equal with the Father. It may be here remarked, that there were three parties to original sin. And there is a triple alliance,—of the world, the flesh, and the devil. And there is a Holy Trinity—the Father, Son, and Holy Ghost.

While man conformed to the will of his Maker, all was harmony, beauty, and innocence. While Adam retained his integrity and was obedient, there was no confusion in the beautiful temple of the universe. Everything went on regularly. There was perfect order. But upon the fall, there came confusion and disorder. Adam gained nothing by his transgression, save a knowledge of good and evil, which was obtained at the expense of forfeiting that which he had. *Death was the consequence of his act.* The Lord would not permit him to remain in the garden, and sent him beyond its gates, on his way to ruin and death. The covenant was broken, and he could continue in Paradise no longer. He must leave the seat of bliss, and once the seat of innocence. The judgment is pronounced. The awful sentence is passed.

He departs, and cherubim, with flaming swords, as sentinels of divine justice, take their station at the east of the garden, to keep the way of the tree of life.

As soon as our first parents transgressed, they endeavored to conceal themselves and escape from the presence and justice of God. They knew that they were guilty, and fled and hid themselves among the trees of the garden. Their efforts to escape were vain. They were found near the scene of their guilt, and brought to punishment. All the parties to the deed were condemned, and each one received a different punishment. *There* were three penalties. The serpent was cursed above all cattle and above every beast of the field. The sentence was pronounced: Upon thy belly shalt thou go, and dust shalt thou eat all the days of thy life[620]. Unto the woman he said, I will greatly multiply thy sorrow and thy conception; in sorrow shalt thou bring forth children; and thy desire shall be to thy husband, and he shall rule over thee. And unto Adam he said: In the sweat of thy face shalt thou eat bread, till thou return unto the ground; for dust thou art, and unto dust shalt thou return[621].

The act of eating the forbidden fruit was a sin of commission. And had not sin been committed, there would have been no redemption; for the covenant would not have been violated, and consequently there would not have been any ground for reconciliation[622]. But the will of God was disobeyed, and had not Christ suffered and died, not one of Adam's race could have entered the holy of holies in the temple of God. In our view, the posterity of Adam gained much mediately from the transgression. God will be justified, and every Christian will "be reconciled, adopted, sanctified," and brought to greater light and glory. The church of Christ has been *substituted* or established on earth, and there is also a church in heaven. Then there is a church militant and a church triumphant. No Mason can be exalted, unless he has taken the Master's degree. The one necessarily precedes the other. The church militant is on earth—the church triumphant in heaven. Had not Jesus died, there would have been no church here and none above. We would have been without a plan of redemption, or the means of regaining the favor of an offended God or his ineffable mercy. True, we have to pass through many trials and difficulties— ravel many dangerous paths in life, and

---

[620] Three things are involved in the curse pronounced upon the serpent: 1st: The stature of the serpent, which many persons supposed to have been erect, was brought down. 2nd: The serpent was to feed upon the dust. 3rd: There was continual enmity to exist between the serpent and mankind.

[621] Genesis 3.

[622] The two great cardinal events in the history of man are the fall and the recovery. Innocence, being lost, was to be restored.

many roads beset with all kinds of temptations, and may possibly lose life eternal, and which is full of glory. But there is much efficiency in prayer—silent prayer and holy meditation. The sinner should often retire alone to pray, and kneel, as it were, in the very presence of his Master. His thoughts and aspirations must ascend to the holy of holies in eternity, where God is manifested in mercy and glory. Answered prayer will enable us to encounter all danger and peril, and to pass safely the gates of death; for we will then be on our way to the temple of the Lord, and pass its arches in search of long lost innocence. The Christian, when he goes down into the grave, will be consoled with the beautiful sentiment: "He that humbleth himself shall be exalted."

In our monitors it is written, that the third degree exemplifies an instance of virtue, fortitude, and integrity unparalleled in the history of man. But the prophet Isaiah gives an affecting picture of virtue, fortitude, and integrity, without a parallel in the universe. He was despised and rejected of men; he came to his own, and his own received him not; he was stricken, smitten of God, and afflicted; he was taken away by distress and by judgment; he was cut off out of the land of the living; his grave was with the wicked, but he was with the rich after his death; his visage was marred more than any man's, and his form more than the sons of men; he was stricken upon various parts of his body; he had done no violence, neither was there any deceit in his mouth; the chastisement of our peace was upon him, and with his stripes we are healed.

The ruling principle of ancient craft Masonry, we believe, is to illustrate biblical truth. Divested of this principle, the institution is deprived of all its beauty and power. But when its mysteries and doctrines are investigated in connection with those contained in Divine revelation, and it is found that they harmonize; we are delighted with their consistency, and astonished at their grandeur, while we feel assured that Masonry may be made a great instrument in spreading the gospel and in convincing the skeptical.

Nearly eighteen hundred and fifty years have elapsed since our Lord appeared upon the earth in his Divine and human character. Sin came into the world soon after the creation of man. The plan of redemption embraced all men in all ages. Upon the ruins of the first estate arose the mediatorial kingdom. "With the rebellion came the surety. The eternal word and eternal life were vouchsafed when the Lamb was slain in the midst of the throne.

In the fourth chapter of the gospel according to St. Matthew, is contained a graphic account of the temptation of our Savior. The prince of evil insidiously attacked the Master, but his Divine integrity and truth could not be made to yield. Jesus was tempted at *three* different places, at *three* distinct times, and in *three* different ways, but how firmly he resisted the suggestions of the devil! The first temptation was in the wilderness. It failed. The devil then took him up into the holy city, and set him on a pinnacle of the temple[623], and there tempted him. The resistance of the Savior seemed to wax stronger, and he said to the devil: "It is written again, Thou shalt not tempt the Lord thy God." And again the evil one "taketh him up into an exceeding high mountain, and showeth him all the kingdoms of the world, and the glory of them ; and saith unto him, All these things will I give thee, if thou wilt fall down and worship me." At this last trial, the Lord became, if possible, more decided and positive, and said: "Get thee hence, Satan: for it is written, Thou shalt worship the Lord thy God, and him only shalt thou serve."

The best of Masons are liable to be tempted. There are many evil persons ready to assail them, even thrice, and at times when they least expect an assault. If tempted, it is our

---

[623] A wing of the temple; that is, a part of the roof of one of its courts. — D'Oyly and Mant's Com., Matthew 4.

duty to repel at once the unlawful act, and resist it with firmness and decision.

The devil is called the tempter in Matthew's gospel; and the word which means tempter or trier, in the original Greek, signifies to pierce through[624]. It would seem, then, that the object of Satan's attack was three-fold—to humble Christ, to prove him, and to know what was in his heart. He would not be humbled by the enemy of mankind, but proved himself firm and steadfast, and Satan knew not what was in his heart.

It is a well known fact, that all the Entered Apprentice Masons in the world cannot make an Entered Apprentice Mason; nor can any number of Fellow Crafts do it; nor can any number of Fellow Crafts make a Fellow Craft. None but Master Masons can confer a degree, and it requires at least *three* Master Masons to make a Master Mason. They must unite and agree in the work, which can be done only in one way. Mankind can only be saved in one way. We must go through the process of regeneration: *Every man in his own order; first Christ, and they that come after him.* Christ tasted of death: so must we. He rose again: so must all the earth. *He knew and obeyed the commandment of the Father, what he should say and what he should speak. Whatever he spoke, therefore, even as the Father said unto him, so he spoke*[625]. The apostle Paul, speaking of Christ, says: If we be dead with him, we shall also live with him; if we suffer, we shall also reign with him[626]. And where is the body of Christ? It is in the real holy of holies. There is the seat of eternal mercy and the abode of cherubim. Knowledge of God or his holy word can only be imparted in one way, and as it is received it can only be imparted. The sinner must ask before he can expect the favor of Heaven; he must seek before he can find it; and he must knock before the door will be opened unto

---

[624] Clarke's Com., Matthew 4:3.

[625] John 12:49-50.

[626] 2 Timothy 2:11-12.

him. He, too, must begin the good work, before the word of God will be regularly and spiritually communicated. Its golden letters spell salvation. He, who would prove himself worthy, must commence in a way to make himself known; for his commencement is the alpha or beginning of wisdom.

We have assimilated the ground floor of Solomon's temple to the earth, the inner chamber to the region of the stars, and the holy of holies to heaven[627]. The Father gave to his only begotten Son the kingdoms of the earth. The Redeemer came down from heaven to the earth—from the holy of holies to the ground floor. And he was above all[628]. He was the Master; and being equal with the Father and the Spirit, had knowledge of all mysteries. He existed from all eternity to make intercession for us. He was born of the Virgin Mary, but conceived by the Holy Ghost. The Holy Virgin is represented under the *three-fold* description of her name, condition, and action. Her name was Mary, her condition a virgin, and her action the conception and birth of Christ[629]. Hiram, the builder, was the son of a widow; and, so far as we are informed, he was the first and only son of that widow.[630] Sanctify unto me all the first born[631]. Every male that openeth the womb shall be called holy to the Lord[632]. A widow, too, is mentioned as an object of peculiar interest in the Scriptures: Judge the fatherless, plead for the widow[633]. Oppress not the stranger, the fatherless, and

---

[627] Vide supra, page 12 and note.

[628] John 3:31.

[629] Pearson on the Creed, p. 265.

[630] It is remarkable that the Bible should contain so little about the life and character of this builder.

[631] Exodus 13:2.

[632] Luke 2:23.

[633] Isaiah 1:17.

the widow[634]. Ye shall not afflict any widow or fatherless child[635]. The Lord preserveth the strangers; he relieveth the fatherless and widow[636].

But Christ calleth himself the Master Builder. While on earth he was constantly going about doing good. He taught in the synagogue, in the highway, and in the market-place. He was continually instructing his disciples—his pious workmen—in the great principles upon which his church was to be founded, the doctrines of the Christian religion. He made known those vast designs which were drawn on his tracing-board, and instructed the world in the plan of his glorious undertaking. He also spoke of an inheritance in store for all who proved themselves worthy. But Judas lost confidence in his Master and betrayed him. He was handed over to his enemies, tried, condemned, and crucified on the earth, on one of the *three* peaks of Mount Moriah, near where the old temple stood. He was, it may be said, literally slain on the ground floor of that temple, for its foundations were made of clay taken from Calvary. And it is a curious fact in the eye of a Mason, that when the Jews cried out against the release of Jesus, Pilate heard them and brought Jesus forth and sat him down in the judgment-seat, in a place that was called *the pavement.* And it was the preparation of the Passover and about the *sixth hour,* which was *midday*[637]. The pavement alluded to, says a compiler, was no doubt a *tessellated pavement* of *Mosaic work,* in front of the palace of Pilate, where the sentence of crucifixion was pronounced.

Pilate, the judge who condemned our Savior to suffer death, protested his innocence. He did not take any part in the execution, but he was privy to the transaction. He was

---

[634] Jeremiah 7:6.

[635] Exodus 22:22.

[636] Psalms 146:9.

[637] John 19:13-14.

reluctant to condemn him, or enter into the conspiracy against him. And it is a signal truth, that he made an attempt to deliver Christ out of the hands of the Jews. After he failed in this, what did he? When Pilate saw that he could do nothing, and that the design of the conspirators would be carried into execution, he took water and washed his hands, saying, I am innocent of the blood of this just person. And then answered they that were concerned in the plot, His blood be on us, and on our children[638].

The Christian world regard the death of our Savior as a murder[639]. He was not tried according to the forms of law. Having passed a mock trial, which eventuated in acquittal, such was the violence of the mob and the timidity of the judge, he was again arraigned. The charge preferred against him was blasphemy, and of that crime he was convicted. There was another accusation, that of treason. The plot to take his life had been made some time before he was taken prisoner. His death had been fully resolved upon from the time he raised Lazarus. Then gathered the chief priests and the Pharisees a council, and said: What do we? For this man doeth many miracles. If we let him thus alone, all men will believe on him; and the Romans shall come and take away both our place and nation. And one of them, named Caiaphas, being the high priest that same year, said unto them, Ye know nothing at all, nor consider that it is expedient for us that one man should die for the people, and that the whole nation perish not. And this spake he not of himself: but being high priest that year, he prophesied that Jesus should die for that nation: and not for that nation only, but that also he should gather together in one the children of God that were scattered abroad. Then from that

---

[638] Matthew 27:24-25.

[639] For a concise view and accurate account of the trial of Jesus, the reader is referred to Greenleaf's *Testimony of the Evangelists* [*op. cit*], Appendix No. 4, p. 520.

day forth they took counsel together, for to put him to death[640].

The first step taken against the Messiah accomplished nothing. Political excitement could not be brought to bear effectually against him. The second effort was to awaken against him a religious animosity, which also failed. Then a certain lawyer interrogated him, tempting him, saying, Master, which is the greatest commandment in the law? The reply of the Savior put him to confusion and silence. Then these *open* attempts against the life of that pure and holy being *all failed.* It was therefore determined to secure his person secretly. He was betrayed by Judas, one of the twelve; charged with blasphemy and also with treason. The Sanhedrim found him guilty of blasphemy, but possessed no power to pass sentence of death[641]. The crime was such that the Roman Governor could not notice it under the law. He was then arraigned for treason, and acquitted. He was arraigned a third time, tried, convicted, and crucified. So he was tried three times before the conspirators accomplished their object.

Every Mason should keep in view the important fact that before Christ was betrayed and taken by his enemies, he retired alone to pray, or hold communion with the Father. He was sorrowful. He anticipated his death. He knew the time was near at hand when he must lay down his life, the just for the unjust. When he reached Gethsemane, he said unto his disciples, Sit ye here, while I go and pray yonder. He retired, and fell on his face and prayed. And he prayed *three* different times the same prayer: O my Father, if it be possible, let this cup pass from me: nevertheless not as

---

[640] John 11:47-53.

[641] Though the Sanhedrim had condemned him, they had not the power to pass a capital sentence; this being a right which had passed from the Jews by conquest of their country, and now belonged to the Romans alone. — Greenleaf, op. cit., Appendix, p. 526.

I will, but as thou wilt[642]. It would seem that he knew that there was no escape through his own earthly strength; he prayed to the Father, who sealed his death. If this cup may not pass from me, except I drink it, thy will be done[643]. In the fervent and agonizing petitions of Jesus, his human nature manifested the deepest distress. The cup of which he drank was full of bitterness. There were none to save him. His own strong arm of Divinity was uplifted for his death: the Holy Spirit was a party to the deed: and the Father willed that he should die. He prayed to the Father in vain. His disciples, when he was betrayed, were taking *refreshment* in sleep: And he cometh unto his disciples and findeth them asleep, and saith unto Peter, What, could ye not watch with me *one hour?*[644] He was seized and carried before Pilate; he was tried, condemned, and crucified. He died on Calvary. A grave was *prepared* for his body. It was a new-made tomb. And where was it? "Come and see where Jesus lay." It was at or near the scene of crucifixion. He reposed at the foot of "the throne of the thunder." The place of the holy sepulcher is supposed by many to be immediately under the dome of the Church of the Holy Sepulcher, and that church is situated on the supposed Mount of crucifixion[645]. He was buried near the place of his crucifixion. Jesus died! His death was a gradual work. It was not accomplished at a single blow; but it was consummated, and he died for all. The star in our checkered pavement would teach the brethren that he died that all might have eternal life. That pavement is an emblem of human life—made up of various thoughts, feelings, wants, affections, sympathies,

---

[642] It was in the cave of Gethsemane, at the foot of the Mount of Olives, that Christ retired, according to tradition, to escape sometimes from the persecution of his enemies and the importunities of his disciples. — 1 Lam. Phil., p. 302.

[643] Matthew 26:36. These words ought to be the epitaph of every life, and the sole aspiration of every created being. — Ibid.

[644] Matthew 26:40.

[645] 1 Pict. Dict., p. 679.

and vicissitudes, like Mosaic work, which is composed of a number of precious and variegated stones, all nicely fitted and blended together. In the midst of that pavement is our emblematical star. Men and brethren! The heavens are shining above you. "A diadem is sparkling in the firmament." A radiant delta is visible in our clouded canopy.

When our Lord cried out with a loud voice and gave up the ghost, the veil was rent in twain from the top to the bottom. There was great confusion on the Mount. Even silence reigned in heaven. Darkness threw her mantle over the earth. There was moaning among his disciples. They knew not what to do. Their Master was dead. Nature was distracted with grief. The earthquake shook the mountains. The rocks were rent, and "opened their dumb mouths," to condemn the guilty murderers. There were voices in the very clefts of the adjacent hills, and they were the voices of condemnation. The rocks uttered groans of lamentation. The earth tasted of the innocent blood, and was filled with grief. And all the people that came together to that sight, beholding the things which were done, smote their breasts, and returned[646]. How dark must have been that hour when the Son of man expired! But his death was a mighty triumph. It was heralded throughout the universe. The world, the flesh, and the devil were overthrown. The song of victory was hymned in eternity. Its lofty notes filled the realms of immensity. The Savior had conquered death and hell. An angel of the Lord had descended from heaven and rolled back the stone from the sepulcher. He rose from the dead. The victorious sleeper leaped from the tomb. The powers of darkness could not hold him there. He tarried for a season on the earth. Having finished his work, he led his disciples to the Mount of Olives, and after pronouncing a solemn benediction, "he was parted from them and carried up into heaven."

---

[646] Luke 23:48.

"Now, lifted as on mighty wing,
He curtain'd his ascent,
And, wrapt in clouds, went triumphing
Above the firmament."

Angels herald him to glory. "They precede his approach, and boldly on his behalf demand entrance into the realms of light."[647] "Lift up your heads, 0 ye gates;" they cry, "and be ye lift up, ye everlasting doors; and the King of glory shall come in." A voice is heard from heaven asking, "Who is the King of glory?" "The Lord strong and mighty, the Lord mighty in battle," is the reply. And again they exclaim: "Lift up your heads, 0 ye gates; even lift them up, ye everlasting doors; and the King of glory shall come in."[648] Again the heavenly keepers inquire: "Who is the King of glory? The Lord of Hosts, he is the King of glory." The golden gates are opened wide, and he enters the New Jerusalem.

He was attended by a splendid procession of angels arrayed in white. He was seen in his ascended state. John saw him; so did St. Stephen and St. Paul. And he ascended from a Mount. He was conducted to the temple on high. He appeared there as a priest. He opened the way to that most holy place. And in heaven there is an everlasting monument erected to the goodness and greatness of God. That monument is his human nature, upon which is delineated an inscription of his sufferings and his death—his mercy and truth. It was reared in honor and in memory of the dying man. It is a most beautiful structure, and is situated at the

---

[647] Bishop Horne, commenting on the 24th Psalm, says: We roust now form to ourselves an idea of the Lord of glory, after his resurrection from the dead, making his entry into the eternal temple of heaven, as of old by the symbol of his presence, he took possession of that figurative and temporary structure which once stood upon the hill of Zion.

[648] That these words have a secondary, if not a primary, reference to the ascension of our Savior, the reader is referred to an able sermon of one of the most eloquent of living divines. — 1 Mel. Ser., p. 345. See also D'Oyly and Mant's Com.

right hand of the throne. There is no virgin there weeping over it. The recording angel is smiling near it. The Lamb's Book of Life is open before her. Her right hand is inscribing upon its enduring pages the deeds of men; her left is pointing to the church on earth, in which is treasured up the memory of Jesus. And time with his scythe is not there; but a beautiful seraph is unfolding the immortal ringlets of that angel, while she enrolls the names of the blessed.

The death and resurrection of Jesus Christ did not restore what was lost. It was necessary that he should be exalted in his human but glorified nature, in order that redemption might be made complete. There may be salvation, in one sense, in this life; but the righteous must die before they can obtain everlasting salvation. And who can rightly estimate the exaltation of the true believer! He is elevated to the most august degree of knowledge and virtue. "He will be filled with all the goodness of God." The devoted follower of the Lamb will know the name of Jehovah; and will be introduced into the presence of the holy priesthood, that council composed of one in three and three in one.

How simple and beautiful is the expression: "Behold! I stand at the door and knock." It implies that he who knocks has a right to be admitted. It, perhaps, implies something more. He who stands at the door and knocks may not be answered the first time he knocks. Behold! I *stand* at the door and *knock*. And who is he that stands at the door and knocks? One who has a right to come in. He is our Grand Master. Let all the affections of the heart receive him and clap their hands for joy. He has a right to the throne, and to preside over the mysteries of the soul. He would raise all the Entered Apprentices and Fellow Crafts to knowledge of himself. He offers pardon to children: "Remember thy Creator in the days of thy youth, while the evil days come not." We may serve our Master profitably in manhood. He would preside over the young and the manly affections, and prepare them for the world to come. There is the hope of glory here, but the fullness of joy must come hereafter. We must all be tried by our works; bear the burdens of the day, and the trials of time; and we will be tried by our words also. There will be a due examination, before we can meet and mingle with the celestial craft. Lord! Raise us all to the Holy Mount and Holy City!

Immediately preceding the temptation of our Lord, John baptized him, and as he went up out of the water the heavens were opened, and the Spirit of God descended upon him. A voice was heard from heaven saying: This is my beloved Son, in whom I am well pleased. The church was in progress. Its builder had descended from the skies. He was chosen of God. No one else could do the work. The attack of Satan was made just after he had been in the *third* heaven, holding communion with the Father. The arch enemy made his assault in a solitary place, and near about the time when the work of redemption was to be finished. He met Christ alone. And there are enemies which never dare to assail us except in solitude. There are unseen dangers around and about us; and it is generally in private that they carry their nefarious designs into execution. They lie in ambush at every avenue of the heart, to tempt our holy affections and destroy our good resolutions.

All the principles and mysteries of our Order were derived from the East. Every genuine lodge hails from that quarter. The Order originated in that land of marvelous things, a "land of beauty and of grandeur too," and a land still burning with divinity. We trace our mystic knowledge to Jerusalem, that ancient seat of light and wisdom. We turn our faces toward it. Let us approach in a proper manner. Let all our steps be regular and upright. Let us go with a sincere desire to subdue our passions and improve our hearts. We should all be prepared before we presume to wear an emblem of innocence.

Hiram, the chief architect of the first temple, was, in all things, obedient to the will of Solomon. As the work progressed, his obedience became more manifest; and he seemed to grow in his integrity, that he might fully accomplish the end of his labor and skill. And Christ was perfect obedience. The Father's will was to be done: "Not my will, but thine be done." The nearer he approached the completion of his ministry, at each advancing step to the dark and bloody hill, though bending beneath the weight of the cross and the sins of the world; he seemed to become more patient and mild. He was obedient even unto death. His death was an act of perfect obedience. We know not what the Almighty had in keeping for our first parents before the transgression; we know not what knowledge was in store for them if they had proved obedient, and had not yielded to an overweening desire to understand the secrets of heavenly wisdom; but whatever was the design of the Almighty, it was apparently frustrated by the commission of sin. It has been suggested by many divines, that if Adam and Eve had not disobeyed the law, none of our race could have obtained an inheritance in the heavenly kingdom. But as to what were the Divine plans, we are totally ignorant; for they constitute a portion of those ineffable mysteries which centre in the Godhead.

Hiram, the architect, possessed great skill and genius. He was a master builder, and after he had finished all his work, he became, if possible, a more exalted personage. He lives in the cherished recollections of the fraternity, and his virtues are perpetuated in the traditional annals of our Order. Our Savior, after he had performed his labor of mercy, and had been put to a cruel death, was exalted to the right hand of God the Father. Jesus lives in the affectionate remembrance of all his followers. David spoke prophetically, when he said: "The Lord said unto my Lord, Sit thou at my right hand until I make thine enemies thy footstool." It was God the Father who said: "Sit thou at my right hand until I make thine enemies thy footstool." To sit, then, at the right hand denotes power, for the Son of God sits at the right hand of the throne. In approaching the east, the south is to the right hand. The south or midday denotes a bright state, a state of light, divine light[649]. The church is described in holy writ as being situated on the south side of a Mount. The prophet Ezekiel tells us that, "in the visions of God brought He me into the land of Israel, and set me upon a very high mountain, by which was the frame of a city on the south." The mountain referred to by the prophet was Moriah.

We have regarded Hiram, the builder, as a type of the Redeemer. We have been able to draw but a faint sketch of his life and character. We leave his portrait to be drawn by some abler artist, whose pencil of genius will display the beauties of that countenance whose light continues to shine upon the craft. The name and virtues of our ancient Master are embalmed in the recollections of the fraternity of Masons. "Though he be dead, he still lives." While we cherish the memory of our departed friend, we look forward full of hope. A light is shining upon the margin of the grave. Whenever we "walk the vault" or rehearse our burial service, we are consoled with the announcement that Christ is the resurrection and the life. "Blessed are they that die in the Lord, for they rest from their labours." Then let us "lift up the hands that hang down, and strengthen the feeble knees." The righteous will be raised to a glorious immortality.

The mystic rites and ceremonies of Masonry prove how clearly and distinctly the types of the Old Testament and the prophecies were read and understood by the fathers in Israel. The analogies which have been enumerated would be otherwise wholly unaccountable, unless we believed that our Order was of modern origin, or was established subsequent to the Christian era. But be it an ancient or a modern institution, it commends itself to our wonder and admiration. It required no common ability to create it. Great genius and talent must have been united in establishing it. And when it is viewed in the light in which we have

---

[649] Heav. Arc., n. 3195.

surveyed it, it will be found a great help in bringing us to knowledge of the holy writings, by inducing us to search them and find out the truths which are allegorically represented in our lodges.

There is much force in the testimony afforded by Masonic traditions in the elucidation of scriptural truth. Our traditions cannot be substituted for the *lex scripta* or the Bible. But if they tend to confirm our belief in those articles of faith common to the church universal, they ought not to be rejected; but, on the contrary, should be preserved and respected by the sons of light. The system of Masonry is so perfect, and its mode of transmitting facts orally so pure, that we may safely affirm, that our traditions have been handed down to us without any material alteration. They cannot be constitutionally altered. They are guarded by the most solemn sanctions; and as a proof that they have not been changed; they are now and ever have been the same the world over. The remarkable uniformity which exists in the Masonic work and ceremonies throughout the earth shows that the traditions or landmarks of the institution have been preserved inviolate. Then, if the Masonic traditions confirm the doctrines of the Bible, or throw any light on matters of scriptural interpretation, they ought to be prized very highly. There are traditions which the great body of Christians, from the beginning, have held to be articles of faith[650]. We would not dare to assert that the Holy Bible does not contain the whole of revealed truth, or every doctrine essential to a perfect plan of salvation. Any tradition, which is at variance with the revealed word, is a false tradition, and should be so regarded. But where tradition corresponds with the Scripture or its true interpretation, it ought not to be rejected. Irenæus says: "The tongues of nations vary, but the virtue of tradition is everywhere one and the same." As to forms, ceremonies, and rites, all the holy fathers contend they are justified by tradition. Every church

---

[650] 2 Palm. on Ch., p. 48. Refers to William Palmer, *A Treatise on the Church of Christ*, London, 1838 (Two volumes).

and every sect, from the foundation of Christianity, has practiced a number of rites and matters of discipline which are not in the Scriptures[651]. Everything is lawful which is not forbidden by the law—which is not contrary to the law, contends the same writer; for where no law is, there is no transgression[652].

And now, a parting word to all the brethren. Hold fast to our traditions: preserve inviolate the landmarks which have come down pure and unimpaired. The principles of our institution are those of truth. They are the principles of our sacred religion, and are everlasting. They existed when the foundations of the earth were laid, and formed an arch more magnificent than the firmament with all its glorious "inlay of stars."

We have endeavored to prove that Freemasonry is a most powerful agent of virtue. Every step in Masonry—every mystery of the Order, like "the things hard to be understood in Scripture," are witnesses of Divine truth. From every dangerous path and every rugged way; from every solemn veil we penetrate; and from every mysterious sign and word of exhortation, we derive the most brilliant illustrations of a glorious[653] destiny. Masonry, viewed as a moral science, must command the highest esteem. It opens to our mental vision a sublime astronomy. There are stars and suns revolving about a great centre in the unseen depths of glory. Above that firmament are crystal waters—some spiritual Jordan, in which the righteous may be baptized anew, on their way to the heavenly city. In that land of light, the soul will find problems of moral science, which it will forever delight to study, and never solve. There it may be ever telling up the sum of happiness, and never finding an an-

---

[651] 2 Palm. on Ch., p. 67.

[652] For the authority of tradition, and the relation between religion and tradition, see 2 Palm. on Ch., p. 69.

[653] See address delivered by the author before Jackson R. A. Chapter No 6. — Proceedings of G. R. A. Chap, of Mississippi, 1847.

swer. How incomprehensible is the mystery of an eternal progress! No plumb-line can sound the depths of mercy; and no compasses can describe immensity, within whose infinite circle there is an infinite triangle, which will continue forever incomprehensible to the student of celestial geometry.

Our Order stands a monument of ancient renown—a massive structure, supported by the pillars of wisdom, strength, and beauty. But if we would enjoy any real satisfaction in looking at the splendid edifice, we must "go down to its very foundation"; we must cross the gulf of time, which is bridged over, and go back to the age in which its "stones were hewn, and visit the graves of the very Masters whose hands fashioned and heaved them into their places." Let us think often upon the mysterious and solemn ties which unite us together as a band of friends, and pledge anew our vows of holy brotherhood, and ever walk uprightly before God and man.

"There is much need; for not as yet
Are we in shelter or repose,
The holy house is still beset
With leaguer of stern foes;
Wild thoughts within, bad men without,
All evil spirits round about
Are banded in unblest device,
To spoil love's earthly paradise.
"Then draw we nearer day by day,
Each to his brethren, all to God;
Let the world take us as she may,
We must not change our road;
Not wondering, though in grief to find
The martyr's foe still keep her mind;
But fix'd to hold love's banner fast,
And by submission win at last."

THE END

APPENDICES

Appendix I

REFLECTIONS A YEAR AFTER DECLARATION OF CONGREGATION FOR THE DOCTRINE OF THE FAITH

Article from L'Osservatore Romano, *March 11, 1985*

Irreconcilability between Christian faith and Freemasonry

On 26 November 1983 the S. Congregation for the Doctrine of the Faith (S.C.D.F.) published a declaration on Masonic associations (cf. *AAS* LXXVI [1984], 300). At a distance of little more than a year from its publication, it may be useful to outline briefly the significance of this document.

Since the Church began to declare her mind concerning Freemasonry, her negative judgment has been inspired by many reasons, both practical and doctrinal. She judged Freemasonry not merely responsible for subversive activity in her regard, but from the earliest pontifical documents on the subject and in particular in the Encyclical *Humanum Genus* by Leo XIII (20 April 1884), the Magisterium of the Church has denounced in Freemasonry philosophical ideas and moral conceptions opposed to Catholic doctrine. For Leo XIII, they essentially led back to a rationalistic naturalism, the inspiration of its plans and activities against the Church. In his Letter to the Italian people *Custodi* (8 December 1892), he wrote: "Let us remember that Christianity and Freemasonry are essentially irreconcilable, so that enrolment in one means separation from the other."

One could not therefore omit to take into consideration the positions of Freemasonry from the doctrinal point of view, when, during the years from 1970-1980, the Sacred Congregation was in correspondence with some Episcopal Conferences especially interested in this problem because of the dialogue undertaken by some Catholic personages with representatives of some Masonic lodges which declared that they were not hostile, but were even favourable, to the Church.

Now more thorough study has led the S.C.D.F. to confirm its conviction of the basic irreconcilability between the principles of Freemasonry and those of the Christian faith.

Prescinding therefore from consideration of the practical attitude of the various lodges, whether of hostility towards the Church or not, with its declaration of 26 November 1983 the S.C.D.F. intended to take a position on the most profound and, for that matter, the most essential part of the problem: that is, on the level of the irreconcilability of the principles, which means on the level of the faith, and its moral requirements.

Beginning from this doctrinal point of view, and in continuity, moreover, with the traditional position of the Church as the aforementioned documents of Leo XIII attest, there arise then the necessary practical consequences, which are valid for all those faithful who may possibly be members of Freemasonry.

Nevertheless, with regard to the affirmation of the irreconcilability between the principles of Freemasonry and the Catholic faith, from some parts are now heard the objection that essential to Freemasonry would be precisely the fact that it does not impose any «principles», in the sense of a philosophical or religious position which is binding for all of its members, but rather that it gathers together, beyond the limits of the various religions and world views, men of good will on the basis of humanistic values comprehensible and acceptable to everyone.

Freemasonry would constitute a cohesive element for all those who believe in the Architect of the Universe and who feel committed with regard to those fundamental moral orientations which are defined, for example, in the Decalogue; it would not separate anyone from his religion, but on the contrary, would constitute an incentive to embrace that religion more strongly.

The multiple historical and philosophical problems which are hidden in these affirmations cannot be discussed here. It is certainly not necessary to emphasize that following the Second Vatican Council the Catholic Church too is pressing in the direction of collaboration between all men of good will. Nevertheless, becoming a member of Freemasonry decidedly exceeds this legitimate collaboration and has a much more important and final significance than this.

Above all, it must be remembered that the community of "Freemasons" and its moral obligations are presented as a progressive system of symbols of an extremely binding nature. The rigid rule of secrecy which prevails there further strengthens the weight of the interaction of signs and ideas. For the members this climate of secrecy entails above all the risk of becoming an instrument of strategies unknown to them.

Even if it is stated that relativism is not assumed as dogma, nevertheless there is really proposed a relativistic symbolic concept and therefore the relativizing value of such a moral-ritual community[654], far from being eliminated, proves on the contrary to be decisive.

In this context the various religious communities to which the individual members of the lodges belong can be

---

[654] One cannot but ponder if the authors may not indeed be eminently qualified in the field of "moral relativism"!

considered only as simple institutionalizations of a broader and elusive truth. The value of these institutionalizations therefore appears to be inevitably relative with respect to this broader truth, which instead is shown in the community of good will, that is, in the Masonic fraternity.

In any case, for a Catholic Christian, it is not possible to live his relation with God in a twofold mode, that is, dividing it into a supraconfessional humanitarian form and an interior Christian form. He cannot cultivate relations of two types with God, nor express his relation with the Creator through symbolic forms of two types. That would be something completely different from that collaboration, which to him is obvious, with all those who are committed to doing good, even if beginning from different principles. On the one hand, a Catholic Christian cannot at the same time share in the full communion of Christian brotherhood and, on the other, look upon his Christian brother, from the Masonic perspective, as an «outsider».

Even when, as stated earlier, there were no explicit obligation to profess relativism as doctrine, nevertheless the relativizing force of such a brotherhood, by its very intrinsic logic, has the capacity to transform the structure of the act of faith in such a radical way as to become unacceptable to a Christian, «to whom his faith is dear» (Leo XIII).

Moreover, this distortion of the fundamental structure of the act of faith is carried out for the most part in a gentle way and without being noticed: firm adherence to the truth of God, revealed in the Church, becomes simple membership, in an institution, considered as a particular expressive form alongside other expressive forms, more or less just as possible and valid, of man's turning toward the eternal.

The temptation to go in this direction is much stronger to-day, inasmuch as it corresponds fully to certain convictions prevalent in contemporary mentality. The opinion that truth cannot be known is a typical characteristic of our era and, at the same time, an essential element in its general crisis.

Precisely by considering all these elements, the Declaration of the Sacred Congregation affirms that membership in Masonic associations "remains forbidden by the Church," and the faithful who enrolls in them "are in a state of grave sin and may not receive Holy Communion."

With this last statement, the Sacred Congregation points out to the faithful that this membership objectively constitutes a grave sin and by specifying that the members of a Masonic association may not receive Holy Communion, it intends to enlighten the conscience of the faithful about a grave consequence which must derive from their belonging to a Masonic lodge.

Finally, the Sacred Congregation declares that "it is not within the competence of local ecclesiastical authorities to give a judgment on the nature of Masonic associations which would imply a derogation from what has been decided above." In this regard, the text also refers to the Declaration of 17 February 1981, which already reserved to the Apostolic See all pronouncements on the nature of these associations which may have implied derogations from the Canon Law then in force (Can. 2335). In the same way, the new document issued by the S.C.D.F. in November 1983 expresses identical intentions of reserve concerning pronouncements which would differ from the judgment expressed here on the irreconcilability of Masonic principles with the Catholic faith, on the gravity of the act of joining a lodge and on the consequences which arise from it for receiving Holy Communion. This disposition points out that, despite the diversity which may exist among Masonic obediences, in particular in their declared attitude towards the Church, the Apostolic See discerns some common principles in them which require the same evaluation by all ecclesiastical authorities.

In making this Declaration, the S.C.D.F. has not intended to disown the efforts made by those who, with the due authorization of this Congregation, have sought to establish a dialogue with representatives of Freemasonry. But since there was the possibility of spreading among the faithful the erroneous opinion that membership in a Masonic lodge was lawful, it felt that it was its duty to make known to them the authentic thought of the Church in this regard and to warn them about a membership incompatible with the Catholic faith.

Only Jesus Christ is, in fact, the Teacher of Truth, and only in him can Christians find the light and the strength to live according to God's plan, working for the true good of their brethren.

Appendix II

CONGREGATION FOR THE DOCTRINE OF THE FAITH

DECLARATION ON MASONIC ASSOCIATIONS

It has been asked whether there has been any change in the Church's decision in regard to Masonic associations since the new Code of Canon Law does not mention them expressly, unlike the previous Code.

This Sacred Congregation is in a position to reply that this circumstance in due to an editorial criterion which was followed also in the case of other associations likewise unmentioned inasmuch as they are contained in wider categories.

Therefore the Church's negative judgment in regard to Masonic association remains unchanged since their principles have always been considered irreconcilable with the doctrine of the Church and therefore membership in them remains forbidden. The faithful who enroll in Masonic associations are in a state of grave sin and may not receive Holy Communion.

It is not within the competence of local ecclesiastical authorities to give a judgment on the nature of Masonic associations which would imply a derogation from what has been decided above, and this in line with the Declaration of this Sacred Congregation issued on 17 February 1981 (cf. *AAS* 73 1981 pp. 240-241; English language edition of *L'Osservatore Romano*, 9 March 1981).

In an audience granted to the undersigned Cardinal Prefect, the Supreme Pontiff John Paul II approved and ordered the publication of this Declaration which had been decided in an ordinary meeting of this Sacred Congregation.

Rome, from the Office of the Sacred Congregation for the Doctrine of the Faith, 26 November 1983.

Joseph Card. RATZINGER
Prefect

+ Fr. Jerome Hamer, O.P.
Titular Archbishop of Lorium
Secretary

M∴W∴Charles Scott, KT, 33°

M∴W∴Charles Scott, KT, 33°, &c.[655], was born in Knox-
ville, Tennessee, on November 12th, 1811. He was a de-
scendant of a Virginia family noted for its production of
many distinguished soldiers and eminent statesmen. He
first begun the practice of law in Nashville, Tennessee,
where he married and soon afterward removed to Jackson,
Mississippi, and there pursued his profession in copartner-
ship with George S. Yerger, who had married his sister.
This firm was eminently successful, and enjoyed distinguished reputation; and the ability and stanch integrity of
Charles Scott, together with his high sense of honor and
amiability of character, commended him so highly to the
people, that in a few years he was elected to the office of
chancellor of Mississippi, and long presided over the superior court of chancery with great ability, and with the universal commendation of both bar and people. It was he
who first rendered the decree in the case of Johnson vs. the
state of Mississippi, establishing the liability of the state for
the payment of the bonds of the Union bank, that case
having been first instituted in the chancery court; and notwithstanding that the popular sensibilities were adverse to
the result, the ability, purity, and sincere integrity which
characterized his decision caused it to be generally received
as a satisfactory emanations of conscientious duty. It was
affirmed by the high court of errors and appeals. In 1859,
Chancellor Scott removed to Memphis, Tennessee, where
he conceived a broader and more prolific field was presented to the practice of his profession, which he then entered
upon with the opening prospects of a brilliant career, but
so soon as the clouds of the war begun to gather along the
horizon, he returned, in 1861, to Jackson, Mississippi, determined to cast his lot with his adopted state in the im-

---

[655] The Masonic Record, Vol. I-II, Nashville, 1868, p. 341.

pending struggle. He had been a devoted friend of the Union, but when Mississippi seceded he promptly yielded to the demands of duty, and his heart and hand became warmly enlisted in her cause. He lived, however, but a short time after his return to Jackson, where he died, and was buried by his beloved Brethren of the Masonic fraternity. Chancellor Scott was a most devoted Mason, and as such had a national reputation. He was for many years Master of Silas Lodge[656], in Jackson, and afterward was Grand Master of the Grand Lodge of Mississippi[657]. Chancellor Scott was not only an ardent, thorough student of the law, but he was also a ripe classical scholar, and was familiar with the standard poets and writers of modern times, particularly surpassing most of his contemporaries in his knowledge of that greatest of all modern poets, Shakespeare. His researches had even extended farther, and much of his time was devoted to sacred writers, while his knowledge of the Bible was thorough and extensive. His studies in this direction had convinced him of all the truths of religion, and he was an exemplary Christian. This sentiment pervaded his whole nature, and quickened a tender consciousness and amiability, which not only rendered him an ornament to society, but especially fitted him for the high office of Chancellor. He was a man of noble candor and knightly courtesy, gentle and affable in his manners, devoted to his friends, unwearied in the performance of duty, and unswerving in fidelity to his high trust. A bright Mason, he cherished the virtue of Charity; a cultivated lawyer, he loved the principles of Justice; an able and upright judge, he promulgated

---

[656] It surely refers to Silas Brown Lodge No 65, of Jackson, chartered on May 6th, 1844. In 1877, it merged with Pearl Lodge No 23, maintaining the latter's name and number. Pearl Lodge No 23 is still an active lodge in Jackson.

[657] 1850.

the purest doctrines of Equity; and a good man, his heart flowed in sympathy and generosity toward his fellowmen. Many of his comrades and friends are still living in Mississippi, and cherish his memory with sincere affection[658].

---

[658] James D. Lynch, *Bench and Bar of Mississippi,* New York, 1881, p. 175.

W∴ Saul M. Montes-Bradley, KT, 32°

Born in Argentina through no fault of his own,—as his lamented friend Larry Nathan Burns used to say: *"Being a gentleman, he was not about to disappoint his mother on such an important occasion for her, regardless of where she chose to give birth"*—Saul Montes-Bradley abandoned the land of his birth for his ancestral home in the 1970s and has hardly ever looked back.

Through the years, he has done extensive research in New England and English lineages, expressed in dozens of articles published in Flintlock & Powderhorn, The Patriot, The Minuteman and other regional and national magazines; genealogies of New England families; research of the early cemetery records of dissidents in South America, and countless lineages for hereditary societies.

Of his *The Bradleys of Essex County Revisited* (TOBF, 2004), Dr. Ralph J. Crandall of the New England Historic Genealogical Society stated: *"This volume will remain the standard work on this international family."*

A seventh generation Mason, he joined the Fraternity in the early 1990s, and has dedicated many years to research in

Masonic subjects, delivering numerous lectures in lodges in Florida and as editor of *The Coconut Trowel* (2001-2006). He is Past Master of Coconut Grove Lodge No 258 (2001), and of Eureka North Shore Lodge No 269 (2008); Past High Priest of Jericho Chapter No 11, Royal Arch Masons (2009); Past Deputy Master of Adoniram Council No 10, Royal and Select Masters; (2010). Past Eminent Commander of Miami Commandery No 13, Knights Templar (2010); Past Master of Kadosh, Valley of Miami, Orient of Florida (2007). He has also served through the years as Lodge Instructor and in various Zone and District Committees of the Grand Lodge of Florida.

He lives in Virginia and Florida with his beloved wife Alexandra and three children and, in addition to his Masonic affiliations, is a member of the New England Historic Genealogical Society; the Maine Historical Society; the North Andover Historical Society; Sons and daughters of the First Settlers of Newbury, Mass.; Sons of the Revolution; Sons of the American Revolution; Order of the Founders and Patriots of America; The Order of the Crown of Charlemagne; Baronial Order of Magna Charta; the Society of the War of 1812.

Recent publications include:

The Bradleys of Essex County Revisited, 2004
When This You See, Remember Me, 2012
Dissident Cemeteries of Buenos Aires, Vol. 1 (1821-1855), 2012
Melgarejo, 2016
Hidalgos, marinos y conquistadores, 2016